JERUSALEM
Problems and Prospects

JERUSALEM
Problems and Prospects

Edited by
JOEL L. KRAEMER

Introduction by
Teddy Kollek

PRAEGER SPECIAL STUDIES • PRAEGER SCIENTIFIC
CBS EDUCATIONAL AND PROFESSIONAL PUBLISHING

Library of Congress Cataloging in Publication Data
Main entry under title:

Jerusalem: problems and prospects.

Includes bibliographical references and index.
1. Jerusalem—Politics and government—Addresses,
essays, lectures. I. Kraemer, Joel L.
DS109.94.J48   956.94'405   80-19418

ISBN 0-03-057733-0
ISBN 0-03-057734-9 (pbk)

The map of Reunited Jerusalem was prepared by Tzipora Segal; all other maps were prepared by cartographer T. A. Bicknell. The maps of The Peel Commission Plan, A Jewish Proposal for Partition, and A British Plan for Partition were published in the *Atlas of the Arab-Israeli Conflict* by Martin Gilbert, copyright © 1974 by Martin Gilbert. The remaining maps appeared in *The Jerusalem History Atlas* by Martin Gilbert, copyright © 1977 by Martin Gilbert. All the maps from both atlases are used by permission of the author and of Weidenfeld & Nicolson, London, and the Macmillan Publishing Company, Inc., New York.

Published in 1980 by Praeger Publishers
CBS Education and Professional Publishing
A Division of CBS, Inc.
521 Fifth Avenue, New York, New York 10017 U.S.A.

© 1980 by the Jerusalem Foundation, Inc.

0123456789 038 987654321

Printed in the United States of America

PREFACE

This book is a collection of studies concerning Jerusalem—its recent history, current problems, and future prospects. The book was conceived a number of years ago when Teddy Kollek, the mayor of Jerusalem, and a group of colleagues realized that despite the proliferation of popular books on Jerusalem, there is an urgent need for a single volume treating topics requisite for understanding the present situation and suggesting options for the future.

The Van Leer Institute in Jerusalem consented to sponsor the project, which was also funded by a contribution from The Jerusalem Foundation. Neither the Institute nor the Foundation has any responsibility for the content of the volume.

An editorial board was formed that included David Farhi, a scholar concerned with Arab affairs and local history; Ron Feinstein, director general of the Jerusalem Municipality; and Yitzhak Gur, personal aide of the mayor, who acted throughout as research coordinator. The editorial board asked experts in various fields to research specific topics, such as proposed solutions of the Jerusalem problem, the Jerusalem Municipality, Israeli policies after the city's reunification, demographic and economic developments since 1967, and the Christian establishment in Jerusalem. It also commissioned comparative studies on local government for heterogeneous populations and on the institutional structure of heterogeneous cities (Brussels, Montreal, Belfast). These studies were undertaken on the assumption that problems arising from ethnic and religious diversity are not unique to Jerusalem, and how such situations are managed elsewhere may offer guidance for Jerusalem; and, conversely, how the Jerusalem experience may contain valuable lessons for others.

The book includes a chapter by Mayor Kollek, which is a revised version of an article originally published in *Foreign Affairs* (July 1977). During the past 15 years the guiding principles that have given direction to Jerusalem were formulated and implemented by Mayor Kollek during one of the most critical periods in the annals of this ancient city. This was surely a fortunate coincidence, rare in history, of the right man in the right place at the right time.

It is not the purpose of this book to offer political or administrative solutions for the Jerusalem question. The authors recognize that any attempt to offer solutions could not possibly take into account all the relevant factors. Moreover, it was obvious that negotiations concerning Jerusalem could not be severed from negotiations between Israel and its neighbors, as the sentiments of the people of the area and of the world at large must be expressed in any settlement. Nevertheless, the authors have permitted themselves, here and there, to raise ideas and to present options that may stimulate thought on the subject.

An academic committee accompanied the early stages of research, including Professor Yehudah Elkana, Professor Menachem Elon, Professor Menahem Milson, Professor Joshua Prawer, Professor Yitzhak Zamir, Mrs. Leah Ben Dor, and Baruch Yekutieli. Professor Bernard Lewis of Princeton University and the Institute for Advanced Study gave unstintingly of his time and always valuable advice. Mrs. Ruth Cheshin, director of The Jerusalem Foundation, contributed her insight, continuing support, and personal interest. Professor Abram Chayes and Professor Charles M. Haar of the Law School of Harvard University, and especially J. Robert Moskin of New York, contributed their long-term editorial assistance. Benis M. Frank prepared the index. And Mrs. Michal Sela aided the editor as research assistant.

This book is dedicated to the memory of David Farhi, colleague and friend, who studied and served Jerusalem and all its inhabitants.

— the editor

CONTENTS

LIST OF TABLES

LIST OF MAPS

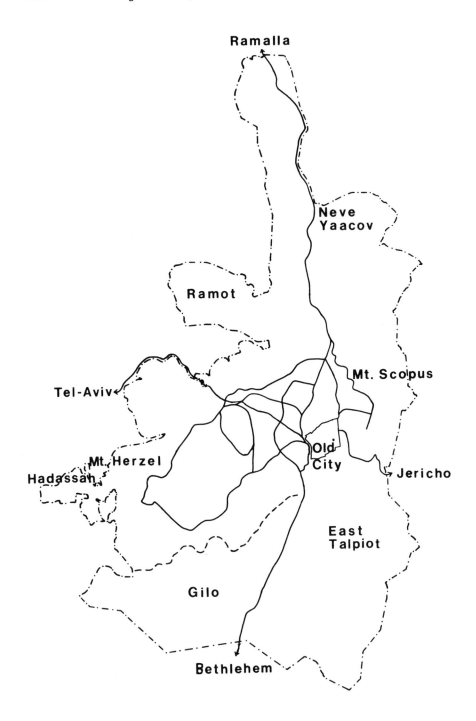

INTRODUCTION: JERUSALEM — TODAY AND TOMORROW

Teddy Kollek

The place of Jerusalem in the process of seeking peace in the Middle East is unique. Its historical, emotional, and international complexities set it apart from other issues that may be solved on the basis of mutually agreed-upon boundaries. The Jerusalem question cannot be decided by drawing a line. The future of Jerusalem cannot be resolved by division.

This does not mean that Jerusalem is an insoluble problem. It means that Jerusalem's people of differing faiths, cultures, and aspirations must find peaceful ways to live together other than by drawing a line in the sand with a stick. It is no solution to rebuild concrete walls and barbed wire through the middle of the city.

The problem of Jerusalem is difficult because age-old and deeply felt emotions are encrusted over the rationality necessary to find solutions. But I am convinced that these solutions can be found by people of goodwill.

To be perfectly candid, what I dread most is that this city—so beautiful, so meaningful, so holy to millions of people— should ever be divided again; that barbed wire fences, mine fields, and concrete barriers should again sever its streets; that armed men should again patrol a frontier through its heart. I fear the redivision of Jerusalem not only as the mayor of the city, as a Jew, and as an Israeli but also as a human being who is deeply sensitive to its history and who cares profoundly about the well-being of its inhabitants.

Jerusalem is, of course, one of the oldest cities. Signs of human habitation have been found dating back at least 4,000 years. In the course of these millennia it has been coveted and conquered by a host of peoples: Canaanites, Jebusites, Israelites, Babylonians, Assyrians, Persians, Romans, Byzantines, Arabs, Seljuks, Crusaders, Mamluks, Ottomans, British, Jordanians, and Israelis. But throughout those thousands of years, Jerusalem has been divided for less than two decades, from 1948 to 1967. It must never again be divided. Once more to cut this living city in two would be as cruel as it is irrational.

Why have all these various peoples sought this city? It has no natural resources; it has no port; it has no material wealth. It has been coveted primarily for spiritual reasons; it was the site of the Temple of the Jews, the site of the Crucifixion of Jesus; and the place from which, according to tradition, Muḥammad rose to Heaven.

The fact that all three great monotheistic religions find meaning in Jerusalem cannot be a random accident. I think the reason is clear. First of all, Jerusalem is a beautiful place set in the mystical Judean Hills, conducive to meditation and thought and wonder at the meaning of life. And second, for all their tensions and exclusiveness, the three great religions are historically deeply interrelated. Jesus came to Jerusalem because he was a Jew who made the pilgrimage to the City of David and the Temple. Muhammad, whose roots were in Mecca and Medina, still the main Holy Cities of Islam, is said to have visited Jerusalem during his night ride because his ideas and his vision were interrelated with Judaism and Christianity. We must live with the reality of these connections. For centuries men have fought and died because of them. But I am not alone in feeling intensely that men can also live in brotherhood because of them.

These very connections make any division of Jerusalem a senseless exercise. The remaining Western Wall of the Temple enclosure, the Church of the Holy Sepulchre, and the Dome of the Rock are all in the Old City within yards of each other. The Dome of the Rock is actually atop the Temple Mount, the very site of the Temple of the Jews.

In 1947, as the British were about to relinquish their Mandate over Palestine, the United Nations, in addition to its partition recommendations, proposed to make Jerusalem an internationalized city. The Jews then accepted internationalization, with a heavy heart, but it was rejected outright by the Arab states, along with the other provisions of the Partition Resolution. Immediately following the passage of the UN resolution, the Arabs initiated hostilities against the Jews of Jerusalem. At the end of the generalized and prolonged fighting that followed, the Arabs held East Jerusalem and the Old City, and the Jews, West Jerusalem.

The Vatican supported internationalization at that time. But the Roman

Catholic Church, although of great influence in the world, is only one element among the more than 30 Christian denominations in Jerusalem. The Catholics, for example, own about 17 percent of the Christian Holy Places. Apart from this, however, for various reasons the emphasis of the Vatican seems over the years to have been greatly modified. Nor is internationalization supported by other leading Christian communities in Jerusalem.

The religious tenets of the Muslims exclude internationalization because they reject the idea that the Temple Mount—the Ḥaram al-Sharīf—should be ruled by infidels. Moreover, internationalization does not accord with Arab political aspirations. As to the Jews, the centrality of Jerusalem in Jewish faith and tradition and the intensity of Jewish feeling about Jerusalem are reflected in the 2,000-year-old prayer repeated throughout the centuries, "Next year in Jerusalem." This symbolizes not only a religious hope but memories of ancient glories under Jewish rule and an unyielding struggle for their revival. All this is expressed for Jews in the word "Jerusalem." The Jewish people cannot give up Jerusalem, nor can they, nor will they ever again, remove their capital from Jerusalem.

But independent of these intense feelings, internationalization will not work for pragmatic reasons. Past experience, whether in Trieste, Danzig, or Shanghai, has shown its unworkability. In the case of Danzig, indeed, it contributed to bringing on a world war.

A city cannot be run by a committee, particularly a city of such complexity and diversity as Jerusalem. Before building a road or a sewage system, the committee members would have to refer back to their foreign offices or to a UN bureaucracy. And who would pay the bills? Jerusalem is not an industrial city; its economy is based on government, education, and tourism, and it does not have the taxing power to pay for itself. Today it is supported by the State of Israel. To this should be added that Israel's experience in the United Nations of recent years has been traumatic, and there is little or no reason to believe that an international body, which presumably would operate under the authority of and reflect various power elements in the United Nations, would be either impartial or effective.

The mayor of Jerusalem does not make foreign policy; that is the function of Israel's national government. But when I look at the future of Jerusalem, there are two premises with which virtually everyone in Israel agrees: that Jerusalem shall remain undivided and that it shall remain the capital of Israel. Most Jerusalemites of every persuasion would agree that, under whatever political solution, the city should remain accessible to all and the rights of every religion to its Holy Places should be preserved.

These two conditions have now existed for 13 years, since the city was so unexpectedly unified after the Jordanians attacked Israel in the June 1967

War. And I think that the history of relations in Jerusalem among Jews, Muslims, and Christians during this decade points to the kind of solution we should eventually evolve for Jerusalem.

Tensions do exist in the city and nobody can deny them. But it was a much less happy city when walls and barbed wire divided it; and it was certainly a more violent city than it is today. We have made progress toward a city of tolerant coexistence in which common interests are emerging, and we have established crucial principles that make continuing progress possible. Four of these principles are

- There shall be free access to all the Holy Places regardless of creed or nationality, and they shall be administered by their adherents.
- Everything possible shall be done to ensure unhindered development of the Arab way of life in the Arab sections of the city and to ensure the Muslims and Christians a practical religious, cultural, and commercial governance over their own daily lives.
- Everything possible shall be done to ensure equal governmental, municipal, and social services in all parts of the city.
- Continuing efforts shall be made to increase cultural, social, and economic contacts among the various elements of Jerusalem's population. And, in fact, civic affairs, law enforcement, infrastructure services, urban planning, marketing and supply, and to a great extent, specialized medical services are centrally provided to all Jerusalemites.

Let me briefly discuss these four principles.

First, the Holy Places: Throughout their occupation of East Jerusalem from 1948 to 1967, the Jordanians reneged on their commitments under the Armistice Agreement to permit Israelis of any religion or Jews of any nationality to have access to the Holy Places under Jordanian control. There was a mass destruction of Jewish synagogues, and other religious shrines were desecrated. There was a ban on the acquisition of land by Christian churches in any part of East Jerusalem.

Since the reunification of the city by Israel, access has been opened to all Holy Places for all religions and sects. Today Christians administer Christian Holy Places and Muslims administer Muslim Holy Places. Israel is a tolerant enclave in a rather intolerant part of the world.

In practice, satisfactory working arrangements have evolved for the Holy Places. The Arabs have independent administration without interference, and Israel maintains sovereignty. International lawyers would no doubt find it a problem to formulate these arrangements in a way satisfactory to both sides. But in practice they exist and work well.

The Temple Mount, a small area of 40 or 50 acres, is the most delicate problem. It is under Arab administration and Israeli sovereignty. After the fire set by a demented Australian fundamentalist Christian to the al-Aqṣā Mosque on the Temple Mount in 1969, the Muslims asked us to help guard this "Holy Enclosure." Previously, we had had no actual signs of Israeli sovereignty on the Temple Mount. But then, at the Muslims' request, we appointed policemen to protect the Muslim Holy Places. No details were discussed, but the police unit guarding the Temple Mount is commanded by a Muslim officer and manned by a mixture of Muslim, Jewish, and Christian policemen. This arrangement is based on a tacit de facto understanding emerging from the necessities of a complicated situation.

In 1976, tension was caused when a group of young Jews attempted to pray on the Temple Mount in violation of regulations. Arab members of the Israeli police force stationed on the Temple Mount arrested the young men and brought them to trial. The magistrate found in favor of the Jewish boys and ruled that there is an inherent Jewish right to pray on the Temple Mount. Sensing a storm, I pressed the government for an immediate policy statement. In response, the minister of police issued a statement forbidding prayers on the Temple Mount. But the crisis was more serious than the government anticipated. Arabs, accustomed to a different judicial tradition, could not believe that a magistrate would make such a decision without prior authorization from a political authority.

A reassuring statement from either the prime minister or the minister of justice perhaps might have been helpful. But the facts that the affair was still in judicial hands and that there is in Israel a clear distinction between judicial and administrative functions were no doubt inhibiting factors. Meanwhile, against the background of the fighting in Lebanon and unrelated tensions in the West Bank, the fat was in the fire. There followed a series of serious demonstrations in the city. Fortunately, however, the vast majority of Jerusalem Muslims did not participate in the disturbances. Subsequently the Israel High Court overruled the decision of the magistrate. To me the whole incident was proof that there is a possibility of living together.

Second, unhindered development of the Arab way of life in the Arab sections of the city and Arab autonomy over their own daily lives: We are a moderate-sized city—in all, 402,000, of whom about 290,000 are Jews, about 96,000 Muslim Arabs, and 16,000 Christians. Of the Christians many belong to national churches and not to great world bodies. The majority are Greeks and Armenians. Latins and Protestants are relative latecomers and fewer. Roughly the same proportion between Jews and non-Jews has continued since the first unofficial census in 1840, when the Jews were first recorded a majority in the city.

We are not trying to create a monolithic melting pot in Jerusalem. What we are trying to do is preserve, in this multicultural mosaic of a pluralistic society, the traditions that have existed in the city for centuries.

If you had walked into the city 100 years ago, you would have found the same patterns. It comprised then only the small area enclosed by the Old City walls, just about 1 square kilometer. Entering through the Jaffa Gate, you would have found an Armenian Quarter, a Greek Quarter, a Latin Quarter, several little enclaves of Copts, Ethiopians, and other Christian groups, a very large Muslim Quarter, and an even larger Jewish Quarter. There was no intermarriage and not much social contact, but relations were, on the whole, reasonable and bearable. The basic idea was that each group felt itself superior to others.

These separate entities still exist today and we have built on them and on that tradition. Jerusalem's Jews consist of old-timers and natives of the city and recent immigrants, coming from over 100 different cultural backgrounds. This great Jewish variety has its own loyalties and aspirations. Among the Christian groups are Arabs, mainly Protestants and some Uniates, who have Arab national loyalties. Sometimes these feelings are very strong because minorities tend to try to give proof of stronger loyalties than secure majorities.

The majority of Christians in Jerusalem have only one desire, namely, to continue their own way of life as they have done for a very long time. The Greek Patriarchs go back to the first century; the Armenians have been here since the fifth century. The Christians in the city measure every government by the freedom given them to run their affairs undisturbed.

We don't interfere with them, their Holy Places, their pilgrimages, or their schools. We help wherever and whenever we are asked to do so. The Jordanians had imposed two restrictive laws. One forced the Christian schools to give equal time to the Bible and the Qur'ān; the other restricted Christian orders or foreigners from buying land or building churches. We have abolished both laws, and in fact four new major churches have since been built or are under construction. Like the Muslims, the Christians have authority over their own institutions and Holy Places. We do everything possible to help them maintain them. Tension among the various Christian denominations, which were rife under some previous regimes, have been reduced, thus enhancing an ecumenical spirit. For example, there are no longer fights concerning the Holy Fire at Easter. If there are problems, there is recourse to Israeli courts, as happened in the case of a dispute between the Ethiopians and Copts.

There is, unfortunately, a wave of intolerance affecting some Muslim countries. Islam seems on the march again, riding on the power and riches of oil, which are expected to revive ancient glories and make amends for Tours and Vienna. The upsurge of Islamic militancy in Iran and other parts of the Muslim world, from Pakistan to Libya, has been accompanied by a spirit of intolerance toward other religions and ideologies. Many have already suffered: the Bahā'īs and Jews in Iran, the Christian Maronites of Lebanon, the black Christians and pagans in the Sudan, and the Jews in Syria.

But to return to Jerusalem, our efforts to help the Arabs preserve their way of life in the city during the past decade have taken many forms. In Jerusalem three Arab dailies are published. This contrasts with the fact that several months before the Six-Day War the Jordanian government decided to suppress the semi-independent newspapers of Jerusalem and replace them by a single government-controlled daily. In no Arab country is the press free to criticize the leadership. In Israel, everyone can criticize the government, and even the Arab press does so in extreme terms; but equally as important, it is in Israel that Arab journalists—to some extent, despite anxiety when traveling to Arab countries—can criticize Arab leaders.

There is freedom to travel. A Jerusalem Arab is free to decide any morning to cross the bridge into Jordan and to go from there to any country. He can go whenever he likes and come back whenever he likes. Every year 150,000 Arabs come to Jerusalem from Jordan, Egypt, Kuwait, and Libya and everywhere else in the Arab world. They carry passports of countries that are at war with us. And they are welcome, because we have undertaken to make the Holy Shrines accessible to everyone.

There is an Arab curriculum in the schools for Arab children, and these schools are entirely maintained by the city. During their final three school years, Arab children have the choice of a course of study designed to qualify them for acceptance by an Arab university in the neighboring Arab countries. This course is acceptable even to the Arab League, and inspectors recognized by the Jordanian Ministry of Education come to Jerusalem to supervise the university entrance examinations. If they prefer, Arab students can take a different course of study during those last three years at school and go to an Israeli university.

The first steps of postsecondary education initiated by a Catholic college in Bethlehem and continuation classes in the Anglican school are also contributing to the raising of Arab educational achievement.

The only change introduced into the former Jordanian curriculum (besides eliminating hate propaganda) provides for Arab children to learn Hebrew. In city schools this is compulsory; in private schools (Muslim and Christian) it is optional but almost universal. At the same time Israel is making special efforts to encourage the study of Arabic.

We have encouraged the growth of economic opportunities. We have built Arab vocational training schools and hope to build more, offering sophisticated subjects, such as electronics, computer technology, and others, that will give Arab youth a chance to improve their standard of living and their self-respect. We are doing what we can to encourage Arab self-confidence and at the same time strengthen the Arab economy in Jerusalem.

And, finally, with few exceptions, the Arabs of Jerusalem are not only citizens of the city but remain citizens of Jordan at the same time. Few have in fact applied for Israeli citizenship and no pressure has been exerted on them to do so. We do not seek nor do we have any interest to break their ties to their families, their heritage, and their culture. On the contrary, we encourage such links. The Arab community of Jerusalem continues its public activities in various fields. Jerusalem houses the Association of Arab Free Professions of the West Bank; it has several Arab clubs, charitable societies, private schools and orphanages, and so on.

All the measures we have taken thus far have been unilateral decisions of the Israeli government and the municipal administration. I have constantly advocated and called on the Arab citizens of the city to share actively in the decision-making process, but so far with little success. Our efforts have been handicapped by the refusal of the Arab leadership to hold political office or to participate openly in the city's elected government. At the same time, many Arabs hold high appointed municipal offices and well over 20 percent of the city's employees are Arabs, while almost all the former Arab municipal employees have continued in their jobs. Thousands of Arabs vote in our municipal elections (without accepting the principle of Israeli sovereignty); but fears lest running for municipal office may be interpreted as accepting Israeli governance have prevented local leaders from standing for election in the municipal administration.

In practice we have overcome this problem in several ways. There is a Supreme Muslim Council that serves as the authority for Muslim affairs under non-Muslim rule. The Council was originally created by the British in 1921, later suspended by the Jordanian government and transferred to Amman, and reestablished in Jerusalem after the Six-Day War. Though it is a self-appointed body not officially recognized by Israeli authorities, we deal with its leaders on day-to-day matters on a de facto basis.

We, on our part, have appointed an adviser on East Jerusalem affairs. He is a Jew, and two of his three assistants are Jerusalem Arabs. They keep in touch with the Arab community in many informal ways, learning its needs and helping to solve its problems.

Communication is also maintained through the ancient system of *mukhtars*, or district leaders, each of whom is responsible for such matters as registering births, deaths, and land ownerships and notarizing documents in his locale. The 60 mukhtars are not democratically elected by their constituents, but they act in the local tradition and perform useful functions. Many of them have created groups of responsible citizens around them—the seeds of democracy. At City Hall we meet with them regularly to discuss the specific needs of their communities, just as we meet with Jewish district leaders.

The Chamber of Commerce of East Jerusalem performs numerous tasks that make possible the free flow of people and goods across the open bridges on the Jordan River. These include providing powers of attorney, authenticating high school diplomas for those wishing to study in Arab universities, and so on. It also serves as a channel through which substantial amounts of Jordanian money are brought in to pay salaries to lawyers, teachers, and others, who in 1967 decided not to resume their work under the Israeli authorities.

In this manner and spirit we do our utmost both to retain flexibility and to reinforce contacts of all kinds with the Arab community of the city.

For some time now, I have envisioned a future structure in Jerusalem under which the city would by governed through a network of boroughs. Each borough would have a great deal of autonomy over its own municipal services and its lifestyle. It would decide its own needs and priorities. It would be modeled not on the boroughs of New York but on those of London, which have their own budgets and a great deal of independence.

Of course, the borough idea is not a panacea. The Arabs will want the Temple Mount to be in their borough, and no Jew would agree to that. But the proposal does suggest an approach under which many of the aspects of everyday life can be delegated to local authorities and the people of the various neighborhoods can feel some increasing control over their own lives and the decision-making process.

By making our efforts permanent, by ensuring their administration of the Temple Mount, and by increasing their local autonomy, we hope to diminish any feeling among Jerusalem's Arabs that their way of life is threatened by Israeli sovereignty. We want to create a secure future for Arabs within the capital of Israel.

The third principle we follow is that everything possible should be done to provide equal municipal and social services in all parts of the city. We are doing this despite the fact that Jerusalem is a poor city. It has no great industrial base. Although presently there is full employment, the people have not been able to accumulate capital. The population of this city of immigrants, both Jews and non-Jews, has grown by 350 percent in 25 years—a record increase! Most of the city's Jews (60 percent) are refugees from Asian and African countries who arrived without means and without useful skills. We also have a great number of elderly people, including aged Jewish immigrants who have prayed all their lives to come to Jerusalem. And we have a disproportionate share of young people in schools—100,000 from nursery schools to the Hebrew University. Our actual labor force is smaller than in other places.

In spite of these difficulties, we have done a great deal to improve local services and to equalize opportunities. We have created jobs. We have made it possible for Arab lawyers, judges, doctors, dentists, and pharmacists to practice their professions without passing Israeli qualification exams. We have permitted corporations and other businesses to operate without the licenses and registrations required by Israeli law. We have extended our social welfare program to East Jerusalem where none existed before. We have opened community health centers in Arab neighborhoods. We have improved schools and built new ones. We have brought roads and electricity to outlying districts for the first time. The East Jerusalem sewage system, which existed only within the city walls, is at least 300 years old and some of it goes back to Roman times. It could not absorb the great new quantities of water we provided, and we are now spending considerable public funds to improve it.

Let me cite one specific example to illustrate some of the problems we face and how we go about solving them. Within the boundaries of Jerusalem, there is an Arab village called Silwān with about 17,000 inhabitants. In 1948, there was no road at all to Silwān. The people used a donkey path that went through an ancient Jewish cemetery. In 1956, the people of Silwān decided they needed a paved road for vehicular traffic and so they poured concrete over the Jewish graves and built a road.

When the Jews returned in 1967, they set about restoring the graves of their grandfathers and great-grandfathers and proceeded to chop up the Jordanian road. The Arabs from Silwān naturally objected vociferously. Within days we made a decision to build an alternative road that would skirt the graves. We allocated $1.5 million, raised the money, and completed the road, preserving the graves and providing Silwān with an alternative road, thus avoiding a possible serious clash.

The fourth principle by which we administer the city is that continuing efforts shall be made to increase cultural, social, and economic contacts among all the various elements of Jerusalemites.

I see the future of the city dependent in considerable part on the close relationships that can develop between its various components. Today we have summer joint youth camps attended by 15,000 youngsters—Jews, Christians, and Muslims. We have art classes for Arab as well as Jewish young people at the Israel Museum. Hundreds of Arab children attend these classes. Now, since the opening of a beautifully designed branch of the Israel Museum Youth Wing in East Jerusalem, it is even easier for Arab children to attend classes because they are close to their neighborhoods. In this branch, there is a majority of Arab pupils. Arabs visit and use Jewish clinics and hospitals. We have built a garden for the blind, on a former battleground, where Jewish and Arab blind now meet. Of course, we are lucky in one respect: There are no racial barriers or even distinctions. You can walk through Jerusalem's streets and find Jews and Arabs working side by side, and you will often not be able to differentiate between them.

Despite all our efforts, it is obvious that the Arabs in Jerusalem still do not accept being included within Israel's frontiers. The Arabs and Jews in Jerusalem do not share a single national consensus, and this creates problems. But both communities share a common love for Jerusalem and a concern for its welfare and peace. The Arabs are in a difficult position. Some, perhaps many, must have been proud when Yāsir ʿArafāt appeared before the United Nations. And yet I believe that most of them do not really expect or wish the Palestine Liberation Organization to solve their intricate problems or regard the PLO ideology as desirable, let alone tenable. This is not because they are pro-Israel or pro-Zionist. Rather, their fundamental goal is to remain in Jerusalem and to preserve the Arab character of their part of the city. That is their loyalty.

During the 19 years of Jordanian rule, Jerusalem experienced an emigration of Arabs. It was a dead-end city and most opportunities were in Amman or in the oil countries. Christians tended to emigrate to North and South America. In order for the Arabs to remain here, they need a flourishing economic life. Today, they have economic prosperity and employment. And because their economy is to a great extent based on cooperation with the Jewish economy, terrorism and the PLO are not in the interests of local Arabs and the continuation of the Arab presence in Jerusalem. I suspect that if the PLO would come to East Jerusalem there would be a great exodus even of leading Arabs from the city.

They face another danger. When the Mufti of Jerusalem fought the British and the Jews in the Palestine of the British Mandate in the 1930s, more Arabs who opposed him were killed by him and his henchmen than were British and Jews put together. About 500 Jews and 150 British lost their lives, while about 3,200 Arabs were killed by their own brother Arabs. The Mufti was the the father of the present-day PLO ideology of a monolithic and militant Palestinian Arab nationalism. Jerusalem's Arabs fear a repetition of such internal terrorism if the PLO were to take over, particularly in the light of what has happened in Lebanon.

It must not be forgotten that the city's Arabs also complained about occupation when the Ottoman Turks, the British, and the "Jordanian Bedouin" were in control—and they called it "occupation" even then! Under Jordanian rule, they felt that Jerusalem was neglected and that Amman was favored over Jerusalem, as indeed it was. The Jordanian government rejected the idea of establishing its capital in Jerusalem after it had decided to annex the West Bank and incorporate it in the Hashemite Kingdom.

Instances of Jordanian neglect, and disrespect, for Jerusalem are numerous. Contrary to expectation and hope, the Jordanian government rejected a plea to establish an Arab university in Jerusalem and instead they built it in Amman. When the Hospital of the Order of St. John of Jerusalem was about to be built, the Jordanians tried to persuade the Order of St. John to build its hospital in Amman. Only after the Order threatened not to build the hospital at all did it finally get the necessary permission to build in Jerusalem. No industry was started in Jerusalem. The largest single enterprise in Jordan-controlled Jerusalem, outside of hotels, was a cigarette factory that employed 12 people. Under Jordan's rule nothing was done to improve Jerusalem and there was widespread unhappiness during that time. People tend to forget such past unhappiness.

In the divided city there was, too, more violence than there is today.

There was intermittent shooting across the border that ran through the city. Every year people were killed or wounded. There was a feeling of claustrophobia in the city then. There was no sense of freedom. Everywhere one went, the street ended abruptly with a sign: "Stop. Frontier. Danger Ahead." Today this is but a faint unpleasant memory of the past for Jew and non-Jew alike.

We do not want to make Jerusalem a parochial city but to restore its ancient glory. We have built a handsome Israel Museum, perhaps the major museum of international art and archeology between the eastern Mediterranean and Tokyo. The Jerusalem Museum of Islamic Art and Culture, opened only a few years ago, is one of outstanding excellence. The Jerusalem Theater has given us a home for the performing arts. There is an Arab theatrical group that performs stories and plays from *Thousand and One Nights* for schoolchildren and by authors such as Nagīb Maḥfūẓ and Friedrich Dürrenmatt for adults. We have built an embryonic center for writers, artists, and musicians at Mishkenot Sha'ananim, to which such world-renowned figures as Simone de Beauvoir, Saul Bellow, Isaiah Berlin, Jorge Luis Borges, Richard Burton, Alexander Calder, Pablo Casals, Marc Chagall, Paul Dirac, Friedrich Dürrenmatt, Erik Erikson, Ernst Gombrich, Sana Hasan, John Hersey, Bernard Lewis, Octavio Paz, Robert Rauschenberg, Arthur Rubinstein, Meyer Schapiro, Stephen Spender, and Isaac Stern have already come and worked and contributed to the cultural life of the city.

We are deeply immersed in city planning to improve the quality of life in Jerusalem. Our present planning focuses upon the Old City and its immediate surroundings. We are developing a green belt around the Old City at great expense. Jerusalem is, I believe, the only city in modern times to create, by purchase, a large central green area such as was preserved by the Boston Common, New York City's Central Park, London's Hyde Park, and the Bois de Boulogne of Paris more than a century ago.

To guide us in our planning, we have established a Jerusalem Committee, a unique group of more than 60 eminent people from all over the world: philosophers, historians, theologians, city planners, educators, architects, writers, artists. They gather in Jerusalem periodically and observe what we are planning and what we are doing. Sometimes they criticize us severely; sometimes they praise us. We take the criticism to heart and carry out practically all their recommendations. As a result, Jerusalem is becoming increasingly a more beautiful city literally day by day.

Despite our good intentions and care, there have been controversies. One was over the building of housing for Jews in East Jerusalem outside the Old City walls. This dispute was hardly justified, as we did not infringe upon any Arab housing. We built mainly on rocky ground newly incorporated into the city. We used no wooded land or land that was employed for agriculture. We removed nothing of value. Our fondest hope is to keep the present population ratio, and this can be maintained without land appropriation in the future.

At the same time, we have provided for Arab expansion too. Jerusalem's Arabs have the highest birth rate in the world and need more and more room in which to live. City-guaranteed mortgages have encouraged several times the amount of annual housing construction that was carried out under Jordanian rule.

We have paid much attention to the beauty of the Old City. We have permitted no changes there. We are rebuilding to scale the Jewish Quarter that was destroyed by the Jordanians in 1948. We have started to replace the forest of television antennas that disfigures the Old City with a central antenna and cables.

We have been improving living space in the poorer neighborhoods. We have planted trees and modernized schools and improved roads and built playgrounds. We have taken special pains with garbage clearance. We have worked hard to make neighborhoods in which young people will not be ashamed to live. We do not want the younger generation to move out.

Another area of controversy has been our eagerness to reveal and preserve the great heritage of Jerusalem's past. We are preserving more than anyone ever thought could be preserved. For this we were condemned by UNESCO, which charged that we were changing the character of Jerusalem with our archeological digs.

Muslims living far from Jerusalem and not knowing the truth may perhaps have been worried by our archeological activities. Some Muslims may even fear that we want to rebuild the Temple and that to this end we would undermine or remove the buildings on the Temple Mount. Their fear is groundless. Jews are not allowed to build the Temple inasmuch as Jewish religious tradition holds that the Temple is already built and is waiting in Heaven for the Messiah to come, when it will descend into its appropriate place. Unless and until the Messiah should come, there is therefore no chance of the Muslim Holy Places being disturbed. What has actually happened is entirely different. More Islamic antiquities have been unearthed by Israeli archeologists in these past 13 years than in all previous history, thus enriching tremendously the world's knowledge of the Islamic past.

We have other complications. For example, we built a road from Mount Zion toward the Dung Gate to relieve traffic in the Old City. In our work, we came upon several levels of remains, remnants of Jewish houses destroyed by Titus in 70 A.D., a Roman road of the second century, the ruins of a large church built by Justinian and on top of that several Crusader towers, and above this again, a 500-year-old Ottoman city wall that badly needed repair because of neglect by the Jordanians. Not only did we change the alignment of the road at substantial cost and inconvenience but also invested much effort and money in preserving the discoveries.

My point is that there is no connection between the complaints about our archeological digs and reality. People abroad devise stories to feed their political propaganda. In reality we are beautifying, restoring, and preserving Jerusalem, not damaging it. The members of the Jerusalem Committee, people of standing, integrity, and independent judgment, came and saw and approved.

Jews care intensely about Jerusalem. The Christians have Rome and Canterbury and even Salt Lake City; Muslims have Mecca and Medina. Jerusalem has great meaning for them also. But the Jews have only Jerusalem and only the Jews have made it their capital. That is why it has so much deeper a meaning for them than for anybody else.

When the city was reunited, all Jews, not only the religious but also the secular, felt the ancient prophecy fulfilled. Jerusalem was our capital even when few were here—for 2,000 years. Since the Muslim conquest only the Crusaders and the British ever made it the administrative capital of the country. On the two occasions when the Arabs could have made Jerusalem their capital, they did not. In the Middle Ages they chose Ramleh, near Lydda on the way to Jerusalem, and in 1948 they chose Amman, which they preferred to Jerusalem.

We do not aspire to find solutions to all the problems of the Middle East in Jerusalem. This is a complicated city with conflicting interests, and it is impossible to satisfy the wishes of everybody.

Sometimes people outside the Middle East ask: What is the relevance of what we are doing in Jerusalem in making the city viable, beautiful, and peaceful to the ultimate question of the sovereignty of the city? We can only look at the situation realistically. If, at worst, Muslim and Jewish differences prove irreconcilable, we will have to live in tension for a long time. All the more reason to care for the city as much as we can to ensure its welfare and well-being in spite of the strains and stresses. If, at best, Jews and Arabs find accommodations that are acceptable to the aspirations of all three faiths, no one would argue that what we are doing for Jerusalem today has been irrelevant.

We want Jerusalem to remain a multicultural city, a mosaic of people. By trying to live together, by joining in many activities, and by equalizing opportunities and social services, we hope to reduce clashes and lower tensions. There are certainly differences of religion, language, cultural attitudes, and political aspirations. But I believe that if the Arabs of Jerusalem are encouraged to feel secure, it should be possible for all to live together in reasonable neighborly relations.

The bottom line is that Jerusalem must never again be divided, with barbed wire through its center, with separate police forces and separate flags. Let it be clearly understood, however, that Jerusalem is and will remain the capital of Israel. Given that axiom, we have proven that others can coexist with us. By contrast, during the 19 years of Arab rule, Jews were totally eliminated and limitations were imposed on Christians.

In this undivided city our objectives are free movement of people and goods, access to the Holy Places for all, the meeting of local needs, reasonable urban planning and development, the reduction of intercommunal conflicts, and the satisfaction of international interests. It is impossible to find a solution that will be fully satisfactory to everyone, and Jerusalem is not unique in this. One cannot make all the people happy all the time. But I feel we can justly claim that under our administration more problems have been solved for more people than under any previous administration.

To enable the city government to carry out the necessary adjustments, it has been suggested that a special Jerusalem law be promulgated, delegating to the city greater autonomy and greater rights, and putting at its disposal additional financial resources, as is done in many countries with regard to their capital cities. This will help provide the elasticity needed to cope with the problems of a multiethnic, multireligious city, with sometimes sudden tension.

Within an undivided city, everything is possible, all kinds of adjustments can be made, all kinds of accommodations can be considered, all kinds of autonomy can be enjoyed, all kinds of positive relationships can be developed.

These have been my ideas for many years, and now even more so with the new reality created by the peace agreement signed between Israel and Egypt. The new reality exists, but it should be stressed that we are at variance with ideas expressed by Egyptian spokesmen, which also reach us from time to time from Jordan, namely, that Jerusalem come under dual sovereignty. It is emotionally inconceivable to divide any city, certainly not Jerusalem, which was a united city from its inception 4,000 years ago until 1948. Nor can this work from a practical point of view. How could one city have two sets of laws, two different courts, different police forces? Within no time there would be frontier barriers, and the walls and the barbed wire would return to where they had been for 19 years. Anyone who really cares for Jerusalem cannot even fathom this situation. Moreover, more than 100,000 Jews now live in areas beyond the former border. On the other hand, Jerusalem has shown in practice that coexistence is possible. In Jerusalem, there already exist many of the aspects of autonomy that the Israeli government has proposed as part of an overall peace settlement. Thus I believe that the ideas expressed here answer this new reality.

In 1967, when attacked by the Jordanians, the Jews were willing to sacrifice their lives for Jerusalem. They would again. Israel gave up Sinai; some Israelis would give up the Golan and some the West Bank and Gaza. But I do not think you can find any Israelis who are willing to give up Jerusalem. They cannot and will not. This beautiful golden city is the heart and soul of the Jewish people. You cannot live without a heart and soul. If you want one simple word to symbolize all of Jewish history, that word would be "Jerusalem."

1

THE JERUSALEM QUESTION

Joel L. Kraemer

First the holy city of one faith, then of two, and thereafter of three, Jerusalem became in the course of history a touchstone of prestige and glory, a symbol of power and supremacy, and therefore a coveted prize in the perennial rivalry of these faiths and the people professing them. At first, the confrontation was between Jews and Christians, then between Christians and Muslims, and most recently between Muslims and Jews.

The Jerusalem question contains two separate elements: sovereignty over the city and the status of the Holy Places.[1] Confusing these issues makes their solution more difficult. When the issue of sovereignty is fused with that of safeguarding the Holy Places, internationalization appears to become a natural solution (as in the 1947 UN Partition Resolution). But these two issues are really quite distinct. The Holy Places may be safeguarded, and access or control of concerned religious communities secured, under an enlightened jurisdiction. The challenge facing a single sovereignty over a unified city is that of providing a satisfactory measure of autonomy for the city's various components. The link between the issue of sovereignty over the city and the question of municipal administration is intimate and the problem consequently complex.

The Jerusalem question did not really exist before the British occupation and Mandate (1917–48). It is true that the City of Peace had been an arena of bloodshed and frequently changed hands for centuries, particularly when Christian West and Muslim East were pitted against each other in holy war; but during the 400 years preceding British administration, in the period of

Muslim Ottoman rule (1517–1917), the city lodged in the secure embrace of a single dynasty.[2]

Although the issue of the Christian Holy Places came up under the Ottomans and became a source of international concern and tension in the nineteenth century, the question of sovereignty over the city was not raised. No one suggested that the Christian Holy Places be torn from the grasp of the Muslim rulers. The Christian powers were content to concede the Holy City to the Muslims, provided these sites be safeguarded and the well-being of Christian residents of the Holy City guaranteed. Solicitude for protection of the Holy Places was often a struggle for prerogatives at these sites, and the endeavor of the Great Powers to extend patronage to their dependent churches and Christian clients was a convenient lever for promoting national interests and meddling in the internal affairs of the tottering Ottoman Empire, with an eye to picking up the pieces when it finally fell.

The situation under the Ottomans was not ideal for non-Muslims, but the Ottoman rulers did exercise a tolerant policy toward non-Muslim Holy Places, within the compass of Islamic regulations. They did not, for instance, officially permit erection of new non-Muslim places of worship. It was during the Ottoman period that the Status Quo vis-a-vis seven Holy Places of Christianity in the Holy Land was confirmed (in 1852).[3] About the same time, access on the part of Jews to the Temple Mount (Ḥaram al-Sharīf) was permitted for an entrance fee or special permit, although Jews were reluctant to exercise this prerogative because of a Halakic prohibition against visiting this holy site.[4]

The Ottoman period followed 257 years of Mamluk rule (1260–1517), during which no foreign invader disquieted the city's tranquility.[5] The Mamluks stamped Jerusalem with a pronounced Islamic character. They stimulated religious life, building mosques, *madrasas* (theological colleges), and Sufi convents, repairing the Ḥaram al-Sharīf mosques, and establishing *waqfs* (religious trusts). The *qāḍīs* (religious judges) enjoyed a high status; the chief judge was appointed by the sultan. Mamluk concern for the Islamic character of Jerusalem was an extension of the religious policy of Saladin and his successors of the Ayyūbid dynasty. Both the Ayyūbids and the Mamluks were reacting to the trauma of the Crusader invasion and the transformation of Jerusalem into a Christian city. Having driven the Crusaders from Jerusalem (1187), Saladin restored to Muslim custody mosques that had been converted into Christian edifices, transformed churches into Muslim institutions, and did his utmost to lend the city an indelible Islamic hue. Heirs and pupils of the Ayyūbids, the Mamluks were trained in holy war against unbelievers and accustomed to official discrimination against the "protected people" (Christians and Jews).

On the other hand, the city of Jerusalem, along with Syria and Palestine as a whole, was neglected physically under the Mamluk sultans of Egypt. The city walls, destroyed in 1219 by al-Mu'azzam 'Īsā, an Ayyūbid sultan of Damascus, were not rebuilt but remained only partially standing throughout the Mamluk period. The resulting perilous situation led to a large-scale evacuation of the city. Poor economic conditions also contributed to depopulation. Jerusalem enjoyed no fertile countryside, had no manufacture to speak of, and was bypassed by important international commercial arteries. For most of the Mamluk period, the city was subordinate to Damascus and thereafter to Cairo, capital of the Mamluk dynasty. Indeed, during the entire period of Arab-Muslim rule (from 638, with interruptions by the Crusaders, until 1917), Jerusalem's status as capital of an independent state—which it had enjoyed until the destruction by the Romans of the Second Jewish Commonwealth—was never restored, and Jerusalem remained a provincial town within great empires having their centers in Damascus, Baghdad, Cairo, or Istanbul.

From the time of the Ottoman conquest of Syria and Palestine at the end of 1516, when Sultan Selim I defeated the Mamluk army, until the nineteenth century, Palestine was a backwater territory of the Ottoman Empire, its population sparse, economy primitive, and roads poor and uncertain. Jerusalem remained a small, neglected provincial town, impoverished and plague-ridden, with no particular political, economic, or strategic importance. As under the Mamluks, the city was remote from principal lines of communication and lacked a sound economic base. It is described in a seventeenth-century firman (imperial edict) as being, along with Hebron, "on the frontier of Arabia (*'Arabistān serhaddinde*), where rebellious Bedouins disturb the peace."[6] The city walls, built by Sultan Süleyman the Magnificent in 1537–41 and standing until the present, were meant to protect the city against Bedouin raids. Not many Turks settled in Jerusalem, nor did Turkish replace Arabic as the common language of daily discourse, though Turkish words seeped into the vocabulary of administration. Distinguished local Arab families (the *a'yān*, or "notables") rose to positions of prominence and influence on the strength of tax farming (*iltizām*) and religious functions, which by and large remained hereditary.[7]

The Ottomans carried on the religious policy of the Mamluks, building madrasas and convents and establishing waqfs. Süleyman the Magnificent had the walls of the Dome of the Rock overlaid with marble and faience.

During this period, the Christian community was split into various sects, and churches were in intermittent conflict owing to disputes over jurisdiction in the Holy Places, particularly in the Holy Sepulchre, called al-Qiyāma ("Resurrection") by the Christians and al-Qumāma ("Rubbish") by the Muslims, and the keys to the church remained in the custody of a Muslim family.[8]

Palestine was not a single administrative unit—it did not become so until the British Mandate—but a composite of several *sanjaks* (provincial districts).

Under the Ottomans, Syria and Palestine were normally divided into three main provinces, with varying administrative borders. These were the provinces (*eyalets* or *vilāyets*) of Aleppo, Damascus, and one or more coastal provinces, based at first on Tripoli, later on Sidon, subsequently on Acre, and finally on Beirut. After the Ottoman conquest, the whole of Palestine, on both sides of the Jordan, was part of the province of Damascus, of which it constituted the sanjaks of Safed, Lajjūn (Megiddo), ʿAjlūn, Nāblus, Jerusalem, and Gaza. In the final period of Ottoman rule, part of Palestine was incorporated in the province of Damascus and part in the province of Beirut, while Jerusalem and its surroundings, previously part of one or the other province, was detached to form a special administrative unit known as the independent *mutasarriflik* of Jerusalem. As such, it was directly subordinate to Istanbul and not to any provincial government.

The nineteenth century was a turning point in the fortunes of Jerusalem (and of Palestine in general), marked by growing involvement of the European powers and greater Ottoman interest in local affairs. England and France, in particular, had political and commercial interests—Palestine was at the crossroads to India and the Far East. The Holy Places became scenes for power struggles among the European countries. The French had been the first to extend their patronage over holy sites and Christian (Catholic) believers by means of a Capitulations agreement signed by Sultan Süleyman the Magnificent and King Francis I in 1535; the Russians claimed to be protectors of Greek Orthodox believers after the Treaty of Küçük Kaynarca in 1774. By the nineteenth century, the British, Austrians, Prussians, Germans, and Italians joined the fray and tried to abolish the privileges gained by the French and Russians.

European powers, notably Britain, aided the Ottomans in their conflict with the rebellious governor of Egypt, Muḥammad ʿAlī, and his son, Ibrāhīm Pasha, and helped them regain sovereignty over Syria and Palestine after almost a decade of Egyptian occupation (1831–40). In an effort to secure the sympathy and support of local non-Muslims and of the European powers in their struggle against the Ottomans, the Egyptians removed discriminating legislation against non-Muslims and instituted a measure of municipal self-government by means of advisory councils wherein non-Muslims participated, thus breaking the virtual monopoly of Muslims in local administration. This was a trend the Ottomans could hardly reverse when they regained control in 1840. In the early 1840s, England and France opened vice-consulates in Jerusalem, and other powers soon followed suit.

The heightened interest and influence of European powers coincided with the beginning of the Ottoman period of reform and modernization, the *Tanzimat* (1839–76). The Tanzimat were aimed at legal and administrative reorganization along European lines. One of the objects of reform was municipal organization. From 1854 to 1858 a municipal council, having a chairman (*reis*) and 12 members, was appointed in Istanbul.[9] A decade later a municipal administrative body began to develop in Jerusalem.

The Ottoman Municipal Code of 1877 required a council for every 40,000 residents of a city, but Jerusalem remained one city, despite the fact that by the beginning of World War I it had twice this number of residents. The Municipal Council always included Christians and Jews, with Muslims making up a majority in the council. There were six members at first and ten in later years. The mayor, who was appointed from among the council members, was invariably from one of the distinguished Muslim Arab families. No true election was held until the Young Turk Revolt in 1908.

Because suffrage was extended only to male, propertied, tax-paying Ottoman citizens, Jews and Christians were not proportionately represented in the council, as most were not Ottoman citizens. Nevertheless, the fact that local Jerusalemite leaders were given representation in the Municipal Council was a step in the direction of democratic government. Moreover, local officials were more apt to attend to the development of the city than was a foreign Turkish governor. The impression that the European-like innovation of a municipality made upon local residents may be gauged from a comment in a letter by a Jewish resident of Jerusalem, a certain Dr. London: "In Jerusalem, where I reside, a Municipal Council has been founded, as in all European cities which conduct themselves in the light of civilization, such as has not existed in Jerusalem from the time Judea went into exile."[10] In what appears as an attempt to give concrete expression to modernization, the Jerusalem Municipality erected a clock tower inside the Jaffa Gate in 1907. It symbolized the attempt of the ancient city to move with the times. After the British occupied Palestine in 1917, it was removed as part of their effort to restore the majesty of the Ottoman period to the Old City.[11]

While the two issues of sovereignty and the Holy Places were kept apart during the Ottoman period, after the Palestine Mandate fell to the British at the end of World War I, the problems of sovereignty and the Holy Places became both intertwined and acute. Jerusalem became the focus in the political-national struggle between the two rival local communities, Jews and Arabs.

The new situation that developed when the Holy Land slipped from the grasp of the Ottomans might be summed up thusly. A Christian country became the occupying power in Palestine (for the first time since the end of the Crusader Kingdom in 1291), establishing its administrative capital at Jerusalem (as had the Crusaders), while the local Jews and Arabs were undergoing an intense phase of national revival.[12] The British permitted Arab and Muslim countries to become involved in the Jerusalem issue (beginning with the Wailing Wall Commission hearings in 1929), thus in effect playing into the hands of the strategy of the Mufti Ḥājj Amīn al-Ḥusaynī and the Supreme Muslim Council. The problem became more impervious to treatment on a local level. The European powers and the United States were primarily concerned with the Holy Places at the beginning of the Mandate period, but by its termination after World War II, when the Palestine problem was taken up by an international forum, the United Nations, the questions of sovereignty and the Holy Places coalesced and were treated as one.

The various British plans proposed for Jerusalem from the time of the implementation of the British Mandate for Palestine were based upon three guiding principles: First, Jerusalem should remain undivided regardless of the solution for all Palestine, with sovereignty over the city being envisioned as either British or Arab. Thus, although the Jerusalem question was inseparable from the broader Palestine problem, the various plans often regarded it as a separate and distinct issue. Second, there should be free access to the Holy Places for members of all concerned religious groups. To ensure this, Jerusalem was occasionally set apart as a separate enclave, as were Bethlehem and Nazareth, where were also located Christian Holy Places. And third, the municipal administration should remain in the hands of the local population, with Muslims to be given preeminence, including the mayoralty, and Jews and Christians, representation in the Municipality.

The proposed solutions were offered against the backdrop of an intensifying conflict between the Zionist movement and the Jewish *yishuv*, on the one side, and the local Arab national movement, on the other. Jerusalem was the main arena wherein this bitter struggle was carried on. From the very onset of the Mandate period the Jewish and Arab communities reacted differently to the various plans concerning Jerusalem (and Palestine in general). The Jews already had a dynamic national organization. Heartened by the Balfour Declaration, they welcomed the British Mandate, although they were soon disillusioned by British policies and what appeared as a retreat, in the face of violent Arab opposition, from the promise of a Jewish national home.

The Arabs, on their part, were galvanized by the fear that the Zionist movement intended to establish a Jewish state in all of Palestine, and they opposed the Mandate from its inception, demanding that Palestine be Arab in character. At first, local Arabs insisted that Palestine be considered an integral part of Syria ("Southern Syria"). The two areas, it was maintained, were never separated throughout history and had intimate national, religious, and linguistic ties. But with the collapse of King Faysal's regime in Syria (1920), attention gradually focused upon Palestine as an independent entity, although the "Southern Syria" concept survived and was occasionally revived by Palestinian Arab spokesmen (and particularly by Syrian political leaders, who refer to Palestine as "Southern Syria" until the present).

The Arab side consistently rejected foreign proposals for settling the Jerusalem question. The Arab demand was a general and principled one, that the country remain Arab, that Jerusalem be placed under Arab control, and that the mayor of the city be Muslim Arab under all circumstances. The

Zionist leadership constantly responded to British and other foreign plans with their own counterproposals. As the European situation deteriorated in the 1930s, and even more so during World War II, the Jews came to the conclusion that there was no alternative to the establishment of a Jewish state. They were occasionally prepared, out of a kind of pragmatic realism based on weakness and desperation, to make what they regarded as great sacrifices to attain a state, for example, acceptance in principle of the Peel Commission's partition plan in 1937 and the Jewish Agency's plan of 1938, surrendering large areas of Jerusalem.

At the same time, Arab antagonism to British rule and to the Zionist movement intensified. The pressing need of the Jews for immigration aroused Arab fears that the country's character would be changed. The UN Partition Resolution of November 1947, with its provision for internationalization of Jerusalem, was not all the Zionists hoped for, and relinquishing Jerusalem was a painful sacrifice made for the sake of peace and in the hope that it would not be a permanent arrangement. (It was to be reexamined by the Trusteeship Council at the end of a ten-year period when the city's citizens would express their wishes in a referendum.)

After 1948, there was not a single Arab camp. There were contradictory interests between most Arab countries and Jordan and between the local Palestinian Arabs and the Hashemite Kingdom. With Jerusalem divided between Jordan and Israel as a result of the 1948 War, the Arab countries (save Jordan and Iraq) had become amenable to the internationalization of Jerusalem so as to keep the city from King ʿAbdallāh and the Israelis. By then, the Israeli side had withdrawn its support of territorial internationalization (but was prepared to accept functional internationalization), or extraterritoriality, of the holy sites. King ʿAbdallāh was unalterably opposed to internationalization from the start, and certainly when half the city was in his hands.

Thus the long parade of proposals, plans, and commission reports ultimately came to naught, and the fate of the city was determined by facts—demographic, political, and strategic—established by the two main local players at the time, the Israelis and Jordanians. Thirty years of plans to solve the Jerusalem question bore no fruit. No foreign power or international body could impose any solution acceptable to the people of Jerusalem themselves, who, with their conflicting national feelings and political interests, were alone in determining the fate of the holy city.

Although none of the plans projected during and after the Mandate period created a settlement of the Jerusalem problem, a number have more than historical interest, particularly those relating to municipal organization (see Chapter 2 by Alisa Ginio). Borough (or arrondissement) systems under a municipal council were proposed in various forms and shapes by Chaim Arlosoroff and B. Campbell (1932), Daniel Auster (1933), and Sir William

Fitzgerald (1945), and provide an intriguing backdrop for Mayor Teddy Kollek's suggestions for a borough system (see his Introduction). And Daniel J. Elazar, in his chapter on local government for heterogeneous populations, also lists a borough system as one of the options for Jerusalem. Other options he proffers envisage a capital district providing extraterritorial status for specific sites and residents; a county having separate municipalities with an overall governing council (see the proposal by Sir William Fitzgerald); a confederation of separate entities united for purposes of municipal administration; or some kind of "consociational arrangement."

While Elazar assesses that an eventual formal institutionalization of hitherto ad hoc solutions is both inevitable and desirable, he estimates that Jerusalem, under its present administration, has managed as well as, and perhaps better than, other modern cities in governing hetcrogcneous populations, and he observes that it already contains many elements of consociationalism. He presents the main dilemma of the Jerusalem municipal government thusly. While in the premodern past unity had to be imposed from above by an overarching autocracy or an imperial power, the dilemma at present is how to achieve unity within a democratic framework. In this respect, he says, one of the impressive achievements of the post-1967 Jerusalem Municipality has been its success in managing to govern a heterogeneous population along reasonably democratic lines.

The record of solving the problems of heterogeneous populations in other cities is rather discouraging, if one wishes to seek solace from this quarter. This conclusion emerges from the chapter by Emanuel Gutmann and Claude Klein on the institutional structure of heterogeneous cities (Brussels, Montreal, Belfast). The internal conflicts in these cities have recently become more severe and solutions more remote. The three cities, particularly Belfast, have much in common with Jerusalem. The conflicts in these cities are facets of a wider struggle, and they are intense and intractable insofar as the crucial issues pertain to primal loyalties: ethnonational divisions and conflicting political allegiances. However, even when parallels are drawn, Gutmann and Klein stress the unique aspects of the Jerusalem situation. The conflicting claims of sovereignty are keener and a national consensus does not exist at all. Moreover, Jerusalem as the site of the Holy Places is the cynosure of millions of believers and the focus of international concern. The authors make the pessimistic assessment that conflicts stemming from national and religious or communal divisions are not significantly relieved by fair administration, nor can they be effectively alleviated by economic advantages accruing from good government.

Thus the demographic and economic boom in the Arab sector of Jerusalem after its annexation by Israel in 1967, documented by Israel Kimhi and Benjamin Hyman in their survey of demographic and economic developments, may compensate to a limited extent for what East Jerusalem residents perceive as an unfavorable political situation. The neglect of the city during 19 years of Jordanian control (reflected in the deliberations of the Municipal Council discussed by Daniel Rubinstein in his chapter) may have been resented by Jerusalemite Arabs, but Israeli rule is resisted (see the chapter by Uzi Benziman), if only passively, for the most part.[13] The exemplary fairness of the Israeli administration may take the sting out of Arab resistance, but neither fairness nor prosperity answers the basic political and national strivings of the Arab population of East Jerusalem.

The means by which the Jerusalem Municipality and the Israeli governing authorities have managed a potentially explosive situation have been signally flexible and pragmatic. This is the dominant theme of Benziman's chapter on Israeli policy in East Jerusalem after reunification. While annexing the territory of East Jerusalem (an act that received no international support), the Israeli authorities granted the residents a considerable amount of autonomy, even bending the law to do so. It is fascinating to read how both sides, by mutual adjustment, established the rules of the game. While pragmatic flexibility has enabled the Israelis to manage a complicated situation, there is realization that the ad hoc measures adopted can hardly become permanent. They were imposed unilaterally, and for a more far-reaching solution Arab attitudes must come into play. On the other hand, the de facto cooperation on many issues, and collaboration in the past between Israel and Jordan, give cause for some optimism that solutions can be found.

Nor can the sentiments of Muslim believers throughout the world be overlooked. And Christian concern for the holy city has been long-standing and fervent (see Saul P. Colbi's chapter on the Christian establishment). The vital difference between Muslim and Christian attitudes may be formulated as follows. The Muslims insist upon sovereignty, at least over Arab Jerusalem, whereas (non-Arab) Christians are mainly concerned with the safety of Christian Holy Places. Although this concern often leads to calls for internationalization, guarantees and safeguards for the religious sites remain paramount.

The status of Jerusalem as a city holy to three faiths has made it the focal point of passionate confrontation. Although Judaism, Christianity, and Islam have in common a shared view of the sacredness of Jerusalem, the position of the city in the consciousness of the three groups is of a different order and value. And the distinctive and divergent, as well as the shared, ought to be brought into perspective.[14]

The Jewish people, throughout history, have remained indissolubly bound to Jerusalem, the heart of their national and religious existence. Israel became a nation when David made Jebus, or Zion, his capital, the City of David, and brought the Ark of the Lord from Kiriath-jearim, after a period of wandering and homelessness, to its permanent resting place in Jerusalem.

Jerusalem thus became the national capital of the United Monarchy.[15] The kingdom was consolidated by Solomon, who founded the First Temple, built a royal palace, and transformed Jerusalem into a religious and political metropolis. The city must have had cultic significance prior to the time of David and Solomon. According to Genesis 14:18, Salem (identified in Psalm 16:13 with Jerusalem) was ruled by Melchizedek, a priest-king of El Elyon (God Most High). And the threshing floor of Arauna, where the Ark came to rest, appears to have been a cultic center. It is not certain, however, that the name "Jerusalem" means "Foundation of (the god) Shalem"—an etymology that has gained scholarly acceptance.

Although we should like to say something positive about the name of this important city, it is so ancient that its meaning is shrouded in philological and historical mystery. With the greatest of reservation it may be suggested that the first element (*Yeru-*) reflects the Sumerian word for city (URU) and that the element *sh-l-m* is an epithet having something to do with the idea of "wholeness, perfection, good order," possibly "peace," and may be an attribute of an unknown god.[16] An ancient folk etymology takes "Jerusalem" to mean the "City of Peace" (see Psalm 122 and especially Hebrews 7:2), and so it has come to be understood by posterity.

Even when the state lost its independence or ceased to exist, Jerusalem remained the capital of the Jewish people. Thus, during the time of the First Exile, after the destruction of Jerusalem and the First Temple by the Babylonians in 586 B.C., Jerusalem was remembered with veneration and envisioned by prophets as the future site of a rebuilt sanctuary and center of a reconstituted commonwealth. During the period of the Roman occupation of Judea (from 63 B.C.) Jerusalem became the metropolis of the Jewish Diaspora.[17] Jews maintained contact with their city by contributions to the Temple (the half shekel and votive donations) and by pilgrimages and settlement in its precincts—as Saul (later the apostle Paul) came from Tarsus in Cilicia to Jerusalem to study at the feet of Rabban Gamaliel (Acts 22:3) and as Hillel came from Babylonia to study with Shemaiah and Abtalion (Talmud, b.Yoma 35b).[18]

Despite the loss of political independence, King Herod the Great accentuated the sacredness of the city by means of a monumental reconstruction of the Temple and its enclosure walls, part of which stand until the present day. Under this Roman vassal-king, Jerusalem reached the peak of its majestic splendor. The Great, or First, Revolt against the Romans (A.D. 66–70) restored Jerusalem as the liberated national capital.

After the catastrophic destruction of the city and the Temple by Titus, Jerusalem became a desolate city occupied by the Roman Tenth Legion, and Judea became "Judaea Capta," as was inscribed on Roman coins commemorating the triumph. When the emperor Hadrian set out to transform Jerusalem into a pagan Roman city, the Jews, under the leadership of Simon bar Koziba (Bar Kokhba), revolted against Roman rule (A.D. 132-135).[19] They succeeded in reconquering Jerusalem, evicted the Romans, and reconstituted the Jewish state. Coins with Hebrew inscriptions were struck bearing the date of "The Redemption of Israel," "The Freedom of Israel," or "The Freedom of Jerusalem." When the revolt was suppressed, Jews were prohibited from dwelling in Jerusalem or visiting there, and the Roman colony of Aelia Capitolina, founded on the Ninth of Ab 135, totally replaced the Jewish city.[20] The Romans also replaced the name "Judea" with "Syria Palestine" as the official name of the country, with the same purpose of obliterating its Jewish identity.[21]

After the fall of Jerusalem, without ever losing its status as national and religious center, the city was lifted to a plane of cosmic and eschatological significance in rabbinic theology. The symbol of national rebirth became also the symbol of universal salvation. This rabbinic doctrine was, of course, anchored in biblical prophecy.[22] In contrast to Jewish apocalyptic and Christian motifs, rabbinic thought gives precedence to the historical-eschatological new Jerusalem over the metahistorical-celestial city. Rabbi Johanan (second century) quotes the Lord as saying, "I shall not enter the heavenly Jerusalem until I have entered the earthly Jerusalem."[23] The earthly city is prior. In the same spirit, in a late *midrash*, the heavenly Jerusalem is said to be patterned after the earthly city, and not the reverse.[24] The sages were consciously reacting to apocalyptic visions of the descent to earth of a resplendent heavenly city. The terrestrial city, in their view, will not descend from heaven but will be constructed by men upon earth. The Jerusalem below is the archetype of the Jerusalem above, and not the reverse.[25]

In both biblical and rabbinic lore and legend, Jerusalem becomes the site of the central events of human history. The Foundation Stone (*even hashetiyyah*) in the Holy of Holies is the navel (*omphalos*) of the universe, where the world was generated. Here, Adam was created. In Jerusalem (Salem), Abraham was blessed by Melchizedek, who promised him victory over his enemies and took from him a tithe from everything. On Mount Moriah, identified in biblical lore with the Temple Mount, Abraham offered his son Isaac upon the altar.[26] And in Jerusalem the final redemption of mankind will take place.

Throughout centuries of exile the Jewish people nurtured hopes of redemption and restoration of their ancient city, mourned its destruction, turned to it in prayer, remembered it at times of joy, and visited it in its desolation. When the modern Jewish national movement was born, it called itself "Zionism" after the ancient name of the city. (Zion first was a part of the city, David's City, and then it came to mean the whole city and by extension the entire land.) The national anthem expressed the hope to return to "the land of Zion and Jerusalem." Jerusalem stands for the whole. For Judaism, veneration for Jerusalem does not hinge upon holy sites sacralized by holy events, real or legendary, but upon the city itself. There is only the Wall, and

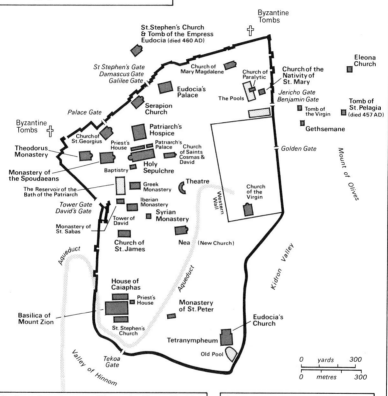

BYZANTINE JERUSALEM
324 AD - 629 AD

In 324 AD Jerusalem came under the rule, from Byzantium (later Constantinople), of the Christian Emperor Constantine. Two years later his mother Helena visited Jerusalem, where she 'located' several Christian sites and relics. The Temple of Venus was destroyed, the Church of the Holy Sepulchre dedicated on the same site in 335, and the Eleona Church built on the Mount of Olives.

The walls of Jerusalem in Byzantine times.

The old Roman aqueduct, kept under repair and continuing to bring water from Solomon's Pools in Byzantine times.

Principal buildings constructed during Byzantine rule.

Byzantine Tombs

St.Stephen's Church & Tomb of the Empress Eudocia (died 460 AD)

Eleona Church

St Stephen's Gate
Damascus Gate
Galilee Gate

Church of Mary Magdalene

Church of Paralytic

Church of the Nativity of St. Mary

Eudocia's Palace

The Pools

Jericho Gate
Benjamin Gate

Tomb of St.Pelagia (died 457 AD)

Serapion Church

Tomb of the Virgin

Palace Gate

Byzantine Tombs

Patriarch's Hospice

Gethsemane

Church of St.Georgius

Priest's House

Patriarch's Palace

Church of Saints Cosmas & David

Golden Gate

Mount of Olives

Theodorus Monastery

Holy Sepulchre

Monastery of the Spoudaeans

Baptistry

The Reservoir of the Bath of the Patriarch

Greek Monastery

Theatre

Church of the Virgin

Tower Gate
David's Gate

Iberian Monastery

Western Wall

Tower of David

Syrian Monastery

Monastery of St. Sabas

Church of St.James

Nea (New Church)

Kidron Valley

Aqueduct

Aqueduct

House of Caiaphas

Priest's House

Monastery of St.Peter

Eudocia's Church

Basilica of Mount Zion

Tetranympheum

St.Stephen's Church

Old Pool

Valley of Hinnom

Tekoa Gate

| 0 | yards | 300 |
| 0 | metres | 300 |

Under Byzantine rule, several Roman families settled in the City, many Christian churches were founded, and the city was rebuilt within its walls. Jews were forbidden to enter the city except on the 9th of Av, when they were allowed to lament the destruction of the Temple. The Empress Eudocia, who first visited the city in 438, allowed the Jews to return. In 614 the Persians, having conquered the city, handed it over to the Jews. But with the return of the Byzantines in 629, the Jews were again expelled.

'On the 15th September, annually, an immense number of people of different nations are used to meet in Jerusalem for the purpose of commerce, and the streets are so clogged with the dung of camels, horses, mules and oxen, that they become almost impassable'.

BISHOP ARCULF OF GAUL
680 AD

© Martin Gilbert 1977

the Wall stands for the Temple, and the Temple for the city in its glory. The rebirth of the Jewish people in their national home and the rebuilding of Jerusalem are intimately related. The one cannot happen without the other.[27]

For Christians, Jerusalem is the scene of the decisive events in the Gospels, particularly in the life of Jesus—his preaching, the end of his ministry, and his passion, resurrection, and ascension. Here was born the earliest church and the first Christian community. Thus historical facts and religious belief generated Holy Places.[28] Holy Places tied to holy events were related to terrestrial Jerusalem. But in Christianity a fundamental ambiguity set in, of literalism versus allegory and of the terrestrial versus the celestial city.

A "deterritorialization" of the sacredness of place is already discernible in the New Testament. It is not the Holy of Holies that is the center, but Christ, and the holy area is the body of Christ and the new community. When Jesus speaks of the impending destruction of the Temple (John 2:19; cf. Mark 14:58 and Matthew 26:61), Christian exegesis understands the Temple to mean the resurrected body of Jesus (John 2:21-22). Mount Zion and the city of the living God are identified with the heavenly Jerusalem (Epistle to the Hebrews 12:22-23). The celestial city is the archetype of the Church (*mater ecclesia*), which is its terrestrial reflection. In contrast to "the Jerusalem of the present" (*hē nun Ierousalēm*), we do not find the future Jerusalem but "the Jerusalem which is above" (*hē anō Ierousalēm*): "the Jerusalem which is above" is "the mother of us all" (Galatians 4:26).[29]

The "holy geography," the marking of Holy Places where sacred events occurred, received a powerful impetus during the age of Constantine the Great, when pagan Aelia Capitolina was transformed into the spiritual capital of the new Christian Roman Empire. Jerusalem was rebuilt as a Christian city. Christian Holy Places were erected on sites of pagan temples in an effort to lend political and religious legitimacy to the new order. Whereas the ruins of Aelia Capitolina had served as mute testimony to the curse resting upon the Jews, the rebuilt Christian city became new proof of the validity of the faith. And the real physical city became a concrete symbol of Christianity's victory over both paganism and Judaism.[30]

The new stress on the physical city, the founding of Holy Places, and the consequent flow of pilgrims and relic collectors provoked an opposite reaction because they ran counter to the profound spiritualizing strain of early Christianity. The spiritual character of the New Jerusalem was taught by Doctors of the Church (such as St. Jerome, St. Augustine, St. Gregory of Nyssa). St. Jerome, for example, who even objected to pilgrimages to holy sites, stated that "the heavenly sanctuary is open from Britain no less than from Jerusalem, and the Kingdom of God is within you."[31] In a later age the Protestant reformers were also to preach that the true earthly Jerusalem exists wherever the perfect Christian life is lived, an idea that pervades Christian hymnology.[32]

While the spiritual symbol of heavenly Jerusalem became the dominant current, visions of a restoration of the real terrestrial city continued to emerge. And ancient Old Testament themes lived on in popular consciousness, awakening a yearning for the real city. The spiritualization of Jerusalem was offset by "sacred topography," the function of the city as a mnemonic of sacred events marked by shrines visited by pilgrims, and especially by the eruption of religious passion at the time of the great "peregrinatio," the Crusades.[33]

The motives of the Crusaders were a blend of pragmatism and idealism, a desire to free the Holy Places (and Christ) from Muslim captivity and an expectation that the Kingdom of Heaven would descend upon Mount Zion and a new world order be founded. When the Crusaders conquered Jerusalem in 1099, they established their capital there, certainly for its symbolic religious value, as, from any practical consideration, it was eminently unsuitable. The city had not been a capital from the time of the destruction of the Second Temple (or the Bar Kokhba revolt), nor was it to be from the end of the Crusader occupation of Jerusalem (1244) until 1917 when the British captured the city from the Muslim Ottoman Turks. Indeed, it was not even a regional administrative center, except for the purely local Ottoman sanjak, or district, of Jerusalem.

Whereas Godfrey of Bouillon was called by the ambiguous title "Advocate of the Holy Sepulchre," his successor Baldwin I proclaimed himself "King of the Kingdom of Jerusalem." Consciously invoking biblical associations, he had himself crowned in the Basilica of the Nativity in Bethlehem and announced a restored Kingdom of David. The Crusader Kingdom was named "Kingdom of Jerusalem," "Jerusalemite Kingdom," and "Kingdom of David." Biblical associations also moved the Crusaders to appropriate the mosques on the Temple Mount, so that the Dome of the Rock became the Temple of the Lord (Templum Domini) and the al-Aqṣā Mosque, the Temple of Solomon (Templum Solomonis).

It is not surprising that holy geography, which flourished in Byzantine Jerusalem, was given impetus during the Crusader period.[34] Jews and Muslims were prohibited from settling in the city. Only after its reconquest by Saladin (in 1187) were they permitted to return. The failure of the Crusades dampened Christian enthusiasm for earthly Jerusalem.[35]

The Christian attitude toward the terrestrial city embodies another ambiguity stemming from the ambivalence of Christianity toward Judaism and the Jews. Before the Jewish revolt of A.D. 66–70, Christianity was a Jewish messianic sect with its center in Jerusalem. When Christianity was transformed from a national sect into a universal Savior-God religion, Jerusalem ceased being the center of the church. It remained the center only for Jewish-

CRUSADER JERUSALEM

Once Jerusalem had been conquered by the Crusaders, as many as 10,000 Christian pilgrims made the journey every year, some from as far away as Scandinavia, Muscovy and Portugal; and each year a small number of these pilgrims decided to remain permanently in the city.

Following the Crusader entry into Jerusalem in 1099, all the Jews in the City were either murdered, sold into slavery in Europe, or ransomed to the Jewish community of Egypt. The Crusaders then brought Christian Arab tribes from east of the river Jordan, and settled them in the former Jewish Quarter, between St. Stephen's Gate and the Gate of Jehoshafat.

■ Principal Crusader buildings.

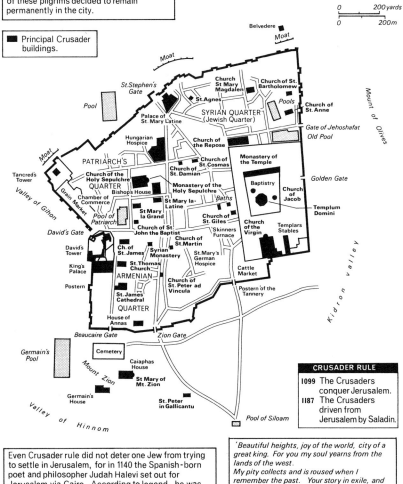

0   200 yards
0   200 m

Belvedere

Moat

Moat

St.Stephen's Gate

Church St Mary Magdalen

Church of St. Bartholomew

St.Agnes

SYRIAN QUARTER (Jewish Quarter)

Pools

Church of St.Anne

Pool

Palace of St. Mary Latine

Gate of Jehoshafat
Old Pool

Hungarian Hospice

Church of the Repose

Mount of Olives

PATRIARCH'S

Church of St.Cosmas

Monastery of the Temple

Church of St. Damian

QUARTER

Church of the Holy Sepulchre

Baptistry

Golden Gate

Tancred's Tower

Bishop's House

Monastery of the Holy Sepulchre

Church of Jacob

Valley of Gihon

Grain Market

Chamber of Commerce

St Mary la-Latine

Baths

Templum Domini

Pool of Patriarch

St Mary la Grand

Church of St. Giles

Church of the Virgin

Templars Stables

David's Gate

Church of St. John the Baptist

Skinners Furnace

David's Tower

Ch. of St.James

Syrian Monastery

Church of St.Martin

St.Mary's German Hospice

King's Palace

St.Thomas Church

ARMENIAN

Cattle Market

Kidron Valley

Postern

Church of St.Peter ad Vincula

Postern of the Tannery

St.James Cathedral

QUARTER

House of Annas

Beaucaire Gate

Zion Gate

Germain's Pool

Cemetery

Caiaphas House

Mount Zion

St Mary of Mt. Zion

CRUSADER RULE

1099 The Crusaders conquer Jerusalem.

1187 The Crusaders driven from Jerusalem by Saladin.

Germain's House

St.Peter in Gallicantu

Pool of Siloam

Valley of Hinnom

Even Crusader rule did not deter one Jew from trying to settle in Jerusalem, for in 1140 the Spanish-born poet and philosopher Judah Halevi set out for Jerusalem via Cairo. According to legend, he was approaching the City Walls when an Arab horseman, leaving by one of the Gates, trampled him to death. As he lay dying he is said to have recited one of his own poems: "Zion, shall I not seek thee".

'Beautiful heights, joy of the world, city of a great king. For you my soul yearns from the lands of the west.
My pity collects and is roused when I remember the past. Your story in exile, and your Temple destroyed....
I shall cherish your stones and kiss them. And your earth will be sweeter than honey to my taste'.
JUDAH HALEVI
c. 1140

Christian sects. These sects faced Jerusalem in prayer. The Church of Jerusalem was extinguished and others, especially that of Rome, rose to prominence in its place. Whereas Jerusalem remained forever the center for Jews and Mecca or Istanbul the center for Muslims, the center of Christendom was transferred to Rome, an expression of its universal mission.[36]

While not becoming the central abode of the authority of the church, Jerusalem was extinguished and others, especially that of Rome, rose to prominence in its place. Whereas Jerusalem remained forever the center for Jews sus developed according to which the New Jerusalem could not pertain to the Jews, nor could they rebuild the city save as potential or actual converts. For the Jews, *Hieroselyma est perdita*—"Jerusalem is lost."

Thus the destruction of city and Temple by the pagan Romans, as well as the exile, were viewed as just divine punishment for rejection of Jesus and as fulfillment of his prophecy that "There will not be left here one stone upon another, that will not be thrown down" (Matthew 24:2; Mark 13:2). Constantine not only gave Jerusalem a Christian aura but renewed (probably in 335, when the Church of the Holy Sepulchre was consecrated) the Hadrianic prohibition against Jews dwelling in or visiting the city. Only on the Ninth of Ab were Jews permitted to visit Jerusalem. The prohibition was later renewed by Emperor Heraclius when he reconquered Jerusalem in 630 (after it had been conquered by the Persians in 614) and restored the Cross to the Church of the Holy Sepulchre. Again, when the Crusaders conquered the city in 1099, the Constantinian prohibitions were renewed.

A rebuilt Jewish Jerusalem consequently becomes a theological embarrassment and evokes an ambivalent response to Israel revidivus. This is relieved on the part of some Christians by severing the modern return from its biblical roots. Yet, for others, a rebuilt Jerusalem and restored Israel are viewed as fulfillment of biblical prophecy. There is, for example, the synoptic apocalypse in Luke 21:20–28.[38] Jesus prophesied the destruction of Jerusalem and its liberation in the latter days when the Messiah comes. The restored Israel and rebuilt Jerusalem are the "beginning of redemption," signs of the coming of the last days, just as for some pious Jews. The difference is that the Christians believe that all Israel will accept belief in Jesus (cf. Paul in Romans 11:26: "And so all Israel will be saved"), who will appear in the Second Coming as the Messiah.[39]

According to Islamic tradition, Jerusalem was the first direction of prayer (*qibla*) of the Muslims.[40] Not long after Muḥammad's emigration (*hijra*) to Medina, however, the qibla was changed to Mecca, and so it has remained until the present. Jerusalem attained its sacred character in Islam on the basis of the tradition of Muḥammad's night journey from Mecca to Jerusalem and his heavenly ascent, believed to have taken place from a site on the Temple Mount (Ḥaram al-Sharīf, "the Noble Sanctuary").[41] The Qur'ān (17:1) speaks of the night journey of "God's servant" from the sacred mosque (in

Mecca) to the farthest mosque (al-masjid al-aqṣā). The verse is unclear as to the location and identity of "the farthest mosque."[42]

In earlier Muslim exegesis the nocturnal journey to the farthest mosque was understood to be to a heavenly place, either in reality or in ecstatic vision. And some older traditions relate the ascension to heaven to the prophetic initiation, thus taking place from Mecca. Later traditions located the farthest mosque in Jerusalem. The identification of the farthest mosque with a site in Jerusalem was not made earlier than the second century A.H./eighth century A.D.

A harmonizing exegesis, which became consensus, fused the two versions. First the night journey to Jerusalem, and then from there the ascent to heaven. It is quite possible that the original intention of the verse was to a heavenly sanctuary, or to celestial Jerusalem. The location of the farthest mosque in a specific place in terrestrial Jerusalem may have been related to the endeavor of the Syria-based Umayyad dynasty to enhance the status of Jerusalem. In any case, it was a Syrian tradition that prevailed here.[43]

The Temple Mount first came to the attention of the Muslims when they conquered Jerusalem in A.D. 638. According to various accounts, the Caliph ᶜUmar ibn al-Khaṭṭāb visited Jerusalem in person; according to one version, he came to the city to accept its surrender by the Patriarch Sophronios, who received from the caliph a treaty guaranteeing safety for the lives, possessions, churches, and crosses of the people of Jerusalem, and stipulating that no Jew was to live with them.[44] A number of texts portray the caliph's visit to the Temple Mount. According to one narrative, ᶜUmar asked a Jewish convert to Islam named Kaᶜb al-Aḥbār where the Rock (that is, the Foundation Stone of the Holy of Holies) was located.[45] When Kaᶜb indicated its location, ᶜUmar asked him where the place of worship he intended to build should be placed. Kaᶜb replied that is should be erected behind (north of) the Rock, so that both qiblas, of Moses and Muḥammad, would be united. ᶜUmar rejected the suggestion as a judaizing tendency and elected to build the mosque in front (to the south) of the Rock.[46]

According to another version of this visit, when ᶜUmar had cleared the holy site of the refuse covering it, which has been deliberately placed there by the Byzantine Christians, Kaᶜb al-Aḥbār informed the caliph that 500 years previously (around the time the Bar Kokhba revolt was suppressed) a prophet foretold what ᶜUmar would do on that day. Kaᶜb then recapitulated the conquests of the city from the time of the Byzantines and ended by stating that God sent a prophet who said, "Rejoice, O Jerusalem. The Redeemer (Fārūq) will come and cleanse you [of the refuse]."[47] In the same spirit, a story is told of a Damascene Jew who greeted ᶜUmar as the Redeemer (Fārūq) who would conquer Jerusalem.[48]

These accounts from Muslim sources and late Jewish apocalypses, as well as a number of Christian sources, suggest that at the time of the Muslim conquest of Syria and Palestine the Jews harbored messianic hopes and regarded the conquest, which freed them of the Byzantine yoke, as a preliminary sign of redemption.[49] In any case, whatever Jewish expectations might have been, the flow of events was such that the Muslims did not permit them to rebuild their Temple but rather appropriated for themselves the traditional sacredness of the spot.

ʿUmar reportedly had a mosque built on the Temple Mount, presumably where the al-Aqṣā Mosque stands today. The Frankish Bishop Arculf, visiting Jerusalem about 670, described a simple wooden mosque built where the Temple once stood "in all its splendor," which may have been this structure.[50] (It may, however, have been built during the period of the Umayyad Caliph Muʿāwiya.) The Dome of the Rock was built by Caliph ʿAbd al-Malik (completed in 72/691–692) over what was believed to be the Foundation Stone, which stood in the Holy of Holies of the Temple, and where, according to Jewish tradition, Abraham offered to sacrifice his son Isaac.

The original significance of the Rock was not to mark the place of Muḥammad's ascension, as it later came to be, for none of the many Quarānic inscriptions in the mosque—a ciborium or reliquary built over a sacred spot—refers to the relevant verse in the Qur'ān (17:1). The Quarānic inscriptions in the mosque adumbrate the significance of the structure. The verses proclaim Islam as the final true revelation. And they are directed in a missionary spirit toward the Christians and Jews, especially the former, inviting them to submit to the faith of Islam, which acknowledges the Hebrew and Christian prophets as precursors. Islam is not pronounced a new faith but the culmination of the faith of the People of the Book. The decorative motifs in the Dome of the Rock consciously use symbols to demonstrate that the enemies of Islam, the Byzantines and Persians, have been subdued. Thus the inscriptions and artistic motifs and the building itself powerfully assert the supreme religious and political might of the faith of Islam.[51]

At first, the Muslim conquerors called the city Īliyā', from Aelia (Capitolina), a name that was preserved by the Byzantines. The name "Jerusalem" was not adopted by the Muslims, although it came to be used (in the form Ūrshalīm) by Christian Arabs. The principal name of the city during the Arab period (638–1099) was Bayt al-Maqdis (cf. Hebrew Bet Hamiqdash), meaning either the Ḥaram al-Sharīf area or the entire city (as in Hebrew). The name al-Quds (cf. Hebrew [ʿIr] Haqodesh), the present-day Arabic name for the city, came into currency in the tenth century and gradually replaced the longer appellation. As its names indicate, the significance of the city was mainly religious. The administrative capital of the country was established in the town of Ramleh, newly founded in place of the Christian town of Lydda, by Süleyman, son of ʿAbd al-Malik, in 705.

The holiness attached to Jerusalem, along with the adoption of sites in the city as sacred, was not unanimous. By the beginning of the second century A.H. (100/A.D. 718), a consensus emerged affirming the sanctity of the mosques of Mecca, Medina, and Jerusalem (al-Aqṣā).[52] But this consensus was achieved after a struggle wherein the surpassing sanctity of Mecca and Medina were stressed and that of Jerusalem downgraded in an effort to discourage excessive veneration for its sanctity. Moreover, Muslim scholars were aware that many beliefs surrounding Jerusalem were of Jewish provenance and attacked them as judaizing heresies. Muṭahhar ibn Ṭāhir al-Maqdisī, a tenth-century Jerusalemite, denied that the Resurrection will take place in Jerusalem—a popular Muslim belief—alleging that this is a Jewish doctrine. Two Ḥanbalī scholars of the fourteenth century also protested against veneration for Jerusalem. Ibn Kathīr claimed that the belief that the Last Judgment would take place in Jerusalem was a local invention to attract tourism. And Ibn Taymiyya wrote a treatise against the exaggerated claims made for Jerusalem, asserting that beliefs concerning the sanctuary and the Rock were of Jewish and Christian origin.[53]

When finally adopted as sacred, the legends regarding Jerusalem's holiness reflect the influence of Jewish and Christian belief and practice, transmitted by converts; for example, the events relating to the Last Judgment, the notion that the Rock is the navel of the universe, is beneath God's throne, is part of paradise, and so on. Even when Jerusalem was given sacred status, it was never given the rank of Mecca and Medina. The pilgrimage (*ḥājj*) to the holy places in Mecca and Medina is a religious obligation and a pillar of the faith, whereas the visit (*ziyāra*) to Jerusalem is a recommended pious act like visits to many other Holy Places.

The stress on Jerusalem's sanctity often reflects the interest of others, as the reaction to the Crusades, to the European preoccupation with the Holy Places in the nineteenth century, and to Zionism and Israel in the twentieth. In the intervals Muslims exhibited limited interest in the city. The fall of Jerusalem to the Crusaders (1099) did not at first have an impact on them.[54] The delayed reaction may be ascribed to several factors: The idea of sanctity had been weakened by those legal scholars who countered excessive veneration for Jerusalem; the veneration was a local phenomenon concentrated in Syria and Palestine; and Jerusalem itself was unimportant demographically, intellectually, and politically.

When Zangī, ruler of Mosul and Aleppo, declared a holy war against the Crusaders (c. 1150), this relaxed attitude changed. The sanctity of the city was stressed so as to mobilize Muslim forces for the holy war. Zangī's son, Nūr al-Dīn, in his campaign to unite Syria, stressed the sacredness of the city and the significance of al-Aqṣā as the navel of the universe and site of the ascension. At this time a genre of literature called *Faḍā'il al-Quds* (''Merits of Jerusalem'') flourished.[55] It had begun earlier at the beginning of the eleventh century, and had been somewhat dormant during the first half century after the Crusader conquest. The trend of sanctification of Jerusalem was intensified by Saladin and reached a high watermark at the time of his reconquest of the city in 1187. But some years later, in 1229, the Muslims lost interest in the city to such an extent that they were willing to surrender it peacefully to Frederick II.

When the European powers began to take active interest in the Holy Places in the nineteenth century, the attention of the Ottoman rulers became riveted upon the city. The establishment of Jerusalem as the capital under the British Mandate once again placed the city in the limelight, and the Zionist movement, which emblazoned Jerusalem on its banner, evoked a reaction among Muslims, who perceived a threat to the sanctuaries of the Ḥaram al-Sharīf.

The annexation of East Jerusalem and unification of the city under Israeli sovereignty after the 1967 June War stirred deep agitation in the Muslim world and within international forums. Again Jerusalem became a focus of Muslim attention, its religious and political significance accentuated, although sporadic voices were raised against the promotion of the city to an overly exalted status.[56] Christians had become inured through centuries of Muslim rule to Muslim sovereignty over Jerusalem and the Holy Places, and Muslims had known Christian rule; but for both Christians and Muslims, Jewish sovereignty was novel and unknown. Although the Israeli authorities were scrupulous in guaranteeing protection of and access to the Holy Places of all faiths, Jerusalem once again became an international issue, a central element in the local and international struggle concerning the future of the Holy Land.

NOTES

1. On the issue of the Holy Places, see E. Lauterpacht, *Jerusalem and the Holy Places* (London: Anglo-Israel Association, 1968), especially Ch. 1, on sovereignty and the Holy Places. See also S. Berkovitz, "The Legal Status of the Holy Places in Israel," thesis submitted to the Senate of the Hebrew University (Hebrew, with English summary) (Jerusalem, 1978). See also B. Collin, *Pour une solution au problème des Lieux Saints* (Paris: Maisonneuve et Larose, 1974); and W. Zander, *Israel and the Holy Places of Christendom* (London: Weidenfeld and Nicolson, 1971).

2. On Jerusalem during the Ottoman period, see for general orientation M. Maʿoz, ed., *Studies in Palestine During the Ottoman Period* (Jerusalem: Magnes Press, 1975); and the useful survey by H. Z. Hirschberg, W. P. Pick, and J. Kaniel (Mershine), in *Jerusalem* (Jerusalem: Keter Publishing House, 1973) (Keter Books; originally published in the *Encyclopaedia Judaica*), pp. 77–142. See also E. Ashtor, "Jerusalem in the Late Middle Ages" (Hebrew), in *Yerushalayim*, vol. 2, 5 (Jerusalem, 1955), pp. 71–116; and U. Heyd, "Jerusalem Under the Mamluks and the Turks" (Hebrew, with English summary), in *Jerusalem Through the Ages* (Jerusalem: Israel Exploration Society, 1968), pp. 193–202. For the nineteenth century, see Y. Ben-Arieh, *A City Reflected in Its Times: Jerusalem in the Nineteenth Century, The Old City* (Hebrew) (Jerusalem: Yad Izhak Ben-Zvi Publications, 1977). A second volume appeared in 1979. See also ʿArif al-ʿArif, *al-Mufaṣṣal fī taʾrīkh al-quds* (Jerusalem: al-Andalus Library, 1961), pp. 263–368.

3. The Ottoman Status Quo did not pertain to Muslim (since the dynasty was Muslim) or Jewish sacred sites. During the British Mandate, two Jewish sites were added to the seven Christian Holy Places covered by the Status Quo—the Western Wall and Rachel's Tomb near Bethlehem; Berkovitz, *Legal Status*, p. 35.

4. Berkovitz, *Legal Status*, pp. 6, 9, 18, 293; Ben-Arieh, *A City Reflected in Its Times*, pp. 138, 176–79. According to Berkovitz, entrance by Jews to the Temple Mount had been prohibited since 1244, when Jerusalem was recovered by the Muslims from the Crusaders. He points out that nothing in Islamic law prohibits Jewish access to the site, and that in the early period of Muslim rule Jewish presence on the Temple Mount is attested, Jews even acting as caretakers at the Dome of the Rock. On these caretakers, at the time of the Caliph ʿAbd al-Malik (685–705), see Mujīr al-Dīn, *al-Uns al-jalī l fī ta'rī kh al-quds wal-khalī l* (Najaf, 1968), vol. 1, p. 281. (Mujīr al-Dīn's work, written in 1394–95, is the most important history of Jerusalem written by a Muslim scholar.) In the twentieth century, Muslims insisted that Jews be prohibited from entering the Temple Mount, and they were prevented from doing so during most of the British Mandate.

5. On the Mamluk period in Jerusalem, see E. Ashtor and H. Z. Hirschberg, in *Jerusalem* (Jerusalem: Keter Publishing House, 1973), pp. 69–76; Ashtor, "Jerusalem in the Late Middle Ages"; and J. Drory, "Jerusalem in the Mamluk Period" (Hebrew, with English summary), in *Jerusalem in the Middle Ages; Selected Papers*, ed. B. Z. Kedar and Z. Baras (Jerusalem: Yad Izhak Ben-Zvi, 1979), pp. 148–84. Mujīr al-Dīn's *al-Uns al-jalī l* has a wealth of material on Jerusalem during this period. See also ʿArif al-ʿArif, *al-Mufaṣṣal fī ta'rī kh al-quds*, pp. 207–32.

6. U. Heyd, *Ottoman Documents on Palestine 1552–1615* (Oxford: Oxford University Press, 1960), p. 76, no. 28.

7. Heyd, "Jerusalem Under the Mamluks and the Turks," p. 194, mentions the distinguished Muslim families of Dajānī, Anṣārī, Khalidī, Nusayba, ʿAlamī, Nashāshibī, and Husaynī; and the Christian notable families of Salāmeh, Tannūs, ʿAṭāllāh, Farrāj, and Kattān. Many members of these families were active in twentieth-century Jerusalem politics.

8. According to Mujīr al-Dīn, *al-Uns al-jalī l*, vol. 1, p. 257, the epithet "al-Qumāma" was applied by Muslims to the Church of the Holy Sepulchre in retaliation for the desecration of the site of "the Stone" (the Foundation Stone of the Holy of Holies) by the Byzantine Christians.

9. B. Lewis, "Baladiyya," *The Encyclopaedia of Islam*, new ed. (Leiden: Brill, 1960-   ), vol. 1, pp. 972–75; and S. J. Shaw and E. K. Shaw, *History of the Ottoman Empire and Modern Turkey*, vol. 2 (Cambridge: Cambridge University Press, 1977), pp. 92–93.

10. Ruth Kark, "Activities of the Jerusalem Municipality in the Ottoman Period" (Hebrew), *Cathedra* 6 (1977): 77.

11. Ibid., p. 92; and see Martin Gilbert, *Jerusalem; Illustrated History Atlas* (New York: Macmillan, 1977), p. 24. (Martin Gilbert kindly called my attention to the motive of the British in removing the clock tower.)

12. J. Prawer, *The Latin Kingdom of Jerusalem* (London: Weidenfeld and Nicolson, 1972), p. 39, observes that only peoples who regarded the Bible as a holy book (the Jews and Christians) made Jerusalem a capital. To be sure, the Muslims also regard the Bible as a holy book but not in the same way as do the Jews and Christians.

13. D. Rubinstein, in his chapter in this volume, treats protestations of discrimination on the part of Jerusalemite Arabs under the Jordanian administration as reflected in deliberations of the Municipal Council. N. Sofer, "The Political Status of Jerusalem in the Hashemite Kingdom of Jordan, 1948–1967," *Middle Eastern Studies* 12 (1976): 73–94, discusses Jerusalemites' claims of discrimination, their demands to make Jerusalem the capital of Jordan, and Jerusalem's role as a center of opposition to the Amman government. (Elie Kedouri kindly called my attention to this article.)

14. Much light is shed on this subject by R. J. Zwi Werblowsky in his "Jerusalem: Holy City of Three Religions," in *Jaarbericht ex Oriente Lux* 23 (1973–74): 423–39.

15. Jerusalem had been a Canaanite city from c. 2000 B.C. It is mentioned in the Egyptian Execration Texts (19th–18th centuries B.C.) and in the el-Amarna Letters (14th century B.C.). In the twelfth to eleventh centuries B.C. it was ruled by the Jebusites, a people of Hittite stock (see Ezekiel 16:3, and cf. II Samuel 11:6). Owing to its isolation and inaccessibility, Jerusalem was not conquered by the Israelite tribes and remained a foreign enclave within their midst. Its neutral position (it was located between Benjamin on the north and Judah on the south) made it ideally suited to be the capital of the United Monarchy.

16. For the etymology "Foundation of (the God) Shalem," see, for example, B. Mazar, "Jerusalem in the Biblical Period," in *Jerusalem Revealed: Archaeology in the Holy City 1968–1974* (Jerusalem: Israel Exploration Society, 1975), p. 1. The suggestion, tentatively offered here, is based upon personal communications by Y. Muffs and H. Tadmor.

17. Philo of Alexandria describes Jerusalem as the metropolis of the Jewish colonies of the Diaspora in *Flaccus*, 46; and *The Embassy to Gaius*, 281.

18. H. H. Ben-Sasson, ed., *A History of the Jewish People* (Cambridge, Mass.: Harvard University Press, 1976), pp. 266–68; and J. Jeremias, *Jerusalem in the Time of Jesus*, trans. F. H. and C. H. Cave (London: SCM Press, 1967), p. 242.

19. On the causes of the Bar Kokhba Revolt, see Y. Yadin, *Bar-Kokhba: The Rediscovery of the Legendary Hero of the Last Jewish Revolt Against Imperial Rome* (London: Weidenfeld and Nicolson, 1971), pp. 19–22.

20. It appears that the prohibition against Jewish settlement in Jerusalem was enforced, but visits to the city by Jews were more difficult to prevent; see A. Linder, "The Roman Imperial Government and the Jews Under Constantine" (Hebrew, with English summary), *Tarbiz* 44 (1975): 136–38, citing, inter alia, R. Harris, "Hadrian's Decree of Expulsion of the Jews from Jerusalem," *Harvard Theological Review* 19 (1926): 199–206. Linder states that the original prohibition dated from Hadrian's visit to Jerusalem in June-July 134, and was confirmed in 135, when Aelia Capitolina was founded. The appellation "Aelia Capitolina" is derived from the name of Hadrian (Publius Aelius Hadrianus) and the Capitoline triad of gods—Jupiter, Juno, and Minerva. Hadrian built a temple dedicated to Jupiter on the site of the Jewish Temple.

21. The Roman province of Palestine was divided by the Byzantines into three provinces: Palestina Prima, Secunda, and Tertia. Conquered by the Arabs (634–640 or 641), Byzantine Palaestina Prima became the *jund* (military district) of Filastin. The Arabs generally referred to the whole area of Syria-Palestine as al-Shām. Under the Mamluks and Ottomans (1260–1917) there was no province or administrative region of Palestine. This only began with the British Mandate and included at first both Cis-Jordan and Trans-Jordan.

22. Sh. Talmon, "The Biblical Concept of Jerusalem," in *Jerusalem*, ed. J. M. Oesterreicher and A. Sinai (New York: John Day, 1974), p. 200.

23. Talmud, b. Taʿanit 5a.

24. Tanḥuma, Pikkude 1.

25. On the rabbinic concept of heavenly Jerusalem, see E. E. Urbach, "The Heavenly and the Earthly Jerusalem in Rabbinic Thought," in *Jerusalem Through the Ages* (Jerusalem: Israel Exploration Society, 1968), pp. 156–71, where the texts cited in the two previous notes are discussed.

26. The meeting of Abraham with Melchizedek and the identification of Mount Moriah with the Temple Mount appear to be projections onto the patriarchal age of ideas about Jerusalem that developed during the period of the monarchy.

27. Talmon, "The Biblical Concept of Jerusalem," p. 202; Werblowsky, "Jerusalem," p. 437.

28. Werblowsky, "Jerusalem," pp. 433, 437–38.

29. Urbach, "The Heavenly and the Earthly Jerusalem," pp. 161–62; Werblowsky, "Jerusalem," p. 430; and W. D. Davies, "Jerusalem and the Land: The Christian Tradition," in *The Jerusalem Colloquium on Religion, People, Nation and Land*, ed. M. M. Tanenbaum and R. J. Z. Werblowsky (Jerusalem, 1972), pp. 115–54 (cited by Werblowsky). The idea that the earthly

city reflects the heavenly underlies the lovely medieval hymn of the Latin rite, sung when a new church is dedicated, beginning with the words: Urbs Jerusalem beata/Dicta pacis visio/Quae construitur in coelis/Vivis ex lapidibus (Jerusalem city blessed/Said to be a vision of peace/And it is built in heaven/Of living stones) (Werblowsky, "Jerusalem," p. 432). These verses appear at the heading of the chapter in Ronald Storrs' memoirs (*Orientations*, definitive edition [London: Nicolson and Watson, 1945]), p. 310, wherein the British military governor mentions his regulation that the buildings in Jerusalem be constructed out of stone—a fascinating application of the idea that the earthly city is a replica of the heavenly.

30. A. Linder, "Jerusalem as a Focal Point in the Conflict Between Judaism and Christianity" (Hebrew, with English summary), in *Jerusalem in the Middle Ages*, pp. 5–26; J. Prawer, "Christianity Between Heavenly and Earthly Jerusalem" (Hebrew, with English summary), in *Jerusalem Through the Ages*, pp. 183–84.

31. Werblowsky, "Jerusalem," p. 431; St. Jerome, Epistle 58 (*Patrologia Latina*, vol. 22, col. 581), cited by Werblowsky.

32. The Protestant movement, however, returned to earthly Jerusalem by means of Old Testament research. Among the ranks of biblically oriented Protestant scholars were many who grasped the significance of Zionism; see Prawer, "Christianity Between Heavenly and Earthly Jerusalem," p. 192; and Werblowsky, "Jerusalem," p. 431.

33. The discussion herein of the Crusades is based upon Prawer, *The Latin Kingdom of Jerusalem*; and S. Runciman, *A History of the Crusades* (New York: Harper & Row, 1964).

34. Prawer, "Jerusalem in Crusader Days," pp. 102–10.

35. Prawer, "Christianity Between Earthly and Heavenly Jerusalem," p. 191.

36. S. G. F. Brandon, *The Fall of Jerusalem and the Christian Church* (London: SPCK, 1968), passim.

37. H. Nibley, in *Jerusalem* (Jerusalem: Keter Publishing House, 1973), p. 317.

38. In this prophecy, as in Matthew 24:2 and Mark 13:2, Jesus predicts that Jerusalem will be destroyed ("and Jerusalem will be trodden down by the Gentiles"), but he adds the words "until the times of the Gentiles are fulfilled."

39. Nibley, in *Jerusalem*, pp. 319–20; D. Flusser, *Jewish Sources in Early Christianity* (Hebrew) (Tel Aviv: Sifriyat Po'alim, 1979), pp. 132–34, 253–54. Flusser cites H. Bietenhard, *Das tausenjährige Reich* (Zurich, 1955), pp. 90–94, and the author's observation that no detailed work on Christian "Zionism" has yet been written.

40. On the sanctity of Jerusalem and its place in Islam, see H. Busse, "The Sanctity of Jerusalem in Islam," *Judaism* 17 (1968): 441–68; S. D. Goitein, "The Sanctity of Jerusalem and Palestine in Early Islam," in *Studies in Islamic History and Institutions* (Leiden: Brill, 1966), pp. 135–48; M. J. Kister, "'You Shall Only Set Out for Three Mosques': A Study of an Early Tradition," *Le Muséon* 87 (1969): 173–96; H. Lazarus-Yafeh, "The Sanctity of Jerusalem in Islam," in *Jerusalem*, ed. J. M. Oesterreicher and A. Sinai (New York: John Day, 1974), pp. 211–25; E. Sivan, "Le charactère sacré de Jerusalem dans l'Islam au xii⁻-xiii siècle," *Studia Islamica* 27 (1967): 149–82; and A. L. Tibawi, *Jerusalem: Its Place in Islam and Arab History* (Beirut: Institute for Palestine Studies, 1969).

41. On the night journey (*isrā'*) and ascension to heaven (*mi'rāj*), see the relevant articles by B. Schrieke and J. Horovitz, based on their earlier studies, in *Shorter Encyclopaedia of Islam*, ed. H. A. R. Gibb and J. H. Kramers (Ithaca, N.Y.: Cornell University Press, 1961).

42. R. Bell and R. Paret, in their comments on this verse, locate the site in Jerusalem; see R. Bell, *The Qur'ān* (Edinburgh: Clark, 1937), vol. 1, p. 263; and R. Paret, *Der Koran: Kommentar und Konkordanz*, 2d ed. (Stuttgart: Verlag W. Kohlhammer, 1977), pp. 295–96 (with relevant bibliography). A. Guillaume suggested a location of the "farthest mosque" in Ji'rāna, a place near Mecca; "Where Was al-Masŷid al-Aqṣā?" *Al-Andalus* 18 (1953): 323–36. This suggestion was dismissed by Paret, "Die 'ferne Gebetsstätte' in Sure 17,1" *Der Islam* 34 (1959): 150–52; and M. Plessner, "Muḥammed's Clandestine 'Umra in Dhū 'l-Qa'da 8 H. and Sūra 17,1," *Revista*

degli Studi Orientali 32 (1957): 525–30. It may be added that the verse is also unspecific as to the identity of "God's servant." In the following verses the servant is Moses, a figure whose ascent to heaven is related in Jewish legend.

43. Busse, "The Sanctity of Jerusalem in Islam," p. 441.

44. Al-Tabari, *Annales*, ed. M. J. de Goeje (Leiden, 1879–1901); First Series, pp. 2405–6, trans. D. R. Hill, *The Termination of Hostilities in the Early Arab Conquests A.D. 634–656* (New York: Crane, Russak, 1971), p. 60. The authenticity of the story of Caliph ʿUmar's visit to Jerusalem is doubted by some scholars; see, for example, Busse, "The Sanctity of Jerusalem in Islam," pp. 443–48. It is, however, accepted as historical by S. D. Goitein, "Jerusalem in the Arab Period (638–1099)" (Hebrew), in *Yerushalayim; Review for Eretz-Israel Research*, ed. M. Ish-Shalom et al. (Jerusalem, 1953), p. 85. Goitein also accepts the authenticity of ʿUmar's visit to the Temple Mount. (A new article on Jerusalem ["al-Kuds"] has been prepared by S. D. Goitein and O. Grabar for the *Encyclopaedia of Islam*, new ed.) The authenticity of the treaty allegedly signed between ʿUmar and Sophronios is open to question; see, for example, S. D. Goitein, "Did the Caliph Omar Allow the Jews to Reside in Jerusalem?" in *Melilah, A Volume of Studies*, vols. 3–4, ed. E. Robertson and M. Wallenstein (Manchester: Manchester University Press, 1950), pp. 156–65. The treaty may rather reflect efforts by the Christians at the time of the Muslim conquest of the city to secure a prohibition against Jewish settlement therein. Jews did, in fact, reside in Jerusalem from the beginning of the Arab-Muslim period. This would have been inconceivable had someone of ʿUmar's stature agreed to the contrary.

45. Ibn ʿAsākir, *al-Taʾrīkh al-kabir* (Damascus, 1912) vol. 1, p. 176. A similar version of this story is given by al-Tabari, pp. 2408–9; trans. by B. Lewis, *Islam; From the Prophet Muhammad to the Capture of Constantinople* (New York: Harper & Row, 1974), vol. 2, p. 3. In both versions of this visit (Ibn-ʿAsākir and al-Tabari) Kaʿb al-Aḥbār is accused by ʿUmar of harboring judaizing tendencies. In al-Tabari's account it is because he removes his sandals (thus acknowledging the sacredness of the spot).

46. In Ibn ʿAsākir's version, Kaʿb attempted to have the caliph build the place of worship on the northern part of the Temple Mount esplanade. This would have been precisely where the Second Temple was actually located according to the theory recently suggested by A. S. Kaufman, "New Light upon Zion: The Plan and Precise Location of the Second Temple," *Ariel* 43 (1977): 63–99. (I am grateful to Jay Hirshfield for calling Kaufman's research to my attention, and to the author for sending me a copy of his article.) According to Kaufman, the true Foundation Stone is the rock over which the Dome of the Spirits or the Tablets (*qubbat al-alwāḥ/arwāḥ*) stands; its name commemorates the two Tablets of the Covenant that rested on the Foundation Stone in the Holy of Holies. One is thus tempted to pose the tantalizing question whether the story of ʿUmar and Kaʿb al-Aḥbār does not reflect, however distortedly, an attempt by Jews and/or Jewish converts to reconstitute the Jewish Temple upon its original site. This line of speculation receives indirect confirmation from a passage in Ch. 31 of the *History of Heraclius* by Bishop Sebeos, a contemporary of these events; *Histoire d' Héraclius par l'Evêque Sebêos*, trans. F. Macler; cited by M. Schwabe, "The Jews and the Temple Mount After the Conquest of Jerusalem by ʿUmar," *Zion (Me'assef)* 2 (1927): 103–4. Bishop Sebeos speaks of plots by Jews who had aided the Arabs and enjoyed their support. The Jews planned to rebuild the Temple of Solomon. Having revealed the place called "The Holy of Holies," they built upon its foundations a place of worship. The Arabs, out of envy, drove them from this place and called it a place of worship for themselves. The Jews then built nearby another place of worship. The tenth-century Karaite author Salman ben Jeruham, in his *Commentary on Psalms* (30:10), states that the Arabs permitted Jews to dwell in Jerusalem, and they prayed for some time in "The Courtyards of the House of the Lord" until they were driven out, on charges of misdemeanor, to one of the gates (of the Temple site) where they prayed; J. Mann, *Texts and Studies in Jewish History and Literature*, vol. 2, *Karaitica* (Philadelphia: Jewish Publication Society, 1935), pp. 18–19. Another account telling of a Jewish place of worship and academy on the Temple Mount is given by

Abraham bar Hiyya (twelfth century) in his *Megillat hamegalleh*, ed. A. S. Poznanski (Berlin, 1924), pp. 99–100. The actual events underlying these reports are obscure; see Ben-Zion Dinur, "A House of Worship and Study for the Jews on the Temple Mount in the Days of the Arabs" (Hebrew), *Zion (Me'assef)* 3 (1929): 54–87, where additional material is cited.

47. Al-Ṭabarī, p. 2409. Muslim tradition understands the epithet "Fārūq" to mean "The One who Separates *(farraqa)* between Truth and Falsehood." The original sense of the byname appears to have been "Redeemer" (cf. Aramaic *parōqā*, and *furqān* in the Qur'ān, which means "deliverance, decision, revelation," from Aramaic *purqān*). On Fārūq = "Redeemer," see P. Crone and M. Cook, *Hagarism: The Making of the Islamic World* (Cambridge: Cambridge University Press, 1977), p. 5; but it is difficult to accept their interpretation that ʿUmar was a messiah, recognized by the Jews, whose apparition was prophesied by Muḥammad. The 500-year period before the conquest of the city by ʿUmar, during which Jews were not permitted to enter it and dwell there, is mentioned by the tenth-century Karaites, Salman ben Jeruham (see note 46), and Sahl ben Maṣliaḥ; M. Schwabe, "The Jews and the Temple Mount After the Conquest of Jerusalem by ʿUmar," p. 99. Schwabe notes that from the original Hadrianic prohibition in 134 to the Muslim invasion of Palestine in 634 exactly 500 years had elapsed; but ʿUmar's visit took place in 638. See also Linder, "The Roman Imperial Government and the Jews Under Constantine," pp. 136–37, note 227. Other Muslim accounts also relate that the area around the Foundation Stone was left in ruins and covered with rubbish by the Christian Byzantines (to fulfill the prophecy of Jesus that it would be desolate forever); see, for example, Abu l-Fidā, *Kitāb taqwim al-buldān*, ed. M. Reinard and M. de Slane (Paris, 1840), p. 241; and Mujir al-Dīn, vol. 1, pp. 180, 227.

48. Al-Ṭabarī, p. 2403. Al-Ṭabarī also relates (pp. 2402–3) that a Jew in Jābiya (ʿUmar's base in Syria) told ʿUmar that God would make the conquest of Jerusalem possible for him. It may be recalled that the Jews of Ḥimṣ (Edessa) in fact helped the Muslims against the Byzantines.

49. B. Lewis, "An Apocalyptic Vision of Islamic History," *Bulletin of the School of Oriental and African Studies* 13 (1950): 308–38; B. Lewis, "On That Day," *Mélanges d'Islamologie; Volume dédié à la memoire de Armand Abel*, ed. P. Salmon (Leiden: Brill, 1974), pp. 197–200; both reprinted in B. Lewis, *Studies in Classical and Ottoman Islam (7th–16th Centuries)* (nos. 5 and 6) (London: Variorum Reprints, 1976). The account of Sebeos (see note 46) suggests Jewish eschatological expectations.

50. Arculfus, *Itinera Hierosolymitana et discriptiones terrae sanctae*, ed. T. Tobler and A. Molinier (Osnabrück: O. Zeller, 1966), vol. 1, p. 145.

51. O. Grabar, "The Umayyad Dome of the Rock in Jerusalem," *Ars Orientalis* 3 (1959): 33–62.

52. This is brought out by Kister in "You Shall Only Set Out for Three Mosques," especially p. 178.

53. Goitein, "The Sanctity of Jerusalem," p. 141; Sivan, "Le charactère sacré de Jérusalem," p. 180.

54. Sivan treats the Muslim reaction to the Crusades in his article "Le charactère sacré de Jérusalem."

55. E. Sivan, "The Beginnings of the Faḍā'il al-Quds Literature," *Israel Oriental Studies* (Tel Aviv) 1 (1971): 263–71.

56. H. Lazarus-Yafeh, "The Sanctity of Jerusalem in Islam," pp. 222–24, cites the Egyptian Maḥmūd Abū Rayya, on whom see G. H. A. Juynboll, *The Authenticity of the Tradition Literature; Discussions in Modern Egypt* (Leiden: Brill, 1969) (cited by Lazarus-Yafeh), pp. 130–37. Like his medieval forerunner, Ibn-Taymiyya, Abū Rayya objected to the Jewish inspiration of beliefs surrounding Jerusalem and to promotion of the city to a status that might rival that of Mecca.

2

PLANS FOR THE SOLUTION OF THE JERUSALEM PROBLEM

Alisa Ginio

After the British army entered Jerusalem in December 1917 under the flag of General Edmund Allenby, Palestine was ruled by the Occupied Enemy Territory Administration (OETA). The OETA elapsed when Sir Herbert Samuel became high commissioner in July 1920, and the British Mandate came into force de facto. Because of objections by the United States and France, the British plan for its Mandate over Palestine was not ratified by the League of Nations until July 1922. In fact, Palestine became a League of Nations Mandate when the Treaty of Lausanne was ratified in September 1923.

One of the most vexing problems confronting the British was the Jerusalem question. After 400 years of Ottoman (Muslim) rule, the British became the first Christian power to rule Jerusalem since the termination of the Crusader Kingdom. In the brief 30-year period of the Mandate, a host of solutions were proposed for the issues constituting the Jerusalem question: sovereignty, supervision, and control over the Holy Places and organization of the Municipality.

From the vantage point of the Jerusalem problem and its proposed solutions, three main periods may be delineated from 1917 until 1948, when the city was divided between Israel and Jordan: (1) From 1917 until 1936, Jerusalem was primarily an administrative problem for the Mandate power. Britain's main concern was to enact the Mandate and to fulfill its commitments toward the Western powers concerning the Holy Places, with minimum local conflict and disturbance by the local population. The Arab riots in 1920, and the large-scale eruption of violence in 1929, sparked by the

Western Wall controversy, indicated that Britain's task would be far from simple. (2) From 1936 until 1939, Jerusalem became the principal object of contention in the struggle between Zionism and the Arab national movement in Palestine. British interest was to remove Jerusalem from the area of conflict. (3) From 1939 to 1945, the period of World War II, the British government considered plans for a long-term policy, but the settlement was postponed until after the war. At the termination of the war, Jerusalem became an international problem.

FIRST PERIOD: 1917 TO 1936

The main plan for Jerusalem during the first phase of Mandate rule was contained in the draft Mandate for Palestine of December 1920, according to which Jerusalem was to be part of the British Mandate of Palestine. At this juncture, while the national conflict between Jews and Arabs was in its incipient stage, the question of partition was not raised and the discussion centered around the problem of administration and control of the Holy Places.

When Britain presented its draft Mandate to the Council of the League of Nations in December 1920, its sponsors tried to take into account the conflicting interests that came to the fore at the Paris Peace Conference, including disagreements over the question of Palestine and sovereignty over Jerusalem and the Holy Places. Nonetheless, France refused to approve the British Mandate over Palestine until its own Mandate over Syria was granted and, at the same time, demanded supervision over the Holy Places. Italy consented to the British Mandate over Palestine but demanded that the claims to the Holy Places be settled by a committee whose chairman would be appointed by the League of Nations.

The Vatican issued an appeal concerning the future of Palestine in order to alter the 1852 Ottoman firman regulating the Status Quo in the Christian Holy Places. Addressing the College of Cardinals on March 10, 1919, Pope Benedict XV proposed that Christians from Malta be permitted to emigrate to Palestine in order to safeguard Latin rights there, and expressed his concern for the fate of the Holy Places should they fall into the hands of non-Christians (an allusion to the Balfour Declaration).[1] The Vatican position on this subject was formulated prior to the ratification of the proposed British Mandate in a letter sent by Cardinal Gasparri to the League of Nations Council on May 15, 1922.[2] The letter stated: (1) The Holy See does not object to granting the Jews of Palestine rights equal to those of other peoples and religions, but it is vigorously opposed to granting privileges or hegemony to the Jews (which, in the view of the author of the letter, the proposed Mandate intended to do). (2) The Holy See is opposed to Article 14 of the Mandate and to Article 95 of the Treaty of Sèvres.[3] These articles refer to a committee for the Holy Places to be appointed by Britain but headed by a chairman nominated by the League of Nations. Its duties would be to delineate the prerogatives of the various denominations and sects in regard to the Holy Places. Cardinal Gasparri feared that a committee of this kind would make decisions on Catholic interests without being authorized to do so by the Catholic Church. Accordingly, the Vatican proposed the establishment of a supervisory committee of consuls.[4]

At the same time, President Woodrow Wilson of the United States promoted the establishment of an international committee for the Middle East whose task would be to learn the wishes of the region's inhabitants. Ultimately, only the two U.S. members of the committee, Henry King and Charles R. Crane, set out for the Middle East. Their report, presented to the Paris Peace Conference on August 28, 1919, made the following recommendations with regard to sovereignty over Palestine and the problem of the Holy Places[5]: (1) Palestine should be included in a Syrian state ruled by Emir Fayṣal and administered under a single mandate—preferably British or U.S. The aim of turning Palestine into a Jewish state should be abandoned. (2) An international or interdenominational committee for the Holy Places should be established with the consent and under the supervision of the mandatory power and the League of Nations. The Jews were unacceptable to both Christians and Muslims as guardians of the Holy Places.

The King-Crane report was shelved because of, on the U.S. side, the U.S. Senate's opposition to the Versailles Treaty and the subsequent policy of "splendid isolation"; and, on the European side, British and French dissatisfaction with the recommendations. United States interests in the Middle East focused upon the protection of U.S. citizens, missionary activities, commercial interests, and the like. To protect these ends, the United States signed a treaty with Britain in 1924 whereby the United States recognized the British Mandate over Palestine in return for gaining for its citizens rights equal to those granted to citizens of League of Nations member states.[6]

Because of these conflicting interests, Britain's plan for its Mandate was not ratified by the League of Nations until July 24, 1922.[7] The articles concerning Jerusalem are numbers 8, 13, and 14.

Article 8 of the draft Mandate states that the immunities and privileges accorded to foreigners under the Ottoman Capitulations (including consular adjudication and protection) would no longer apply in mandatory Palestine. However, at the conclusion of the Mandate they would be restored in their entirety or with modifications determined by the states concerned. Article 13 makes the mandatory government responsible for the Holy Places, preservation of existing prerogatives, and guaranteeing free access and freedom of worship, while maintaining order. It also expressly affirms that the mandatory government would not interfere in the organization and management of those Holy Places belonging exclusively to the Muslims.

Article 14 requires the mandatory government to appoint a special commission to determine rights and claims concerning the Holy Places and relating to the various religious communities.

On July 31, 1922, Lord Balfour presented a memorandum to the League of Nations Council proposing the formation of a commission on the Holy Places, which would include three subcommittees: one Christian (to include representatives of all the various Christian sects, including the Armenians, the Ethiopians, and the Copts); a second Jewish (presided over by a U.S. Jew and including a Jew from Palestine, one from Britain, and one from Portugal to represent the Sephardi Jews); and a third Muslim. However, the mandatory government contended that, in the absence of proper representation for the Greek Orthodox sect, such a committee was unfeasible. Consequently, Article 14 of the Mandate was never implemented. In effect, supervision of the Holy Places was left to the mandatory government, which perpetuated the Ottoman Status Quo; and on September 15, 1924, a mandatory decree removed all matters connected to the Holy Places from the jurisdiction of Palestinian courts and entrusted them to the high commissioner, whose decision would be final.[8]

Five years after the final ratification of the Mandate, Britain was constrained to attend once more to the problem of the Holy Places, this time not because of foreign concerns but because of a dispute between Jews and Muslims concerning prerogatives at the Western Wall. The incident that sparked the dispute and ensuing riots was of minor significance—the Jews set up a portable partition to separate male and female worshippers on the eve of the Day of Atonement (September 24, 1928)—but the Muslims regarded this change in the status quo as an initial step in a Jewish plot to take possession of the Temple Mount (Ḥaram al-Sharīf). The Muslim leadership, spearheaded by the Mufti Ḥājj Amīn al-Ḥusaynī, mounted a campaign against any alteration of the status quo, and an exchange of conflicting claims ensued. In the summer of 1929 the tension erupted into assaults by Muslims upon Jews in Jerusalem and elsewhere (especially Hebron and Safed).[9]

Fear of the Jewish menace to Muslim Holy Places in Jerusalem arose at the beginning of the nineteenth century.[10] This fear stemmed from the growing strength of Jerusalem's Jewish community in the preceding century. Toward the end of the Ottoman period, a number of cases of litigation concerned the status of the Jews at the Western (Wailing) Wall. The purely religious issue took on prime political importance only after the British occupation.

This preeminence found expression in efforts to elevate Jerusalem's status in the Muslim world and in the renovation of the Ḥaram al-Sharīf mosques, which became the basic focus of the Supreme Muslim Council's policies beginning in the 1920s. Following years of Ottoman neglect, these efforts involved large-scale publicity campaigns, the dispatch of delegations, fund raising, and extensive renovation work in the mosques. The systematic campaign was built around a presentation of the religious menace to Muslim centers in Jerusalem posed by the Zionists. It was not by chance that the campaign was directed particularly at those Muslim-populated countries then under British rule (such as India, Egypt, Iraq) in an attempt to arouse them to exert pressure on the British government. In the late 1920s, the effort culminated in the establishment of national committees to protect the Muslim Holy Places in Jerusalem, the 1929 riots over the Western Wall, testimonies before the Wailing Wall Commission, and the convening of the Pan-Islamic Congress in Jerusalem (December 1931). The Palestinian Arabs endowed the Jerusalem issue with an uncompromisingly religious overtone.

This stress on Muslim religious interests in Jerusalem paved the way for general Arab and Muslim concern over the Palestine issue as a whole and Jerusalem in particular. It provided the foundation for the Arab contention that the world's Muslims were bound to help the Muslims of Jerusalem, who, as the representatives of Islam, were charged with safeguarding the city's character and its Holy Places.

The outbursts of violence in 1929 led to the establishment of the Wailing Wall Commission. On January 14, 1930, acting on the recommendation of the Permanent Mandates Commission, the League of Nations Council decided to establish an international committee to examine the claims and prerogatives of Muslims and Jews with regard to the Western Wailing Wall in Jerusalem. Formed under Article 13 of the Mandate, after Article 14 remained a dead letter, the committee was charged with examining the question of the Western Wall to the exclusion of the other Holy Places. The committee's three members were nominated by Britain and were confirmed by the secretary-general of the League of Nations.[11]

Appearing before this commission, the Jews presented historical claims with regard to religious practices at the Wall. The Muslims, including Muslim representatives from outside Palestine, challenged the jurisdiction of the British mandatory authority, claiming that according to Article 13 of the Mandate, the matter was under the jurisdiction of the *sharīʿa* court and, in any event, the Jewish Holy Places were not covered by the Ottoman Status Quo of 1852. In light of this argument, the committee decided to extend the administrative principles of the Status Quo to the Western Wall, regard it as a Holy Place for both sides, and ordered existing practices maintained.

Despite the communal strife in Jerusalem, the mandatory government was opposed at the time to partition of the city. Partition proposals had been presented as far back as 1932[12] by Chaim Arlosoroff, head of the Jewish Agency's political department, on the strength of a conversation with the southern district commissioner, B. Campbell. Arlosoroff's principal proposals included the following: The municipal region of Jerusalem would be divided into two boroughs: Western Jerusalem, the newer part of the city, which was mostly

Jewish, and the Old City, largely Arab. Each borough would have a council of its own, empowered to impose taxes. Both borough councils would come under the United Municipal Council of Jerusalem, having coordinating and supervisory powers.[13]

It is clear that British policy regarding the Jerusalem Municipality was to preserve the status quo (Arab hegemony) by the following means: From 1934 onward, the electoral wards for the Municipality were delineated on a territorial basis, but the election committees prepared the lists of candidates on a communal-denominational basis. Each ward was designed to include a majority of one community or another, and the candidate of the ward was to be a member of that majority community.[14] Also, the addition of further electoral wards (such as the new Jewish suburbs of Beit Hakerem, Qiryat Mosheh, and Talpiyyot) was strictly supervised and balanced out by the addition of adjoining Arab villages, such as Liftā.[15]

THE CRISIS OF 1936–39 AND REASSESSMENT OF POLICY

The intensification of the Arab-Jewish conflict obliged the British government to reassess its policies on sovereignty over Jerusalem and intercommunal relations in the city. During the years 1933–36, the Jewish population in Palestine grew significantly as a result of immigration caused by the Nazi rise to power in Europe. At the same time, the evolution of Arab nationalism and the growing interest and involvement of Arab countries contributed toward a sharpening of hostility on the part of Palestinian Arabs toward the Jewish population and the Mandate.[16]

The political situation in Palestine entered a crisis with the outbreak of violence in 1936 under the leadership of the Arab Higher Committee (presided over by al-Ḥājj Amīn al-Ḥusaynī, the Grand Mufti of Jerusalem). The crisis atmosphere led to the constitution of the Royal Commission for Palestine under Lord Peel. It began to function in November 1936 and presented its report in July 1937.[17] In view of the irreconcilable differences between the Arab and Jewish national movements, the commission concluded that the Mandate was unworkable and recommended that it be terminated. The Royal Commission proposed the partition of Palestine into two states— Jewish and Arab, with the Arab state including Trans-Jordan. The commission also attempted to remove Jerusalem and its Holy Places from the arena of the Arab-Jewish conflict by proposing that the Jerusalem-Bethlehem enclave, plus a corridor to the sea including Lydda and Ramleh and reaching as far as Jaffa, remain under permanent British Mandate. The British government would become the trustee of the Holy Places under a new League of Nations Mandate. With regard to municipal administration, the commission proposed retaining the existing law, which gave the vote to males aged 25 and over (pro-

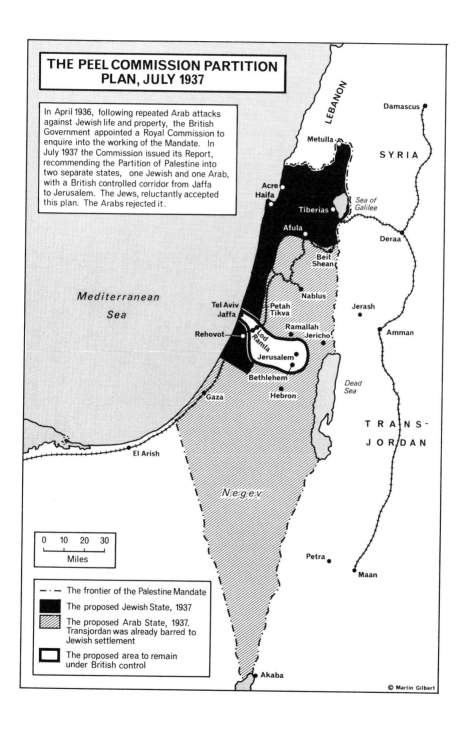

THE PEEL COMMISSION PARTITION PLAN, JULY 1937

In April 1936, following repeated Arab attacks against Jewish life and property, the British Government appointed a Royal Commission to enquire into the working of the Mandate. In July 1937 the Commission issued its Report, recommending the Partition of Palestine into two separate states, one Jewish and one Arab, with a British controlled corridor from Jaffa to Jerusalem. The Jews, reluctantly accepted this plan. The Arabs rejected it.

LEBANON

Damascus

SYRIA

Metulla

Acre
Haifa

Tiberias

Sea of Galilee

Afula

Deraa

Mediterranean Sea

Beit Shean

Nablus

Jerash

Tel Aviv
Jaffa

Petah Tikva

Ramallah

Jericho

Amman

Rehovot

Lod
Ramla

Jerusalem

Bethlehem

Gaza

Hebron

Dead Sea

TRANS-
JORDAN

El Arish

Negev

0 10 20 30
Miles

Petra

Maan

Akaba

— · — The frontier of the Palestine Mandate

█ The proposed Jewish State, 1937

▨ The proposed Arab State, 1937. Transjordan was already barred to Jewish settlement

▢ The proposed area to remain under British control

© Martin Gilbert

viding they paid municipal taxes) and delineated electoral wards on a geographical basis.

While recommended by the British government in a White Paper of July 1937, the Royal Commission Report was received with mild enthusiasm by public opinion. Among those who attacked it in the House of Lords was Viscount (formerly Sir) Herbert Samuel, who proposed that the League of Nations should safeguard the Holy Places. The debate in the House of Commons led to a resolution authorizing the cabinet to seek approval of the League of Nations before drafting a definite plan.

The League's Mandate Commission, which convened on July 30, 1937, was not enthusiastic about the idea of partition, but it was prepared to adopt the plan in view of the British declaration that the Mandate could not be extended. It was also ready to accept an extension of the British Mandate over Jerusalem.

Emir ʿAbdallāh of Trans-Jordan reportedly was receptive to the partition plan, as the recommendation that the Arab area of Palestine be united with Trans-Jordan meant that the territory under his control would be increased. Though there was wavering support for partition among some Palestinian Arabs, particularly the National Defense Party of the Nashāshībis, the majority reacted with vehement hostility. Two factors discouraged local Arab support for partition: coercive terrorism and rejection by outside Arab countries. The Arab Higher Committee, under the chairmanship of Ḥājj Amīn al-Ḥusaynī, rejected partition outright and was supported by other Arab countries, even allies of Britain such as Iraq and Saudi Arabia.

Representatives from Syria and Palestine, along with delegates from Egypt, Iraq, Lebanon, and Trans-Jordan, attended the Arab National Conference in Balūdān, Syria, in September 1937, at which the participants took an oath to liberate Palestine and attain Arab sovereignty over all Palestine. Palestinian and Syrian nationalists agreed among themselves on a violent course of action. The strong stand taken by Arab countries on the partition issue, and the fact that Nūrī al-Saʿīd, an Iraqi minister, testified before the Royal Commission concerning internal Palestinian affairs, constituted an important stage in the "pan-Arabization" of the Palestine issue.[18]

The Twentieth Zionist Congress, convened in Zurich in August 1937, debated the issue of partition. The reception by the Zionist leaders was ambivalent but, on balance, more positive than negative, in the spirit of a half a loaf being better than none. With an eye to the pressing need to provide a refuge for Europe's Jews, Chaim Weizmann advocated conditional acceptance of the principle of partition, though he found the details of the scheme unpalatable. Menachem Ussishkin led the opposition, contending that the Jewish state proposed by the Peel Commission was nonviable. Berl Katznelson, a leader of Mapai, the Labor Zionists, argued that without Jerusalem the Jewish state would be a body without a head. At the end, a Weizmann-

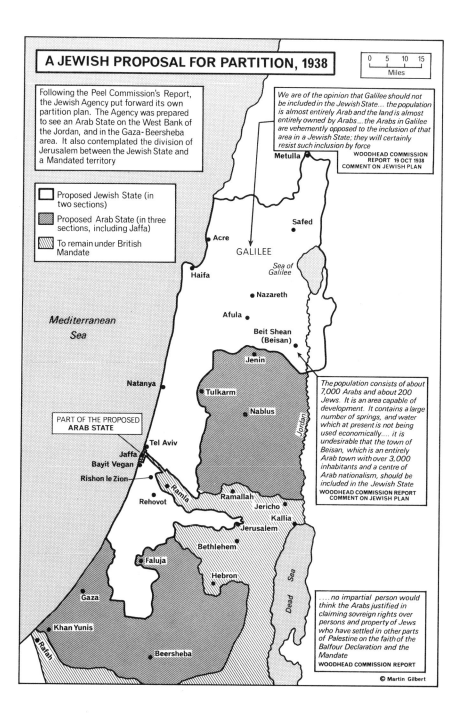

A JEWISH PROPOSAL FOR PARTITION, 1938

0 5 10 15
Miles

Following the Peel Commission's Report, the Jewish Agency put forward its own partition plan. The Agency was prepared to see an Arab State on the West Bank of the Jordan, and in the Gaza-Beersheba area. It also contemplated the division of Jerusalem between the Jewish State and a Mandated territory

We are of the opinion that Galilee should not be included in the Jewish State.... the population is almost entirely Arab and the land is almost entirely owned by Arabs.... the Arabs in Galilee are vehemently opposed to the inclusion of that area in a Jewish State; they will certainly resist such inclusion by force
WOODHEAD COMMISSION REPORT 19 OCT 1938 COMMENT ON JEWISH PLAN

☐ Proposed Jewish State (in two sections)

▨ Proposed Arab State (in three sections, including Jaffa)

▧ To remain under British Mandate

Metulla

Safed

Acre

GALILEE

Haifa

Sea of Galilee

Nazareth

Afula

Mediterranean Sea

Beit Shean (Beisan)

Jenin

Natanya

Tulkarm

Nablus

PART OF THE PROPOSED **ARAB STATE**

Jordan

Tel Aviv
Jaffa
Bayit Vegan
Rishon le Zion

Ramla

Rehovot

Ramallah

Jericho

Kallia

Jerusalem

The population consists of about 7,000 Arabs and about 200 Jews. It is an area capable of development. It contains a large number of springs, and water which at present is not being used economically.... it is undesirable that the town of Beisan, which is an entirely Arab town with over 3,000 inhabitants and a centre of Arab nationalism, should be included in the Jewish State
WOODHEAD COMMISSION REPORT COMMENT ON JEWISH PLAN

Bethlehem

Faluja

Hebron

Dead Sea

Gaza

Khan Yunis

Rafah

Beersheba

....no impartial person would think the Arabs justified in claiming sovereign rights over persons and property of Jews who have settled in other parts of Palestine on the faith of the Balfour Declaration and the Mandate
WOODHEAD COMMISSION REPORT

© Martin Gilbert

inspired resolution was passed. The Zionist Congress rejected the actual partition scheme of the Royal Commission as unacceptable, but it did empower the Zionist Executive to negotiate with Britain in order to determine the precise conditions for the establishment of a Jewish state.[19]

The Jewish Agency advanced a proposal of its own to the Palestine Partition Commission under Sir John Woodhead. The commission was appointed by the British government in March 1938 to work out details of the proposed partition.[20] The Agency's memorandum of August 1938, concerning the partition of Jerusalem, spoke of dividing the city into two parts: New Jerusalem to the west of the Old City walls, together with Mount Scopus, would be attached to the Jewish state; the quarters within and to the east of the walls would constitute the area of the Jerusalem enclave and be placed under a new British Mandate.[21] (The boundary lines were delineated on a map attached to the Woodhead Commission's report, and in Appendix A to the Jewish Agency proposal.)

Also, the proposal made mention of two municipal councils that would share existing municipal property and the possibility, but not necessity, of integrating municipal services (water, sewage, and electricity), using the existing networks. Finally, it was proposed to turn the entire city into a single customs zone, with the possibility of passport control at the boundaries. As examples to prove the feasibility of this form of coexistence, the memorandum cited towns on the Swiss-German-French borders, on the Canadian-U.S. border, and the city of Shanghai.

A different response came from Menachem Ussishkin in a memorandum presented to the Palestine Partition Commission in July 1938.[22] Ussishkin first explained his objections to the partition proposal (which he had earlier presented to the Twentieth Zionist Congress), presenting historical and ideological arguments to prove that it ran counter to Zionist objectives. His main objection was to the partition of Jerusalem, claiming that a divided municipality could exist if it were a large city like Shanghai or a small town whose citizens lived in harmony, but not as a small city in which various communities were hostile toward one another.

Another private plan was that of an engineer by the name of M. Hecker, whose proposal was presented in response to Colonial Secretary Ormsby-Gore's statement before the League of Nations Mandates Commission describing the considerable difficulties involved in partitioning the city.[23] Hecker tried to prove that it was indeed feasible to partition the city. Jewish Jerusalem (which he suggested calling "Zion") would include the new city west and north of the walls, to which he proposed attaching a number of places of religious or historical importance to the Jews. The site of prayer at the Western Wall would be shifted to an area to the west of its southern extremity. In addition, an effort should be made to establish homogeneous areas, for which purpose both sides would have to make certain sacrifices, such as abandoning those houses and quarters located in an alien area. It would also be feasible to separate the water supply and the sewage network.

The U.S. government claimed that under Article 7 of its 1924 treaty with Britain, it was entitled to be consulted, but it raised no objections to changes in the Mandate.[24] The Vatican's comment on the possibility of New Jerusalem being included in the Jewish state was made by Monsignor Malusardi, the Vatican's undersecretary of state, in his expression of regret over "the removal of any portion of Palestine from Christian control." However, the Vatican appreciated the British quandary, and the Pope accepted the idea in view of "the present effort in the cause of international appeasement."[25]

Although the Woodhead Commission was appointed by the British government to work out the details of the partition plan, its report, published in October 1938, summarized three alternate plans that had been analyzed (coded A, B, and C) and concluded that none was feasible. The commission utterly dismissed the idea of partitioning Jerusalem and concluded that, from the administrative viewpoint, it should be considered a single city and a single customs zone with a single water and sewage network. Thus, without the cooperation of the rival communities, partition was impractical. Furthermore, it was observed that Jerusalem was holy to all three monotheistic religions. Thus Jerusalem would remain in a mandatory zone as a separate enclave.

The Jerusalem enclave is identical in all three plans. Its northern border lies to the north of Rāmallāh. The southern border lies to the south of the Aqir Royal Air Force base and includes Bethlehem (combining strategic and religious considerations). The enclave includes Lydda airport and the road leading to it, and a corridor to the sea between Jaffa and Rishon le-Zion. Nazareth is also a mandated zone in all three plans.[26]

Following the Woodhead Commission's report, the British government rejected the partition idea in a White Paper presented to Parliament in November 1938. The British government then turned directly to the parties involved and convened parallel Anglo-Arab and Anglo-Jewish consultations in London (the St. James Conference), but they bore no fruit. The conference sessions were broken off on March 17, 1939, and two months later the British advanced their own plan in a White Paper (May 17, 1939).[27] It affirmed that Palestine was not included in the territory referred to in the exchange of letters between Sir Henry McMahon and Sharīf Husayn of Mecca, and thus was not to become an Arab state, adding that, although Britain did have commitments to the Jews, it was not committed to a Jewish state, per se. Britain intended, within ten years, to establish in Palestine a state inhabited by both Jews and Arabs. Jerusalem would therefore be the undivided capital of the state of Palestine. Furthermore, the state would be linked to Britain by a treaty that would, inter alia, guarantee freedom of access to the Holy Places (Article 7) and protection of minorities and their rights. Jewish immigration would be limited to 75,000 during the next five years and sale of land to Jews would be

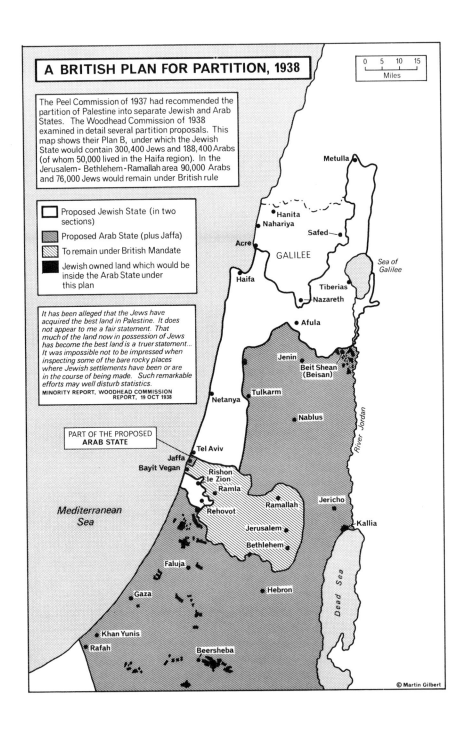

A BRITISH PLAN FOR PARTITION, 1938

The Peel Commission of 1937 had recommended the partition of Palestine into separate Jewish and Arab States. The Woodhead Commission of 1938 examined in detail several partition proposals. This map shows their Plan B, under which the Jewish State would contain 300,400 Jews and 188,400 Arabs (of whom 50,000 lived in the Haifa region). In the Jerusalem-Bethlehem-Ramallah area 90,000 Arabs and 76,000 Jews would remain under British rule

- Proposed Jewish State (in two sections)
- Proposed Arab State (plus Jaffa)
- To remain under British Mandate
- Jewish owned land which would be inside the Arab State under this plan

It has been alleged that the Jews have acquired the best land in Palestine. It does not appear to me a fair statement. That much of the land now in possession of Jews has become the best land is a truer statement... It was impossible not to be impressed when inspecting some of the bare rocky places where Jewish settlements have been or are in the course of being made. Such remarkable efforts may well disturb statistics.
MINORITY REPORT, WOODHEAD COMMISSION REPORT, 19 OCT 1938

PART OF THE PROPOSED **ARAB STATE**

0   5   10   15
Miles

Metulla

Hanita
Nahariya
Safed
Acre
GALILEE
Haifa
Sea of Galilee
Tiberias
Nazareth
Afula
Jenin
Beit Shean (Beisan)
Tulkarm
Netanya
Nablus
River Jordan
Tel Aviv
Jaffa
Bayit Vegan
Rishon le Zion
Ramla
Rehovot
Ramallah
Jericho
Kallia
Jerusalem
Bethlehem
Mediterranean Sea
Faluja
Gaza
Hebron
Dead Sea
Khan Yunis
Rafah
Beersheba

© Martin Gilbert

52

restricted. The Zionists regarded the White Paper as a betrayal of British promises, and the Arabs were also discontented because immigration was not halted altogether.

Examining the text of the White Paper in June 1939, the League of Nations Permanent Mandates Commission confirmed that it did not fulfill the conditions of the Mandate. A majority of the commission's members were in favor of partition, while a minority (Britain, France, and Portugal) expressed support for the White Paper policies.

1939-48: INTERNATIONALIZATION OF THE JERUSALEM PROBLEMS

During World War II, for obvious reasons, no major new plans for a solution of the Jerusalem issue were forthcoming. During the war the British government reviewed the policy of the 1939 White Paper and reexamined partition plans so as to determine future policy. Near the end of the war, a dispute over the Jerusalem Municipality caused the high commissioner to attempt to solve this stubborn controversy, which reflected the broader conflict. The war and its aftermath produced a situation that made a continuation of the Mandate untenable and the idea of partition inevitable. At the same time, there was a change in the international arena. Britain emerged from the war weakened, and the exit of the British from Palestine became a mere question of time. Concurrently, the United States gained stature as a world power, and the United Nations became the forum for solving international crises. At this phase, the question of Palestine and Jerusalem became an international problem.

As early as July 1943, the British War Cabinet discussed the Palestine question on the basis of the assumption that the White Paper principles would have to be abandoned in favor of a return to the possibility of partition. A ministerial committee under Herbert Morrison was asked to present its proposals to the cabinet. Among the supporters of partition were Lord Moyne, the resident British minister in Cairo, and Sir Harold MacMichael, British High Commissioner for Palestine since 1938. The plan adopted by the Morrison ministerial committee, and supported by MacMichael, proposed that Palestine be divided into four parts: a Jewish state, an Arab territory, the state of Jerusalem (Jerusalem, Bethlehem, Rāmallāh, Lydda, Ramleh, and the Rosh Ha{c}ayin springs, under British supervision), and the Negev and the {c}Arava. This plan, however like many others, never received operative attention.[28]

Toward the end of the war, the conflict in Jerusalem revived following the death of the city's Arab mayor, Muṣṭafā al-Khālidī, on August 24, 1944. The Jews, citing their majority in the city's population, demanded a Jewish mayor.

The Muslims objected, invoking historical precedent. In the meanwhile, Daniel Auster, the Jewish deputy mayor, officiated as acting mayor in the face of Arab protests. The British High Commissioner, Viscount Gort, wrote to the colonial secretary on February 5, 1945, warning that the present calm was illusory and proposing the appointment of two British members to the Municipal Council (''to protect the Holy Places''); annual rotation in the post of mayor; and if the first two proposals failed, the establishment of a committee headed by a British official. On February 14, the colonial secretary approved this line of action.[29] On March 21, the high commissioner advanced a plan that included the first two proposals. The Jews accepted it on condition that the mayoralty be rotated every two years, with the first mayor being Jewish and the third British. But the Arabs rejected the plan categorically and held a protest strike on March 24, 1945. Because they also boycotted Municipal Council meetings, the council lacked a quorum and was effectively paralyzed.[30]

On July 11, 1945, the high commissioner took two steps. First, he issued a decree terminating the tenure of office of the Jerusalem Municipality and authorizing the district commissioner to appoint a committee (under Article 61 of the Municipalities Order) of six British officials to supervise the municipal administration and maintain regular municipal services in the city. (This committee administered the city up to the end of the Mandate.) Second, he appointed the chief justice in Palestine, Sir William Fitzgerald, as a one-man commission ''to enquire and report on the local administration in Jerusalem, and to make recommendations in relation thereto.'' Fitzgerald's report[31] included the following points:

- It was assumed that the Mandate would continue, with Britain exercising sovereignty over Palestine as a whole, and therefore over Jerusalem.
- The 1934 Municipalities Ordinance, which tried to adapt British traditions of local government to Palestinian conditions, was a failure. The British system was based upon majority rights, whereas Jerusalem required an entirely different type of administration. (The Jews claimed that as a majority they were entitled to the rights that British political tradition grants to the majority, although they were prepared to make certain concessions in view of Jerusalem's unique status.)[32]
- The Arabs cited precedent, contending that the Jews, by settling outside the Old City, had conceded Arab preeminence. Fitzgerald rejected this claim, affirming that a citizen has the right to live in any part of his country unless the law expressly forbids it.
- The problem was how to preserve the city's sacred traditions while facilitating the existence of a modern city, with all the urban municipal services required for its 151,000 inhabitants.[33]

The solution advanced by Fitzgerald was to distinguish between the "Jerusalem of tradition," sacred to millions of Jews, Christians, and Muslims, and the other portions of the city, along the following lines:

- Jerusalem of tradition is indivisible, and Fitzgerald was not prepared to regard it as just any municipal area. He proposed that it be treated as an "administrative county" under the supervision of an "administrative council" modeled on the London County Council.
- With regard to municipal administration, he proposed that the city be divided into boroughs (likewise on the London model). The city could be divided into two boroughs: one predominantly Arab and the other Jewish, with "clearly defined boundaries," "each with a different outlook on life, with different aspirations, and interests."
- Areas not included in the above-mentioned boroughs but belonging to the city's planning zone would come under the direct responsibility of the "administrative council." Each borough would be empowered to engage in urban planning within its own area of jurisdiction, subject to the approval of the administrative council. The city's area of jurisdiction could be altered by decree of the high commissioner.
- Each borough would be administered by a council and a mayor. The council's 24 members would be elected by the existing electoral wards (where appropriate), with two members for each ward. The number of council members was doubled, as was the number elected in each ward. Each voter would be entitled to choose two candidates. There would also be a reassessment of the franchise. (Fitzgerald was prepared to concede that after the first elections held under his present proposals, there could be changes in the franchise, according to the decision of each borough.) The mayor would be selected by the council members at their first session. However, "as the mayor will exercise executive functions, it might be advisable to give the High Commissioner the right to veto the election of any individual to the mayoralty."
- The boroughs' spheres of jurisdiction were delineated as follows: (a) Each borough would be empowered to impose taxes on its residents. The administrative council would not be able to impose taxes, but it could assess each borough for the necessary sums, which each would collect at its own discretion. (b) Education would be the exclusive concern of each borough. (c) In health and social services, local powers would be granted to each borough. (d) In the engineering and public works spheres, powers would be granted to each borough. (e) The administrative council would lease water rights to each of the boroughs. (f) The Electricity Corporation would sign a supply contract with each borough. (g) Each borough would be responsible for the sewage network in its own area; however, respon-

sibility for the general sewage system would devolve upon the administrative council.

- The administrative council members would be composed of the following: (a) Representatives of each borough, to be chosen annually by the borough council from among its own members. (b) Two representatives, neither Jews nor Arabs, appointed by the high commissioner to represent "the traditional historical interests" connected with Jerusalem, which the mandatory government was morally and legally obliged to protect. (c) The chairman of the council, who would be appointed by the high commissioner. (Fitzgerald suggested that his title be "the Jerusalem administrator.") The district commissioner's extensive powers of veto, granted by mandatory law, should be restricted in view of the total change of attitude toward the municipal government.
- Each borough would be authorized to take action with regard to the Holy Places within its area of jurisdiction, subject to the approval of the administrative council, but the latter would also be subject to the powers granted to the high commissioner regarding the Holy Places.

By the time Fitzgerald presented this detailed report, World War II had come to an end and the Jewish-Arab conflict had again broken out violently as a result of the problem of the Jewish refugees and displaced persons in Europe. The tempest swept the report aside, and it was never given operational attention.

By 1945, the immigration quota of 75,000, established in the 1939 White Paper, had been filled, and Jewish immigration was therefore to end unless the Arabs agreed otherwise. In an attempt to deal with the problem of Jewish refugees in Europe, an Anglo-American Committee of Inquiry was appointed.[34] Its report, published on May 1, 1946, recommended that Palestine should be neither a Jewish nor an Arab state. The committee did not recommend partition. Instead, it suggested that as long as the intercommunal hostility persisted the Mandate be continued, pending execution of a trusteeship agreement under the United Nations. This recommendation was justified by its proponents on the basis of concern for the Holy Places and their fate at the hands of the warring parties. Continuation of the existing situation meant, of course, that Jerusalem would remain the capital of Palestine.

In response to the report, both Jews and Arabs called for the establishment of a state of their own. Nevertheless, a technical committee was appointed to work out details of the proposal. Headed by Herbert Morrison of Britain and Ambassador Henry Grady of the United States, the committee advanced a proposal (publicized on July 30, 1946) that was a compromise between the partition plans and the plans designed to maintain Palestine as a single political entity.[35] It suggested the cantonization of Palestine (a plan that was ascribed to Ernest Bevin) with an autonomous Jewish province, an autonomous Arab province ("which will enjoy a large measure of autonomy under a central government"), and two zones under the direct rule of a central government headed by the British high commissioner. One of these zones would be the Jerusalem-Bethlehem enclave, without an outlet to the sea. (The other was the district of the Negev.) The Jerusalem District would have a council whose "powers would be similar to those of a municipal council. The majority of its members would be elected, but certain members would be nominated by the High Commissioner." This form of administration was designed to protect the interests of the three religions at the Holy Places.

The Morrison-Grady plan was rejected by the Jewish Agency, which objected to details of the partition proposal, principally those sections dealing with the question of immigration. Considering the pressing need to provide a refuge for the Holocaust survivors, the Jewish Agency executive, meeting in Paris on August 1, 1946, proposed a partition plan calling for the establishment of a viable Jewish state in an adequate area of Palestine, alongside an Arab state, and called for the immediate admission of 100,000 Jewish immigrants to Palestine.[36] Although Jerusalem was not specifically mentioned in the program, the Jewish Agency's proposal expressed a readiness to cede the "central plateau" to the Arabs and proposed guarantees for the Holy Places. This vagueness has given rise to the unwarranted conclusions that no claim was laid to Jerusalem or that it was to be part of the Arab state.[37]

The Arabs also rejected the Morrison-Grady plan and called for the termination of the Mandate. In fact, both sides rejected the British invitation to discuss the Morrison-Grady proposals.

Because the United States also refused to support the Morrison-Grady plan, on April 2, 1947, British Prime Minister Clement Attlee placed the Palestine question on the agenda of the UN General Assembly. On May 15, 1947, an 11-country UN Special Committee on Palestine (UNSCOP) was appointed.[38] At the conclusion of its deliberations, it submitted a majority report and a minority report, the majority report being approved by the General Assembly, with minor changes, on November 29, 1947. It proposed the partition of mandatory Palestine into three entities: a Jewish state, an Arab state, and an international zone. The city of Jerusalem would be proclaimed an international zone—a separate political entity (corpus separatum)—administered by the United Nations, and the problem of Jerusalem would thereafter be transferred to the UN Trusteeship Council. The extent of the corpus separatum would be from north to south, Shuᶜfāt-Bethlehem; from east to west, Abū Dīs- ᶜEin Kārim. It also proposed to establish an economic union for all three bodies (the two states and the corpus separatum). The international administration proposed under this plan blurred the distinction between sovereign political government and local government.

The majority plan did not specify details of the city's administration. It merely stated that the city's governor would be appointed by the UN

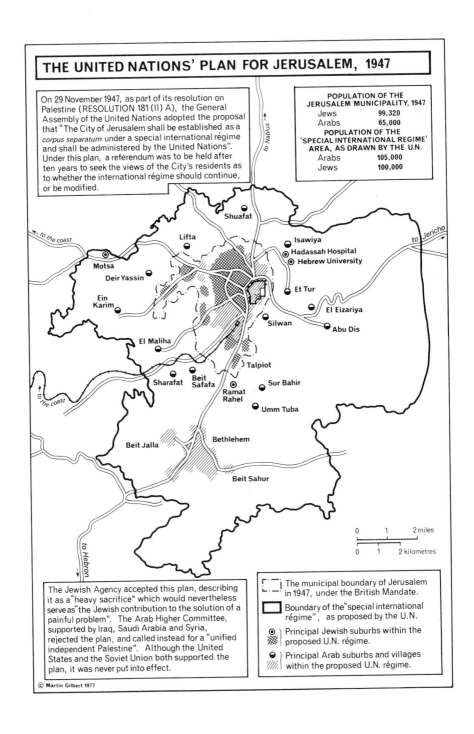

THE UNITED NATIONS' PLAN FOR JERUSALEM, 1947

On 29 November 1947, as part of its resolution on Palestine (RESOLUTION 181 (II) A), the General Assembly of the United Nations adopted the proposal that "The City of Jerusalem shall be established as a *corpus separatum* under a special international régime and shall be administered by the United Nations". Under this plan, a referendum was to be held after ten years to seek the views of the City's residents as to whether the international régime should continue, or be modified.

POPULATION OF THE JERUSALEM MUNICIPALITY, 1947	
Jews	99,320
Arabs	65,000

POPULATION OF THE 'SPECIAL INTERNATIONAL REGIME' AREA, AS DRAWN BY THE U.N.	
Arabs	105,000
Jews	100,000

to Nablus

to the coast

to Jericho

Shuafat

Lifta

Isawiya

Hadassah Hospital

Hebrew University

Motsa

Deir Yassin

Ein Karim

Et Tur

El Eizariya

El Maliha

Silwan

Abu Dis

Talpiot

Sharafat

Beit Safafa

Ramat Rahel

Sur Bahir

Umm Tuba

to the coast

Beit Jalla

Bethlehem

Beit Sahur

to Hebron

| | 0 | 1 | 2 miles |
| 0 | 1 | | 2 kilometres |

The Jewish Agency accepted this plan, describing it as a "heavy sacrifice" which would nevertheless serve as "the Jewish contribution to the solution of a painful problem". The Arab Higher Committee, supported by Iraq, Saudi Arabia and Syria, rejected the plan, and called instead for a "unified independent Palestine". Although the United States and the Soviet Union both supported the plan, it was never put into effect.

The municipal boundary of Jerusalem in 1947, under the British Mandate.

Boundary of the "special international régime", as proposed by the U.N.

Principal Jewish suburbs within the proposed U.N. régime.

Principal Arab suburbs and villages within the proposed U.N. régime.

© Martin Gilbert 1977

Trusteeship Council and he would be responsible to it; that he must be neither a Jew nor an Arab; and that he must not be a citizen of either of the two Palestinian states or a resident of Jerusalem. The governor was to be responsible for the city's administration, including the conduct of external affairs, and for the Holy Places—thus providing international guarantees for their protection—and the Ottoman Capitulations would be abrogated. The plan also proposed a special international police force to be recruited from outside Palestine and to include neither Jews nor Arabs. It said that citizens of both states would have the right to reside in Jerusalem and vote for its elected bodies. Finally, the proposal stated that both an elected legislature and a judicial body would be established on lines determined in the trusteeship agreement. In December 1947, the Trusteeship Council nominated a working committee to prepare proposals for the status of Jerusalem.

The UNSCOP minority report, supported by India, Iran, and Yugoslavia, proposed the establishment within three years of a federal state in Palestine, composed of an Arab and a Jewish province. Jerusalem was to be the federal capital, and it would have two municipalities: one Arab, for the area within the Old City walls and the Arab neighborhoods outside them, and the other Jewish, for the Jewish Quarter within the Old City walls and the Jewish neighborhoods outside them. The two municipalities would possess administrative powers as agreed upon by the federal government, and the various municipal services such as water, sewage, fire brigade, traffic, and telephone and telegraph facilities would be shared. Finally, a permanent international body would be established to protect the Holy Places. This proposal was rejected by the General Assembly's ad hoc committee.

On November 29, 1947, the General Assembly accepted the Partition Resolution, on the basis of the ad hoc committee's report, calling for the partition of Palestine into two states and the internationalization of Jerusalem. The Arab states rejected the resolution, which they considered an illegal trespass on the rights of the Palestinian Arabs. The Jewish representatives accepted the Partition Resolution. Though they were averse to internationalization of Jerusalem, they accepted it for the sake of peace and international agreement.

Once the Partition Resolution was approved, it devolved upon the UN Trusteeship Council to provide a statute for the city of Jerusalem. The draft statute for the city of Jerusalem prepared by the Trusteeship Council's Working Committee affirmed that the city would be a corpus separatum within the Shuʿfāṭ-Abū Dīs-Bethlehem-ʿEin Kārim boundaries and would exist in this format for ten years.[39] A resident of Jerusalem was defined as any person residing in the city on November 29, 1947; others would have to reside for an interim period before they acquired the status of residents. Jerusalem citizenship would be exclusive, that is, a person could not be both a citizen of Jerusalem and a national of either the Jewish or the Arab state. Elections would be free and by secret ballot, and the franchise would be extended exclusively to Jerusalem's citizens (not to residents). The city's administration would be composed of the governor, a legislative council, a judicial body, and a general secretary. The governor and the general secretary would be nominated by and responsible to the Trusteeship Council.

Three proposals were advanced with regard to the composition of the legislative council: ethnic representation, religious representation, and general representation of all the voters. The committee's chairman, Benjamin Gerig of the United States, then advanced a compromise proposal: a 40-member council with 18 Jewish members, 18 Arab members, 1 or 2 members who were neither Arabs nor Jews, and the rest to be chosen by the general electorate from a list of 6 people nominated by the governor from among those residents registered as neither Jews nor Arabs.

While the working committee's discussions were in progress, fighting broke out in Palestine, and the Jewish section of Jerusalem came under siege from February 1948 onward. It was therefore decided that after the termination of the Mandate on May 15, 1948, a special municipal commissioner would be sent to discharge municipal functions until December 31, 1949. The person chosen to take up this post was Harold Evans, but as a Quaker he refused to accept a military escort to this post and preferred to wait in Cairo "until peace was restored." Accordingly, Pablo Azcárate y Florez, who was already in Palestine, was appointed temporary special municipal commissioner, but his efforts remained fruitless. The city's Jewish section was organized as a municipality, headed by Daniel Auster; the Arab section was under the rule of the Arab Legion. Evans resigned, and the post of special municipal commissioner was abolished.[40]

A similar fate overtook the draft statute for Jerusalem. It was put to the vote on May 14, 1948 and defeated. With the Mandate at an end, Jerusalem remained a corpus separatum but possessed neither statute nor governor.[41]

At this stage, the problem of Jerusalem was transferred to the General Assembly, which appointed Count Folke Bernadotte, president of the Swedish Red Cross, as UN mediator for Palestine (May 17, 1948). On June 11, he succeeded in negotiating a cease-fire, and on June 28 and 29 he presented preliminary proposals to the two sides.[42] Under the first of these, Jerusalem would become part of the Arab state, with municipal autonomy for its Jewish community and, needless to say, special arrangements for protecting the Holy Places. Israel's provisional government emphatically rejected any deviation from the November 29, 1947 resolution. King ʿAbdallāh of Jordan was positively disposed to Count Bernadotte's proposals, as Jerusalem was to be placed under his control. The Arab League opposed the plan and called for a single state in the whole of Palestine.

Meanwhile, the siege of Jewish Jerusalem was lifted, and in Israel calls were voiced for the annexation of the western portions of the city.[43] On August 2, 1948, those portions were placed under military administration, with Dov

Joseph as military governor. (On February 2, 1949, Israel replaced the military government by a civil administration, and when Israel and Jordan signed an agreement on armistice lines for Jerusalem on March 16, 1949, Jordan did the same. On January 23, 1950, while the 1950 draft statute for Jerusalem was being submitted to the United Nations, the Israeli parliament, the Knesset, affirmed that Jerusalem was and would remain the capital of Israel.)

On September 17, 1948, while on his way to the high commissioner's residence, Count Bernadotte was assassinated by Jewish extremists. However, his final report, which had been completed before his death, was presented to the General Assembly. With regard to Jerusalem, it proposed UN rule and supervision, with local autonomy for Jews and Arabs within the area determined in the General Assembly resolution of November 29, 1947, and the demilitarization of the city with free access by land and air for all parties. The report did not omit mention of the Holy Places, stressing that they should be protected after having suffered during the fighting.

Among his other proposals, Bernadotte also suggested the establishment of a conciliation commission responsible to the United Nations and operating upon its instructions.[44] Such a committee was indeed established (consisting of France, Turkey, and the United States), and UN Resolution No. 194 (III) of December 11, 1948 instructed it to submit "detailed proposals for a permanent international regime for the Jerusalem area which will provide for the maximum local autonomy for distinctive groups consistent with the special international status of the Jerusalem area."

On January 24, 1949, the Palestine Conciliation Commission took up its quarters in Jerusalem's high commissioner's residence, and on September 1, 1949, it presented draft proposals for an international regime for the Jerusalem area. Its plan proposed a permanent international regime for the Jerusalem area, within the boundaries determined by the November 29, 1947 resolution.[45] The Jerusalem region would be divided into two zones—Jewish and Arab (the latter to be administered by Jordan, being the "responsible authority of the Arab zone")—but the boundaries between them were not drawn precisely, as "the demarcation line . . . is intimately connected with the final settlement of the Palestine problem. . . ."

The plan further suggested that the United Nations be represented by a commissioner and a deputy commissioner, to be appointed for a five-year term. The commissioner would keep the peace, supervise the demilitarization of the city, and guarantee free access to the Holy Places.[46] The commissioner would be assisted by an appointed 14-person committee—consisting of 5 Arabs and 5 Jews nominated by "the responsible authorities" of the Jewish zone and the Arab zone and 2 Jews and 2 Arabs "who shall endeavour to ensure by his choice equitable representation on the Council of distinctive

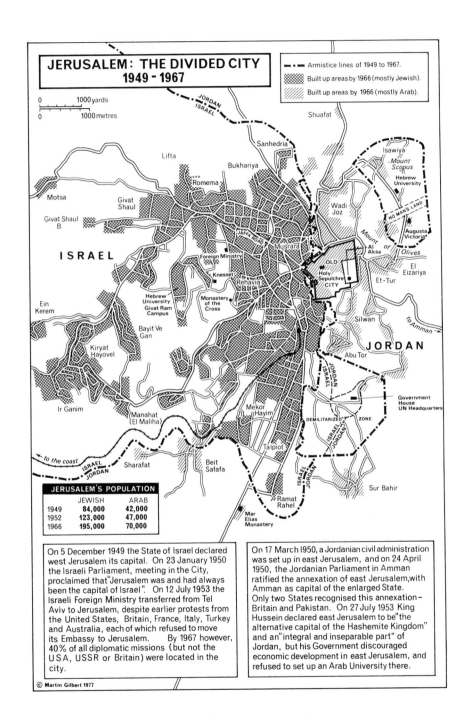

JERUSALEM: THE DIVIDED CITY 1949 - 1967

— · — Armistice lines of 1949 to 1967.

▨▨ Built up areas by 1966 (mostly Jewish).

▨▨ Built up areas by 1966 (mostly Arab).

0 ___ 1000 yards
0 ___ 1000 metres

JORDAN
ISRAEL

Shuafat

Sanhedria

Lifta

Bukhariya

Isawiya

Mount Scopus

Hebrew University

Romema

Motsa

Givat Shaul

Givat Shaul B

Wadi Joz

NO MAN'S LAND

Augusta Victoria

ISRAEL

JAFFA ROAD

Foreign Ministry

Musrara

Mount of Olives

Al Aksa

El Eizariya

Knesset

OLD Holy Sepulchre CITY

Et-Tur

Ein Kerem

Rehavia

Hebrew University Givat Ram Campus

Monastery of the Cross

Silwan

to Amman

Bayit Ve Gan

JORDAN

Kiryat Hayovel

Abu Tor

JORDAN ISRAEL

Ir Ganim

Manahat (El Maliha)

Mekor Hayim

Government House UN Headquarters

DEMILITARIZED ZONE

Talpiot

ISRAEL JORDAN

to the coast

ISRAEL JORDAN

Sharafat

Beit Safafa

Sur Bahir

ISRAEL JORDAN

JERUSALEM'S POPULATION

	JEWISH	ARAB
1949	84,000	42,000
1952	123,000	47,000
1966	195,000	70,000

Ramat Rahel

Mar Elias Monastery

On 5 December 1949 the State of Israel declared west Jerusalem its capital. On 23 January 1950 the Israeli Parliament, meeting in the City, proclaimed that "Jerusalem was and had always been the capital of Israel". On 12 July 1953 the Israeli Foreign Ministry transferred from Tel Aviv to Jerusalem, despite earlier protests from the United States, Britain, France, Italy, Turkey and Australia, each of which refused to move its Embassy to Jerusalem. By 1967 however, 40% of all diplomatic missions (but not the USA, USSR or Britain) were located in the city.

On 17 March 1950, a Jordanian civil administration was set up in east Jerusalem, and on 24 April 1950, the Jordanian Parliament in Amman ratified the annexation of east Jerusalem, with Amman as capital of the enlarged State. Only two States recognised this annexation – Britain and Pakistan. On 27 July 1953 King Hussein declared east Jerusalem to be "the alternative capital of the Hashemite Kingdom" and an "integral and inseparable part" of Jordan, but his Government discouraged economic development in east Jerusalem, and refused to set up an Arab University there.

© Martin Gilbert 1977

minority groups in the Jerusalem area''—that would function in the spheres of legislation, public services, preservation of antiquities, and economic supervision. In addition, special courts would be established at two levels. This entire structure would be erected on top of the existing Arab and Jewish administrative structures, so as to bridge the gap created by the city's partition. Existing administrative agencies, Jewish and Arab, would continue to function.

At the time the Conciliation Commission presented its report, the Soviet bloc and the Arab states (except for Jordan and Iraq) supported territorial internationalization. Worldwide Catholic public opinion was inclined toward territorial internationalization, while Protestants supported functional internationalization. The commission's proposals, which adopted neither principle, were therefore subject to widespread criticism and were rejected by the General Assembly's ad hoc committee.

Moshe Sharett, then Israeli foreign minister, reiterated the Israeli view, which concurred with functional internationalization of the Holy Places but opposed territorial internationalization.[47] He proposed that the UN secretary-general be instructed to reach agreement with Israel on ensuring protection for the Holy Places in the western section of the city. The secretary-general could also appoint a representative to take up residence in Jerusalem and supervise implementation of this agreement. This proposal, however, was not adopted by the General Assembly's ad hoc committee.[48]

The Arab position on internationalization was complex. While all Arab states opposed internationalization at the time of the 1947 Partition Resolution, by the time the Palestine Conciliation Commission gave its report in September 1949, a polarization on the issue within the Arab world had taken place. This stemmed from the fact that Jordan had taken effective control of the Arab part of Jerusalem. Thus the Jordanians, like the Israelis, had an interest in resisting territorial internationalization.

Contacts between the leaders of the Jewish community (subsequently Israel) and King ʿAbdallāh were initiated well before 1948 and continued until close to the king's assassination in 1951. These meetings dealt with the Jerusalem issue as part of an overall settlement of the Palestine question, whereby the country would be partitioned, with Israel occupying one part and the Arab regions being annexed by the Hashemite Kingdom of Jordan. This tacit agreement was the basis for the talks that transpired between Israel and Jordan throughout 1948, particularly toward the end of the year.[49]

These talks, which culminated early in 1949 (at the time of the Rhodes armistice negotiations), led to a polarization of the Arab view on Jerusalem. On the one hand, King ʿAbdallāh countermanded any attempt to internationalize the city. His policy rested upon the understandings and practical agreements he had succeeded in reaching with Israel regarding the division of the city between the two states, and it had managed to gain partial support among

Palestinian Arabs, as well as the backing of the other Hashemite Kingdom, Iraq. At the opposing pole were the vigorous support for internationalization common to all the Arab states, above all Egypt, and the reserved support of some Palestinian Arabs (the Mufti's followers). The background to this support for internationalization was primarily opposition to the extension of ꜤAbdallāh's kingdom to the west of the Jordan River and to Jerusalem. From the point of view of the Arab states, the internationalization of Jerusalem was preferable to any kind of agreement between ꜤAbdallāh and Israel that would lead to full sovereignty of the two states over the two portions of Jerusalem (and of Palestine).

Consent to the internationalization of Jerusalem (with the exception of Jordan and its supporters) was essentially a reversal of the Arab position. This came about at the end of 1948 in response to talks between Israel and Jordan. However, the first prominent expression of this view was heard only early in 1949, when representatives of the Arab states met with the Palestine Conciliation Commission in Lebanon.[50] Support for the internationalization of Jerusalem was the only weapon left to the Arab states (and part of the Palestinian community) to attain their aim, which was to remove both halves of Jerusalem from the control of Israel and Jordan. Examples of the Arab arguments in favor of internationalization can be found in the speeches of the Egyptian and Syrian representatives to the United Nations on December 6 and 9, 1949.

In general, Arab support for the internationalization of Jerusalem was presented as the "noble" concession of their sanctified rights to the city in order to save Jerusalem from destruction and partition and to forestall the danger of damage to sites sanctified to hundreds of millions of believers throughout the world. This view became firmly established as the official policy of all the Arab states (with the exception of Jordan and Iraq) in the course of 1949, with the principal backing coming from Egypt. The weak point in the case presented by the supporters of internationalization was, obviously, their abandonment of the "Arab character" of the city. In consequence, there was an attempt to demand that the Arab League be granted extensive powers within the international administration, thus guaranteeing a concrete Arab foothold in the city's government.[51]

Extracts from the Jordanian press in this period generally expressed opposition to internationalization (and support for partition of the city), which was Jordan's policy after it established control over the eastern section of the city. The newspaper *al-DifāꜤ* contended that the Soviet Union, which supported internationalization, would exploit an international regime to penetrate the city and regain privileges there, as successor to the Russian czar, who was protector of the Orthodox churches.[52] *Filasṭīn* presented the principal Jordanian argument against internationalization, namely, that such an arrangement would permit the Jews to gain total control of the city.[53]

An important episode in the internal Arab disagreements over internationalization was the Lausanne Conciliation Conference, held in the spring and summer of 1949.[54] By that time, ʿAbdallāh had already succeeded in removing his Palestinian opponents, organized in a force called "al-Jihād al-Muqaddas," from the Jerusalem area, leaving him free to conduct negotiations on the city's future by means of the special committee (in accordance with the Rhodes Armistice Agreements) and in various direct meetings between the sides.[55] The Jordanians had great difficulty in dealing with administrative and economic problems in eastern Jerusalem, primarily because of the presence of many refugees from Arab quarters taken over by Israel. These refugees looked forward to returning to their property and were thus suspicious and hostile toward continued partition of the city along the existing boundaries and ʿAbdallāh's consent to their final separation from their property and homes.

King ʿAbdallāh's firm decision to reject internationalization and agree to divide the city with Israel is clearly presented in the commentary by al-Difāʿ on September 15, 1949 (following the failure of the Lausanne talks and publication of the recommendations for the internationalization of Jerusalem). This article presents every possible argument, from the Jordanian viewpoint, opposing international supervision. This same view was also expressed with great vigor by the premier of Jordan, Tawfīq abu l-Hudā, and by ʿAbdallāh.[56] When the Arab League debated the issue, Jordan presented itself as the protector of the city's "Arab character,"[57] while trying to dismiss the greatest drawback involved in consenting to the city's partition, namely, relinquishing those Arab quarters that were in Israeli hands.

In discussing the proposals of the Palestine Conciliation Commission, the General Assembly's ad hoc political committee weighed an Australian draft resolution, which called for territorial internationalization of the corpus separatum within the November 29, 1947 boundaries. The area would be administered by the United Nations via the Trusteeship Council and under the Jerusalem statute, whose preparation was now to be completed. This plan was unacceptable to both Jordan and Israel. A Dutch-Swedish proposal for functional internationalization of the Holy Places was submitted on December 25, 1949, but it was not passed by the General Assembly. The proposal spoke of functional internationalization under the supervision of the United Nations and its commissioner. The Palestine governments would provide guarantees regarding the Holy Places.[58]

The predominant Protestant position favored functional internationalization. A proposal was advanced by the Archbishop of Canterbury on October 31, 1949, calling for territorial internationalization of the Old City and the adjoining commercial area, the Mount of Olives, Mount Scopus, Terra Sancta, and the Bethlehem road, and international supervision of the Holy Places in Jerusalem, Bethlehem, and Nazareth. The parts of the city that did not come under international supervision would be granted to Israel.[59]

The Catholic view favored territorial internationalization.[60] The Vatican's position was that it was possible to agree to the establishment of a Jewish state if Jerusalem were internationalized. Its assumption was that the existence of the Christian community in the city and the return of refugees would be more feasible in an internationalized city. The Vatican's position influenced Catholic political support for the partition plan. In his Encyclical of October 24, 1948, following the assassination of Bernadotte, the Pope called on his congregants to pray for the cessation of hostilities; free access to the Holy Places and freedom of worship to be ensured by international guarantees; and the bestowal of "an international character to Jerusalem and its vicinity." In his Encyclical of April 15, 1949, against the background of the signing of the armistice agreement between Israel and Jordan in April 1949 and coinciding with the vote on Israel's membership in the United Nations, the Pope reaffirmed the views he expressed the previous October. He demanded that Israel guarantee long-established Catholic prerogatives in Jerusalem and called for the full internationalization "of Jerusalem and the other Holy Places" and freedom of pilgrimage.[61]

In keeping with UN Resolution No. 303, which had been passed by the General Assembly on December 9, 1949, the Trusteeship Council set about preparing the statute for Jerusalem.[62] A working paper was drawn up by Council President Roger Garreau.[63] The text of the proposal appears in Garreau's report. According to his proposal, the Jerusalem area would be divided into three parts: an Israeli zone, under the supervision and administration of the State of Israel; a Jordanian zone, under the supervision and administration of Jordan; and an international zone, under collective UN sovereignty.

Garreau stated that the international area would be administered by the governor of the Holy Places (to be appointed by the Trusteeship Council), who would supervise the demilitarization of the city and the Holy Places. The Haram al-Sharif was excluded from the international zone because it was being administered by Jordan, a Muslim state. The governor would be assisted by an elected municipal council, chosen by the city's inhabitants in general elections, as well as an advisory general council for interdenominational problems and three committees for the Holy Places. The area would also have an international police force; two levels of adjudication (judges would be appointed by the supreme justice, who would himself be chosen by the Trusteeship Council); and its flag would be that of the United Nations. This administration would be in effect for a ten-year period.

In the end, however, the Garreau committee's plan was dropped by the Trusteeship Council, which decided to submit its own report to the General Assembly accompanied by the text of the statute it had approved, Garreau's reports, and the reply of the Israeli government dated May 26, 1950. It also delivered to the Assembly the appeals of the Armenian Patriarchate, the U.S.

National Council of Churches, and the Neturei Karta, all in favor of internationalization.[64]

The Jerusalem statute, as finally ratified by the Trusteeship Council on April 4, 1950, confirmed Jerusalem's status as a corpus separatum[65] to be divided into three zones: an Israeli zone, a Jordanian zone, and an international zone under collective UN sovereignty. The area would be demilitarized for ten years, after which its fate would be decided by a referendum and a decision of the Trusteeship Council. The area would be declared a free trade zone, and immigration into it would be restricted (according to the absorptive capacities of the various communities) and subject to the supervision of the legislative council. Administration of the area would come under the governor of the Holy Places (nominated by the Trusteeship Council), who would supervise the city's demilitarization and administer the Holy Places (that is, preserve the Status Quo) with the assistance of three committees for the Holy Places.

The governor's role would be supplemented by a municipal council elected by the city's citizens in general elections, a general council, a council for intercommunal problems, an international police force, a juridical system, and a legislative council. Twenty-five members of the latter body would be elected by four electoral colleges on the basis of religious affiliation: eight Jews, eight Muslims, eight Christians, and a single representative for those citizens not belonging to any of the other three electoral colleges. In addition to these 25 members, the legislative council would have no more than 15 appointed members, making a total of 40. This council would approve the city seal and its flag. The administration of the city would be implemented by a chief secretary, to be appointed by the Trusteeship Council. However, the governor of the Holy Places would appoint a prosecutor-general, as well as the other components of the administrative system.

This statute met with objections from both Jordan and Israel. Jordan refused even to discuss internationalization.

The Israeli position was presented in a letter dated May 26, 1950 from Abba Eban, then Israeli representative to the United Nations. It stated that democratic principles support the right of the citizens of Jerusalem to choose the administration they find desirable. As Jerusalem possessed a tradition and political bodies linked with Israel, democratic institutions must not be overthrown in favor of imported authoritarian rule. Jerusalem's severance from Israel was also unthinkable for economic and security reasons. However, Israel was prepared to assist the United Nations in fulfilling its commitments with regard to the Holy Places, as long as the United Nations abandoned political and secular coordination and dealt with religious matters alone. It was feasible to adopt internationalization of the area of the Holy Places, rather than territorial internationalization. According to the Israeli view, internationalization lay within the power and responsibility of the General Assembly.

A UN representative could supervise the Holy Places—safeguarding the rights of the various religions there, ensuring their upkeep, and facilitating access for pilgrims—and Israel promised to cooperate with such a representative.

The Trusteeship Council decided to take no further steps before receiving instructions from the General Assembly. And inasmuch as General Assembly decisions require a two-thirds majority, which was not gained, the proposal was defeated. A further discussion in July 1952 also failed to produce any results.

In May 1954, after serious outbreaks of shooting had occurred in Jerusalem, the Vatican asked the French government to use its good offices to protect the Holy Places. The consuls of France, Britain, and the United States established a committee that recommended, first of all, the demilitarization of the area that encompassed all the Holy Places and the manning of the area with an international police force. After this recommendation was rejected, a plan was proposed to create an area in which artillery and mortars would be forbidden. However, Israel and Jordan, both of which opposed the idea of internationalization, reached an agreement between senior officers, and the French initiative was withdrawn.[66]

Meanwhile, the actual political situation in Jerusalem was altered: The city, which had remained divided between Israel and Jordan along the March 16, 1949 armistice lines until the Six-Day War, was then reunited under Israeli rule.

NOTES

1. H. Eugene Bovis, *The Jerusalem Question 1917-1968* (Stanford, Calif.: Hoover Institution Press, 1971), pp. 6-7: C. Rackauskas, *The Internationalization of Jerusalem* (Washington, D.C.: Catholic Association for International Peace, 1957), p. 9. On the Status Quo in the Christian Holy Places, see S. P. Colbi, "The Christian Establishment," this volume.

2. The cardinal's letter appeared in the *New York Times*, June 16, 1922.

3. Article 95 of the Treaty of Sèvres (August 10, 1920) (Cmd. 964, p. 26), quoted by the Peel Commission, Cmd. 5479 (1937) pp. 30-31, par. 33, endows, under Article 22 (of the League of Nations Covenant), "to entrust, by application of the provisions of Article 22, the administration of Palestine" to a mandatory, who would be "responsible for putting into effect the declaration originally made on November 2, 1917 by the British Government [the Balfour Declaration], and adopted by the other Allied Powers." The Treaty of Sèvres was never implemented. In 1923 Turkey signed the Treaty of Lausanne, which does not mention the Mandate.

4. On the Vatican position, see Bovis, *The Jerusalem Question*, pp. 6-7, 10-12.

5. George Antonius, *The Arab Awakening* (Beirut: Khayat's College Book Cooperative, 1938), pp. 443-58.

6. Bovis, *The Jerusalem Question*, pp. 19-20; and Cmd. 2559.

7. Great Britain, Parliamentary Papers, Cmd. 1785, Mandate for Palestine, pp. 2-9.

8. Palestine (Holy Places) Order in Council, 1924, *Palestine Official Gazette*, no. 123, p. 814; cf. UNSCOP Report, Ch. 3, p. 36.

9. Y. Porath, *The Emergence of the Palestinian-Arab National Movement 1918-1929*, vol. 1 (London: Frank Cass, 1974), pp. 258-73.

10. Ibid., pp. 258-60.

11. International Commission for the Wailing Wall, London, H. M. Stationary Office, 1931. See Paul L. Hanna, *British Policy in Palestine* (Washington, D.C.: American Council on Public Affairs, 1942), pp. 92-108. Hanna discusses in particular the Passfield White Paper of October 1930, which was based on the report of the Commission of Inquiry of Sir Walter Shaw (Cmd. 3539) and the report of Sir John Hope Simpson. See also Y. Porath, *The Palestinian Arab National Movement 1929-1939: From Riots to Rebellion*, vol. 2 (London: Frank Cass, 1977), pp. 3-8.

12. And even earlier, at the beginning of the 1920s by Jewish personalities. Aharon Eisenberg of Reḥovot related a discussion held on the subject at a meeting with Rāghib al-Nashāshibī; see D. Rubinstein, this volume.

13. Chaim Arlosoroff's letter to Herbert Samuel, dated January 7, 1932, and notification of the letter to Campbell on January 19, 1932. On April 18, 1932, Campbell contradicted his own proposal by stating: "The government views with disfavor any proposal for the partition of Jerusalem." He attached his hopes to the changes that would be introduced by the new municipal ordinance. Despite his statement, the Jewish Municipal Committee continued to discuss the feasibility of establishing a separate Jewish Municipality. Emissaries were sent to Damascus and Beirut to investigate the situation there, and their reports were discussed. But the matter was shelved for fear that discussions on a separate Municipality would detract from the demands for changes in the municipal constitution, which was then the most urgent matter on the agenda in view of official proposals for a new municipal ordinance. (See "Jerusalem Municipality" File no. 9953, Sect. S/25 [the Jewish Agency Political Department] in the Zionist Archives in Jerusalem.)

In 1933, Daniel Auster submitted his comments on the proposed municipal ordinance (see Sect. A/297, File no. 21, the Daniel Auster Archives, the Zionist Archives). He pointed out a number of defects in the proposal and made the following suggestions: (1) the mayoralty should be rotated between Jews and Arabs; (2) electoral wards should be drawn without territorial continuity but should be homogeneous from the religious viewpoint; (3) the city should be divided into boroughs "with internal autonomy," and "a Municipal Council consisting of the representatives of all these boroughs" should be established (he employed the English word "boroughs" and the French term "arrondissements").

14. File G/5/34 in the archives of the mandatory government's chief secretariat notes (no. 76) that the wards were laid out in a manner designed "to avoid the creation of any large minorities in any one electoral ward." A list of the wards may be found in the above file (Appendix X, File no. 3).

15. Files no. 9728, Sect. S/25 and 5876, Sect. S/25, concerning the subject of Jerusalem, in the Zionist Archives.

16. Bovis, *The Jerusalem Question*, p. 21.

17. Palestine Royal Commission Report, Cmd. 5479, July 7, 1937; Hanna, *British Policy in Palestine*, pp. 126-40.

18. Porath, *The Palestinian Arab National Movement*, pp. 228-32.

19. Walter Laqueur, *A History of Zionism* (New York: Schocken, 1976), pp. 518-21; and Christopher Sykes, *Crossroads to Israel 1917-1948* (Cleveland and New York: World, 1965), pp. 173-76.

20. Palestine Partition Commission, Sir John Woodhead, Cmd. 5854.

21. The Jewish Agency memorandum to the Palestine Partition Commission, "Jerusalem Under Partition," August 1938.

22. Memorandum to the Palestine Partition Commission, submitted by M. Ussishkin, Jerusalem, July 22, 1938.

23. Proposals for the Institution of a Hebrew Jerusalem Municipality, Daniel Auster Archives, A/297/125, in the Zionist Archives.

24. State Department memorandum, October 14, 1938.

25. British Foreign Office Documents FO 371/21879 and FO 371/4890, August 1938, in the State Archives.

26. ESCO Foundation for Palestine, Inc., *Palestine: A Study of Jewish, Arab and British Policies* (New Haven, Conn.: Yale University Press, 1947), vol. 2, pp. 862-75, with maps.

27. Palestine: Statement of Policy, Cmd. 6019.

28. Gabriel Cohen, "Harold MacMichael and the Question of the Future of Palestine" (in Hebrew), *Hamizrah Hehadash* (The New East) 25 (1975): 52-68.

29. British Foreign Office Document FO 371/45410, no. 192, in the State Archives. The second proposal would have left both Jews and Arabs in the minority, whereas, as things stood, their strength was equal, each having 6 out of 12 members of the Municipal Council. On April 20, Gort reported to the colonial secretary (FO 371/45410, no. 627) on an Arab proposal to divide the city between the old and new sections. He added that he had yet to receive concrete details.

30. Document no. 19, File S/25/5877, in the Zionist Archives, which contains details of the negotiations that preceded the high commissioners's March proposals and his order of July 1945, the response to them, and the Jewish policy of noncooperation with Chief Justice Fitzgerald.

31. Report by Sir William Fitzgerald on the Local Administration of Jerusalem, August 28, 1945.

32. The Jews, in fact, refused to appear before Chief Justice Fitzgerald. He presented their views from his own personal knowledge, relying as well on "a year's-long correspondence between them and the government."

33. Fitzgerald reports that they included 92,000 Jews, 32,000 Muslims, and 27,000 who were neither Jews nor Muslims—the majority of whom were Arabs, however.

34. Great Britain, Foreign Office Report, Cmd. 6808.

35. Proposals for the Future of Palestine (July 1946-February 1947), Cmd. 7044.

36. *New York Times*, October 24, 1946; *The Political Problem of Palestine: An Analysis of Proposed Solutions* (Jerusalem: Jewish Agency for Palestine, July 1947); and *The Jewish Plan for Palestine, Memoranda and Statements Presented by the Jewish Agency for Palestine to the UNSCOP* (Jerusalem: Jewish Agency for Palestine, 1947).

37. Cf. Bovis, *The Jerusalem Question*, pp. 40, 134; and Sykes, *Crossroads to Israel*, p. 303.

38. See UNSCOP report to the General Assembly, A/364, Sect. 5 and 6, and especially Sect. 3, pt. 3, of the General Assembly resolution: Resolution 181 (11), pt. 3, pp. 146-50. The countries were Australia, Canada, Czechoslovakia, Guatemala, India, Iran, Holland, Peru, Sweden, Uruguay, and Yugoslavia.

39. Draft Statute for the City of Jerusalem, T/118, January 26, 1948.

40. Bovis, *The Jerusalem Question*, pp. 56-59.

41. The Jewish Agency objected to the draft statute for Jerusalem (see UN Document T/123, February 17, 1948), defining as undemocratic the proposals that only citizens of Jerusalem, and not residents, be included in the electorate and that elections be held on an ethnic basis. It also had comments concerning the sections dealing with adjudication, finances, and general matters.

42. UN Document S/863, June 28, 1948.

43. On May 15, 1948, the Jerusalem Municipal Council issued such a call to the provisional government. See Dov Joseph, *The Faithful City* (New York: Simon & Schuster; Tel Aviv: Schocken, 1960), pp. 298-99; M. Benvenisti, *Jerusalem: The Torn City* (Minneapolis: University of Minnesota Press, 1976), pp. 6-7. See also *Official Gazette* (in Hebrew), no. 12, August 2, 1948.

44. The mediator's report, UN document A/648.

45. United Nations Conciliation Commission, UN Document A/973 1949. The ten-year limitation of the November 29, 1947 resolution had been deleted.

46. Holy Places being those regarded as such on May 14, 1948 (Article 15 in UN Document A/973).

47. *New York Times*, September 17, 1949.

48. Reactions to the proposals of the Conciliation Commission, UN Document A/1222, p. 36.

49. Benvenisti, *Jerusalem*, pp. 7–23; ʿAbdallāh al-Tall, *Kārithat Filasṭin (The Palestine Disaster)* (Cairo: Maṭbaʿ at Miṣr, 1959), pp. 344–46.

50. The newspaper *Filasṭin*, March 23, 1949, on the internationalization of Jerusalem.

51. Ibid.

52. *Al-Difāʿ*, April 28, 1949, on the internationalization of Jerusalem.

53. *Filasṭin*, June 6, 1949, on the internationalization of Jerusalem.

54. *Filasṭin*, June 23, 1949, on Lausanne—internationalization of Jerusalem; July 20, 1949, on partition and internationalization.

55. ʿAbdallāh al-Tall, *Kārithat Filasṭin*, p. 365; M. Benvenisti, *The Torn City* (Hebrew edition) (Jerusalem: Weidenfeld and Nicolson, 1973), pp. 58–65.

56. *Al-Difāʿ*, October 18, 1949, on the Jordanian position; and October 20, 1949, King ʿAbdallāh's address.

57. *Al-Difāʿ*, October 27, 1949.

58. Bovis, *The Jerusalem Question*, pp. 76–80.

59. Ibid., pp. 74, 84, 136.

60. A good presentation of the Roman Catholic view on internationalization at the time is given by Rackauskas, *The Internationalization of Jerusalem*.

61. See the Encyclical "In Multiplicibus," *New York Times*, October 24, 1948, "International Character to Jerusalem and Its Vicinity"; quoted also by Rackauskas, *The Internationalization of Jerusalem*, pp. 69–71. The Encyclical "Redemptoris Nostri" appeared in *New York Times*, April 16, 1949; Rackauskas, *The Internationalization of Jerusalem*, pp. 71–72. The original texts of the two encyclicals were published in *Oriente Moderno* 28 (1948): 172–74; and 29 (1949): 52–53. Pope Paul VI reiterated the demand for the internationalization of Jerusalem on June 26, 1967, after the city's reunification (*New York Times*, June 27, 1967). However, the Vatican's call was far less vigorous in 1967 than it had been in 1918 and 1947, apparently because of the numerical decline of Jerusalem's Christian population in the course of 19 years of partition and the change in the numerical ratio of Christian states in the United Nations, both of which could have prevented the presence of a strong Christian body within the corpus separatum. On July 11, 1967, the Vatican declared (*New York Times*, July 13, 1967) that it was withdrawing its old demand for internationalization of the city and was studying Israeli proposals for granting immunity and invulnerability to the Holy Places, a status similar to that granted to foreign embassies. See also Benvenisti, *Jerusalem*, p. 264.

62. See UN Assembly Resolution no. 303 of December 9, 1949 for details: a permanent corpus separatum within the borders of the November 29, 1947 decision; the Trusteeship Council was asked to prepare a status for Jerusalem.

63. Bovis, *The Jerusalem Question*, pp. 82–84.

64. The declared policy of the highly Orthodox, anti-Zionist Jews of the Neturei Karta was to oppose a Zionist municipality (preferring a mixed municipality) and a Zionist state. See *Hahomah*, May 13, 1945; November 19, 1947; July 21, 1948; and October 19, 1949.

65. See UN Document A/1286.

66. Benvenisti, *The Torn City* (Hebrew edition), pp. 71–73.

3

THE JERUSALEM MUNICIPALITY UNDER THE OTTOMANS, BRITISH, AND JORDANIANS

Daniel Rubinstein

FORMATION OF THE MUNICIPALITY IN THE NINETEENTH CENTURY

Prior to the middle of the nineteenth century, Jerusalem was not an integrated unity with corporate municipal institutions but a conglomeration of heterogeneous quarters lacking an overarching municipal authority or administration. Indeed, even after urban government was introduced, the development of the city as a corporate entity with a representative elected council was a gradual protracted process.

The founding of the Jerusalem Municipality took place in 1863 by a special firman.[1] (According to some, it was founded in 1864 at the time of the Law of Vilāyets.) The Municipal Council included five appointed members: three Muslims, one Christian, and one Jew. Actually, the first functioning council was not appointed until 1867. Its budget was narrow and its scope of action limited. The groundwork for the organization of the Jerusalem Municipality was laid during the period of Egyptian occupation under Ibrāhīm Pasha (1831–40). Among the political and social reforms introduced by the Egyptians was the establishment of consultative municipal bodies (*majlis*, or *dīwān, al-shūrā*) to advise the governor (*vali*). In Jerusalem (and elsewhere) Christians and Jews participated along with Muslims in these councils. During the early nineteenth century, before the Egyptian occupation, a dīwān had functioned in Jerusalem, made up of religious functionaries and having rather limited powers. When Egyptian rule was terminated in

1840, the Sublime Porte retained the provincial councils as advisory bodies to the local governor.

The Jerusalem Municipal Council had to act in concert with other authoritative bodies. It received authorization from the Sublime Porte in Istanbul and from the governor of the Jerusalem *mūtasarriflik*. Moreover, the council did not function independently of foreign consuls and representatives of foreign religious communities. It is noteworthy that a number of foreign consuls protested the foundation of the Municipality, suspecting that their own prerogatives would be curtailed; other consuls were supportive and helped it function during the period of its modest first steps.

The first flutter of municipal activity in the 1860s was intensified in 1871 with the passage of a law on the general administration of the Ottoman provinces. In 1877, with the promulgation of the Provincial Municipal Code, the jurisdiction and functions of the Jerusalem Municipality were further augmented. The main points of the code were as follows:

- Establishment of a single local authority in towns with less than 40,000 inhabitants. In larger towns, councils would be established for the various quarters, none of which was to exceed 40,000 inhabitants (this section was of importance later, when attempts were made to take advantage of it as a justification for partitioning Jerusalem). The Ottoman government apparently inserted this provision to prevent the creation of power centers in the large cities.
- The municipal councils were to consist of six to twelve members elected for four-year periods, with half coming up for reelection every two years.
- The franchise was limited to male Ottoman citizens over age 25 who paid a certain minimal sum in taxes on their property.
- The candidates were to be Turkish-speaking Ottoman citizens aged 30 or over who paid a certain minimal sum (larger than that required of voters) in municipal taxes on their property.
- The duties of the Municipality were as follows: erection and maintenance of public buildings, roads, markets, hospitals, and water supply; planning and supervision of building; registration of births and deaths; supervision of eating places and places of entertainment, bakeries, slaughterhouses, and public washrooms; as well as police and defense duties.
- The Municipality's financing was to come from grants from the central government and a series of municipal taxes.
- The mayor was chosen from among those elected to the council; his salary was to be paid by the Municipality (the other councillors served without pay).

This Ottoman legislation was modeled on French law, and a number of amendments were made until the British occupation of Palestine. The number of councillors also changed. (They were elected on one occasion only, in 1908; for the rest of the Ottoman period, they were appointed.) Later Arab policy toward Jerusalem's Municipality had for its principal basis the precedents laid down with the establishment of the Ottoman municipality. These precedents referred to representation on the Municipal Council (in other words, a majority of Muslim members, with limited representation for Jews and Christians), a Muslim mayor, election procedures, the franchise, the powers of the Municipality and its duties, municipal taxation, and so on.

Despite the fact that a majority of Jerusalem's residents were Jews when the Municipality was established, the Ottoman period saw the creation of a series of precedents limiting their participation in urban politics:

- A relatively large proportion of Jerusalem's Jewish inhabitants were not Ottoman citizens and were consequently prevented from taking part in the elections (it is also possible that they displayed no particular interest in doing so). A similar situation prevailed on a smaller scale among the Christians.

- A considerable portion of Jewish property in the city was registered in the name of communal organizations (*kolelim*) or Jewish philanthropists residing abroad, who could not be considered property owners entitled to take part in the elections.

- The mayoralty became, in effect, the preserve of several notable Arab families (for example, Ḥusaynī, Khālidī, ʿAlamī, and Daʾūdī).

- Because the residents of the Old City were exempt from paying municipal taxes, it was determined that persons living within the Old City walls were entitled to vote even if they did not pay the minimal tax. In the course of the years, Jewish and Christian residents left the Old City for the new neighborhoods (where they had to prove possession of property and payment of municipal tax in order to vote), with the result that the Muslim electorate gained preference and additional weight.

- The principle of a Muslim majority on the Municipal Council, with partial representation for Jews and Christians, was maintained until the end of the Ottoman period. (The last council consisted of ten members: six Muslims, two Christians, and two Jews—Christian representation being divided between the Catholics and Orthodox and Jewish representation between Ashkenazim and Sephardim.) At the same time, the first municipal elections (1908) showed that the Jewish votes could affect the election of Muslims because of the principle whereby all voters cast ballots for all candidates, although representation was denominational and communal.[2]

THE PERIOD OF THE BRITISH MANDATE

British Military Government (December 1917 to June 1920)

When the British entered Jerusalem on December 9, 1917, Mayor Ḥusayn al-Ḥusaynī surrendered the city to the conquering army. A few weeks later al-Ḥusaynī died, and the British military government appointed his elder brother, Mūsā Kāẓim al-Ḥusaynī (formerly Ottoman governor of Yemen), to fill the post. The last Ottoman Municipal Council consisted of ten members: seven Muslims, two Jews (one Sephardi, the other Ashkenazi), and one Christian. Shortly after the occupation began, in January 1918, the British appointed a temporary council consisting of two representatives from each community. Ronald Storrs, the military governor of the Jerusalem district, introduced an innovation by appointing deputy mayors—one Jewish, the other Christian—who were to act alternately as mayor in the mayor's absence. Storrs does not mention whether or not the two deputies had equal status.[3]

The six municipal councillors reflected the city's religious, national, and communal divisions: Mūsā Kāẓim al-Ḥusaynī (the mayor) and Saᶜd al-Dīn al-Khālilī were the Muslim representatives; Yaᶜqūb Farrāj, a Greek Orthodox (deputy mayor), and Yūsuf Albīnā, a Catholic, represented the Christians; David Yellin, an Ashkenazi (deputy mayor) and Yitzḥaq Eliachar, a Sephardi, represented the Jews. This provisional council altered the representational balance that had been customary during the Ottoman period, when the Muslims always constituted an absolute majority of the council's members. At the same time, the Jews constituted only one third of the representatives, although they were now an absolute majority of the city's population. In later years, the Muslim representatives would frequently note that the Jews constituted a majority of the population as far back as the previous century but were nevertheless not proportionately represented because they realized that there was no justification for such an arrangement in Jerusalem.[4]

In the course of 1918, the first year of British military rule, it became evident that the Arabs were adopting a clearly political posture in their attitude toward the Jerusalem Municipality, its domination, and above all, the post of mayor. This was the year in which Jerusalem became the administrative capital of the whole of Palestine, and the struggle for control of the Municipality immediately became part of the political struggle over the Balfour Declaration and the Zionist aim of building a Jewish National Home in Palestine. National and political tensions in the Jerusalem Municipality first appeared at the beginning of 1918, when fighting was still in progress in the north of Palestine, as the Turkish propaganda network warned that the British were turning the Jews into the masters of the country in order to humiliate and repress its Arab population.[5] British policy held that a municipal authority, which served all the citizens, should have no interest in serving political ends.

Mayor Mūsā Kāzim al-Husaynī inaugurated his period of office by launching into ramified political activity as a front-line leader of the Palestinian-Arab national movement, which was campaigning against preparations for granting Britain the Mandate over Palestine. (After its ratification, it will be recalled, the Mandate included the Balfour Declaration.) In his two years as mayor, al-Husaynī headed several demonstrations of a political nature, which culminated in the 1920 Passover riots following the Nebi Mūsā celebration. These demonstrations ultimately led to his dismissal by Storrs, who appointed Rāghib al-Nashāshibī in his place.[6] The mayor's political activities are understandable when one considers that Jerusalem's Arab elite already headed the Palestinian national movement. The political activities of the mayor of Jerusalem also became a central issue in later years, during the terms of Rāghib al-Nashāshibī, Husayn al-Khālidī, Daniel Auster, and Mustafa al-Khālidī.

The fundamental Arab view concerning the Jerusalem Municipality (and, of course, the whole of Palestine) found unambiguous expression in a letter from Jaffa's Muslim-Christian Society addressed to General Sir Gilbert Clayton, chief political officer of the Military Administration, in November 1918.[7] The letter stated that Jerusalem is considered the Holy Place of all nations, as was acknowledged by General Allenby in the *Palestine News* no. 8. The world Christian population is 750 million; the Muslims exceed 350 million; whereas the Jews do not exceed 14 million. The letter's implication regarding control of the city is clear. Thus the justification for Arab claims to control over Jerusalem based on the fact that local Arabs represent the entire Muslim world appears from the very start of British rule, and it can be found in almost all subsequent Arab documents dealing with the Jerusalem issue.

During the early days of British rule, Arab activity in municipal affairs and Mūsā Kāzim al-Husaynī's participation in political demonstrations were partly a response to Jewish demands, including the appointment of Jews to at least half of the seats on the Municipal Council, a Jewish mayor, and the introduction of Hebrew into official use in the Municipality, in keeping with General Allenby's first order concerning the three official languages (English, Arabic, and Hebrew) to be used in the country.[8] The Jewish deputy mayor, David Yellin, did introduce Hebrew at this time, but it was actually used very little; council meetings, for example, were conducted in Arabic until 1927.[9] Mūsā Kāzim al-Husaynī refused to introduce the Hebrew language into the Municipality, and his followers later contended that this was the true reason for his dismissal.[10]

The 1920s

With the establishment of Palestine's civil administration under High Commissioner Herbert Samuel (summer of 1920), an advisory council was convened. It was an appointed representative body, and one of the first items on its agenda was the Municipalities Law. (The council consisted of four Muslims and three Christians, making a total of seven Arabs, three Jews, and ten British officials.) The Arabs in the advisory council generally favored retention of the Ottoman Municipal Law, and the mandatory government supported this view (barring a few amendments), while the Jewish representatives called for certain modifications of the law, their principal aim being greater democracy.[11] With the agreement of a majority of the members of the advisory council, the government later (1926) published a new municipalities ordinance. One of its innovations (in contrast to the Ottoman law) was the enfranchisement of persons paying a municipal tax, even if they were not property owners but merely tenants.[12] The need for this modification arose as a result of the changes in municipal taxation (the imposition of an apartment tax) introduced by a decision of an official committee that considered the subject of municipal taxation at the end of 1920.[13] This subject was of decisive importance in Jerusalem, where many Jews had become municipal taxpayers and consequently acquired the right to vote. The Arabs were, of course, aware of the significance of this change.[14]

One provision of the new law was the requirement that voters must be "Palestinian citizens" (in place of "Ottoman citizens"). As a result of prolonged delays in enacting a Palestinian Citizenship Law, the municipal elections had to be put off until the spring of 1927. These delays stemmed from political events that are not within the scope of this chapter (the 1921 riots, the 1922 White Paper, the deliberations of the Mandates Commission, delays in completing the Lausanne Peace Treaties, and so on). However, this period (1920–26) witnessed political developments among Palestine's Arabs that were to have a powerful influence upon Arab views regarding the publication of the 1926 electoral law and the conduct of the April 1927 elections to Jerusalem's Municipality.

The most important of these political developments was the establishment of the Supreme Muslim Council in Jerusalem in 1922. The Palestinian Arabs were divided between supporters of the council under the Grand Mufti of Jerusalem, Ḥājj Amīn al-Ḥusaynī, and the opposition to al-Ḥusaynī, headed by Jerusalem's mayor, Rāghib al-Nashāshībī. (Al-Nashāshībī, it will be recalled, consented to take up his post in place of Mūsā Kāẓim al-Ḥusaynī, who was dismissed by the British government in 1920.)

The profound rivalry between the two camps created differences, largely of a tactical nature, in their attitudes toward the form of the municipal elections. The key question was whether the elections were to be held on a communal basis (that is, each community electing its own representatives exclusively, not influencing elections in other communities) or on a general basis, with candidates elected according to the number of votes gained in the entire city. And if the elections were to be held on a communal basis, there was the question of whether they should be organized according to religious, ethnic, national, or regional divisions. The British advanced a compromise plan whereby the communal distribution of the electorate (Jews, Muslims, and Christians) would serve as the basis for the number of councillors elected to represent each community, but the entire city would constitute a single electoral ward, and the election of representatives would be carried out on a general, rather than communal, basis.

The supporters of the Supreme Muslim Council (the Ḥusaynīs) called upon the government to conduct independent elections within each community and determine the number of representatives for each community by the percentage of its voters on the electoral roll. The Ḥusaynīs presented this demand in order to prevent rivals, the Nashāshībīs, from benefiting from Jewish votes.[15] The opposition, under Rāghib al-Nashāshibī, naturally rejected this demand, assuming that the nationalist views of their rivals would result in Jewish support for their own camp. Thus dissension within the Arab camp produced two views on the mode of determining municipal representation. The mandatory government, for its part, determined a form of electoral procedure and communal representation that resembled those in force during the Ottoman period.

The Jews likewise kept up constant pressure on a number of issues.[16] For example, they demanded a considerable extension of the franchise (votes for women, reduction of the voting age, repeal of a tax increase, and so on); that the mayor be elected rather than appointed; that the Municipal Council's term of office be shortened; and that the council be granted greater powers. The Arab position rested on vigorous opposition to any such efforts toward greater democracy. Furthermore, because of the constant Jewish pressure, a few Arabs even displayed a certain degree of readiness to partition the city, with the separation of Tel Aviv from Jaffa as a model. Aharon Eisenberg of Reḥovot tells of a conversation on this subject with Rāghib al-Nashāshibī.[17] Such a solution, however, does not appear to have been seriously considered at the time. Jewish pressure for greater representation on Jerusalem's Municipality Council was accompanied by demands for more Jews to be employed by the Municipality, contracts to be issued to Jews, development of the Jewish neighborhoods, more extensive use of Hebrew in the Municipality (hitherto, its use was very limited), and so on. However, this pressure does not appear to have created tensions in the Municipality prior to the 1927 elections; most of the clashes occurred later during the 1930s.

It should also be pointed out that, parallel to the discussions being conducted in the 1920s over the structure of the Jerusalem Municipality, with its particular set of problems, extremely comprehensive work was being done in relation to regional local government in Palestine. A committee conducted prolonged discussions (1923–25) on the powers of the district committee for education, health, transport, and other matters, though it had express instructions from the high commissioner to refrain from dealing with the urban municipalities.[18]

The 1927 Municipal Election

Following a key based on the electoral register, the 12 seats on the Municipal Council were allocated as follows: five to the Muslims, four to the Jews, and three to the Christians. The rivalry between supporters of the Supreme Muslim Council and their opposition, and the Ḥusaynis' desire to displace Rāghib al-Nashāshibī, led to unique attempts to establish Jewish-Arab cooperation during the election campaign. Jewish Supreme Court Justice Gad Frumkin tells of overtures made to him by supporters of the Mufti. And Jamāl al-Ḥusaynī and Jamīl al-Ḥusaynī approached Colonel F. H. Kisch (head of the political department of the Zionist Executive in Jerusalem) with proposals for an agreement whereby the Arabs would refrain from voting for Agudat Israel candidates if the Jews would refrain from voting for al-Nashāshibī.[19] The Ḥusaynis approached the Zionist leadership with a political formula whereby the two sides would cooperate so that each could defeat its own internal rivals.[20] At the same time, the Mufti of Jerusalem made Gad Frumkin other tempting offers with regard to certain Jewish demands. In addition, Arab camps addressed public appeals to the Jewish voters.[21]

The Ḥusaynis failed primarily because the Jews of Jerusalem succeeded in forming a prearranged slate of only four candidates (Y. Ben-Zvi, H. Solomon, Y. Eliachar, and A. Shammaᶜ) for their four places in the Municipal Council. The five Muslim seats and the three Christian seats were contested by rival slates of candidates presented by the Ḥusaynis and the Nashāshibis. In this manner, the Jews were free to choose between the Arab lists. They voted for Rāghib al-Nashāshibī and contributed to the defeat of the Ḥusaynis. The Ḥusaynis' attempt to reach agreement with the Jews became public, and the publicity may have contributed to their downfall among the Arab voters too.[22] Arab election propaganda tied together administrative issues in the work of the Municipality with national and political issues.

The elections lasted three days (April 5–7, 1927) and were conducted in separate polling stations for each community. They resulted in the election of six Nashāshibī candidates (three Muslims and three Christians) and two of the Mufti's candidates (both Muslims). As mentioned, the Jewish voter was not called upon to choose between his own candidates, but he played an important, if not decisive, role in choosing between the Arab candidates. This led to a change in the electoral system during the 1930s.

The Supreme Muslim Council carried on extensive activities on the issue of the Jerusalem Municipality during the 1920s. The Palestinian Arabs, primarily the Ḥusaynīs, undertook a series of activities in Palestine and abroad to highlight Jerusalem's Muslim and Arab character. The civil Municipality was under the control of the Nashāshībī opposition, but the Grand Mufti of Jerusalem and the Supreme Muslim Council operated in the religious (and, of course, the political) sphere by raising contributions, carrying out imposing renovations in the Ḥaram al-Sharīf mosques, establishing public committees, and sending delegations to the world's Muslim communities.[23] These activities undoubtedly helped to draw public attention in Palestine and abroad to the issue of Jerusalem. Two of their consequences were the 1929 riots over the issue of the Western Wall and the inquiry commissions established in their wake. The international committee established to decide the question of rights at the Wall (July 1930) heard Muslim representatives from outside Palestine (Egypt, Lebanon, Iraq, and Persia), along with local advocates of the Muslim cause. In general, it can be affirmed that the issue of an equitable and efficient municipal administration in Jerusalem was of a lower priority to the Arabs than the communal issue of control of the Municipality, which had broader political and national ramifications.

Important municipal matters, such as the boundaries of the city's area of jurisdiction and the status of the deputy mayors, received little consideration, but the Arab view on these issues did find expression in the 1920s and was highlighted further in the 1930s. Prior to the 1927 elections, a number of Arab quarters and villages were attached to the Municipality, and the Jewish representatives suspected that the motive behind this move was to undermine the city's Jewish majority.[24] When the city was hit by an earthquake in 1927, the mayor was on vacation and his Christian deputy (Y. Farrāj) was ill. As a result, a Jewish deputy mayor, H. Solomon, acted as mayor of the city for the first time.[25] Although the Christian deputy's position was not expressly defined in any formal document, he enjoyed a more favored status than the Jewish deputy. This problem, however, grew acute only at a later date. On the language question as well, new procedures were inaugurated in the course of the 1920s, and the Arabs went on the defensive as the Jews strengthened their foothold in the city administration.

The Pro-Jerusalem Society, established during the period of military government by Sir Ronald Storrs, played an unusual role in municipal activity during the 1920s.[26] Because political motivations interfered with practical activity on the municipal level, this society was active in many spheres of city life and, thanks to its unique apolitical character, provided a framework for Arab-Jewish contact and cooperation. Aided by contributions from members of all religions in the city and the country as a whole, as well as by Storrs' efforts to raise money abroad, the society financed such projects as proposals for urban planning, preservation of historical sites (including the renovations of the Ḥaram al-Sharīf mosques), fostering folkcrafts, the establishment of a committee to decide on names for streets and squares, a chess club, and other activities that fall within the sphere of a municipal authority. The society functioned for eight years and prudently managed to avoid incidents between Jewish and Arab representatives.

The 1930s

As the national and political conflict in Palestine grew more acute, the Jerusalem Municipality became a central issue in the confrontation. The Municipality's activities throughout the 1930s were marked by crises and mishaps. In contrast to the relative calm prevailing in Palestine through most of the 1920s, from the 1929 riots onward the country witnessed a series of events that had a marked impact on the functioning of Jerusalem's Municipality. These events and the official responses to them can be summed up as a general heightening of the national conflict in Palestine. As has been seen, from the onset of the British Mandate the composition and character of Jerusalem's Municipality were one of the most important elements in the overall Arab-Jewish confrontation.

Municipal elections were scheduled to be held early in 1931, after the close of the four-year term of the council elected in 1927. In view of the political circumstances, the British government extended the term of office of the existing Municipal Council, while preparing a new electoral law for the Municipality. In the meantime, on a visit to London in 1930, Mayor Rāghib al-Nashāshībī issued a number of nationalist statements, thus provoking a strong reaction on the part of the Jewish councillors. Early in 1931, the four Jewish councillors announced that they were boycotting council meetings, and for almost four years (until the 1934 elections) the Municipality functioned without its Jewish members. As the Jews constituted no more than one third of the council members (four out of twelve), the legally required quorum was nevertheless maintained. There is not much Arab documentation on this episode, as the Jewish boycott did not prevent the Municipality from functioning, and the situation was in fact quite convenient from the Arab viewpoint.[27]

From 1931, all sides awaited the new elections and followed the preparations for the new electoral law. In the course of 1932 and 1933, British officials held consultations on the new law with individuals and groups from both sides. Preparation of the new law dragged on because of the tensions and disturbances that again swept the country in 1933.

The new law, the 1934 Municipal Ordinance, granted some of the Arab demands for communal-based elections, to prevent voters from one community from influencing the representation of another. The system called for dividing the city into 12 electoral wards, each of which contained a majority of one community or another.[28] It also provided for an electoral committee based on parity for the three religions: a Muslim mayor, with a Christian and a Jewish deputy, the latter having special status. The special status of the Jewish mayor was the source of vigorous disagreements between Mayor Ḥusayn al-Khālidī and his Jewish deputy, Daniel Auster, especially in 1936, when al-Khālidī served as a member of the Arab Higher Committee. Arab objections did not relate to the system itself but rather to the definition of who was eligible to vote and thus to the proportion of Jewish representatives in the Municipal Council. After calculating the numbers of voters from the various communities in Jerusalem, the British administration came to the conclusion that the Jews were entitled to a majority of the elected representatives. At that time (March 1934) the Jerusalem district commissioner appointed the Electoral Committee for Jerusalem and briefed its members on their duties as determined by law.[29] While the electoral register was being drawn up, the Arabs naturally insisted on principles that would guarantee them a majority in the electorate. For example, the acting Mufti, Amīn al-Tamīmī, complained that residents of a quarter within the Old City walls were not registered because they had not paid taxes. He demanded retention of the practice whereby inhabitants of the Old City were entitled to vote regardless of tax payments because the *waqf* owned most of the property there.[30] At a later period (1945), Ḥusayn al-Khālidī explained what he considered to have been defects in registering Jewish voters in 1934, raising the following complaints: (1) The British were wrong in permitting the new law to reconfirm their earlier (1926) decision to enfranchise tenants and not exclusively property owners, as the Ottoman law had stipulated. This decision had increased the proportion of Jewish voters. (2) The 1934 elections witnessed an unreasonable increase in the number of Jewish voters, because of the enfranchisement of Jews not legally entitled to vote and suspicions of falsifications. (He accused the Electoral Committee for failing to require that Jewish voters prove they were indeed entitled to vote.) (3) As the size of the electoral wards was not uniform, the new form of elections gave the Jews an inequitable increase in power.[31]

The Mufti Ḥājj Amīn al-Ḥusaynī also complained about the manner in which the city was divided into wards. In his view, the presence of Jews within Arab wards prejudiced the Muslims' exclusive right to choose their representatives. He maintained that the elections should be held on a purely communal basis and complained that those Muslim voters living in Jewish or Christian wards were in effect deprived of the chance to vote for the representatives of their community.[32]

Even before the elections were held, the decision on the number of voters to be included in the electoral register and the division of the city into wards determined the new distribution of representatives on the Municipal Council: six Jews, four Muslims, and two Christians.[33] Despite the effort to conduct the elections on a purely communal basis (within the wards), this time as well, the few (124) Jewish voters residing in Ward 1 had the choice between al-Nashāshibī and al-Khālidī, and they opted for the latter.[34]

The results of the 1934 elections were a victory for the Mufti's followers and a defeat for the Nashāshibī opposition. The postelection clashes between the two rival Arab camps highlighted their views concerning the status of the Municipality, its character, and functions. After losing the elections, the Nashāshibīs challenged the results, going so far as to take the matter to court.[35] The opposition's complaints about the elections are of interest. In a memorandum to the high commissioner, Ḥasan Ṣidqī al-Dajānī, one of the leaders of the opposition, claimed that the appointment of a follower of the Mufti as mayor of Jerusalem would upset the equilibrium between the country's Arab factions and suggested that the mayoralty of Jerusalem was a kind of "preserve" of the Nashāshibī opposition.[36] His second contention affirmed that a Ḥusaynī at the head of the Jerusalem Municipality would encourage Arab nationalist extremism, which indicates the considerable political weight attached to the post. In response to the Nashāshibīs' complaints, there was a vigorous organized reaction by the supporters of al-Khālidī (and the Ḥusaynīs), particularly from the areas around Jerusalem.[37]

The elections at the end of 1934 made it clear to the Arabs that their control of Jerusalem's Municipality was drawing to an end. They seemed likely to lose their majority on the Municipal Council as well as the mayoralty. After the constitution of the council, two deputy mayors were appointed, one Jewish (Daniel Auster) and the other Christian (Y. Farrāj). The powers of the Jewish deputy were defined in separate talks that the high commissioner held with Moshe Shertok (Sharett) and Ḥusayn al-Khālidī[38]; but after taking up his post, al-Khālidī tried to evade implementing the agreement by denying that Auster was first deputy.[39]

The Municipal Council's first year of office passed more or less peacefully, with the principal issues being the official languages to be used in the Municipality[40] and the problem of allocating jobs and contracts to Arabs and Jews. In April 1936, after the onset of the Arab general strike, al-Khālidī sent a letter to the district commissioner stressing the stability of the Municipality's activities and noting that intercommunal relations were good. He promised to resolve the language issue and to regularize the division of contracts between Jews and Arabs.[41]

The Crisis (1936–1939)

Consistent with their response to the Mūsā Kāẓim al-Ḥusaynī and the Rāghib al-Nashāshibī episodes in 1920 and 1930, the Jews at the time of the 1936 general strike complained of the political and nationalistic activities of the Arab mayor of Jerusalem, al-Khālidī.[42] Naturally, the Arab general strike

led to disruptions in the functioning of the Municipal Council,[43] which ir-
ritated the Jews. Al-Khālidī's response to their complaints indicates the principles underlying the Arab view of the Municipality's functions.[44]

Generally outlined, these principles were:

- The mayor of Jerusalem was obligated to serve all the residents of his city,
  but he could not function under political restrictions. This was also the
  contention of his predecessors, Mūsā Kāẓim al-Ḥusaynī and Rāghib al-
  Nashāshībī, who played key roles in the leadership of the nationalist
  Palestinian Arabs in their struggle against Zionism, and this was the
  background to earlier confrontations with Jerusalem's Jewish population.
- The Jewish councillors opposed the mayor because of national and political
  disagreements; in other words, the Jews themselves endowed the
  mayoralty with national and political significance, whereas al-Khālidī
  believed that they should relate only to the manner in which he fulfilled
  his duties as mayor.
- No changes should be made in the law, for example, reducing the quorum
  required for council meetings, which would permit the council to function
  even if the Arab councillors did not attend meetings (during the strike).
- The city's services should not be divided on a communal basis, with the
  Jews carrying out work in the Jewish quarters and the Arabs doing the
  same in Arab quarters. The basis for the appointment of workers ought to
  be economic. (Because Arab labor was cheaper, most municipal jobs were
  performed by Arabs.)

In the summer of 1936, with the disturbances growing more acute and
the strike at its height, the Jews submitted complaints to the mayor concerning
the functioning of the Municipality.[45] Al-Khālidī replied with a series of
statements in which he attempted to prove that he and the Municipality were
functioning properly. At the same time he rejected any attempt by the Jews to
interfere with what he regarded as his political status, which he considered to
be unrelated to the functioning of the Municipality.[46] Even after the termination of the strike, calm was not restored to the Municipality, and Jewish councillors clashed with the mayor over a number of issues, such as the status of the
Jewish deputy mayor, the language issue, and allocation of municipal contracts and jobs.[47] Al-Khālidī always took care to respond to the Jewish
charges, frequently stressing his integrity as the servant of all the inhabitants
of the city.[48]

In August 1937, al-Khālidī went on leave and, by order of the British
district commissioner, his duties were fulfilled by Daniel Auster.[49] When al-
Khālidī returned at the end of August, however, he was arrested by the British
as a member of the Arab Higher Committee and was deported to the
Seychelles in the Indian Ocean on November 1, 1937. As a result, Auster con-

tinued to serve as acting mayor—the first time he did so for any extended period—filling the post until the end of August 1938. There were many Arab protests against this step.[50] Al-Khālidī's deportation and the arrest of another Arab councillor (Ibrāhīm Darwīsh) created a Jewish majority in the Municipal Council. But the Arab councillors boycotted the meetings, and in the absence of a quorum the council was effectively paralyzed. In May 1938, the high commissioner appointed a committee to investigate means to reactivate the Municipal Council. It found that the status quo, whereby the council consisted of six Jews and six Arabs, had to be maintained, at least until the end of its term of office. In accordance with the Municipalities Ordinance, which permitted the high commissioner to appoint councillors in place of those absent, Muṣṭafā al-Khālidī (a High Court judge) was nominated as councillor and mayor on October 1, 1938. The high commissioner also appointed Ḥusayn abū Saʿūd to replace Ibrāhīm Darwīsh. The committee also recommended the appointment of a British municipal secretary.

Municipal elections were to be held at the end of 1939. The Arabs were aware that the current population balance and the new criteria for drawing up the electoral register would give the Jews an absolute majority and exclusive control of the Municipality. Hence they objected to elections being held in their previous format and reiterated their familiar arguments, including the following key sentence: "The mayor of Jerusalem must be a Muslim, at all times and under all circumstances."[51] They requested that the elections be postponed because of the absence of those Arab candidates and voters who were under detention, had been deported, or had fled during the disturbances, and claimed that the economic crisis (which had primarily affected the Arab community during the disturbances) had resulted in many Arabs defaulting on their taxes and thereby losing the right to vote. It should be recalled that in the course of 1939 it was principally the Jews who undermined the functioning of the Municipality, following publication of the White Paper.[52] Be that as it may, the outbreak of war led to a postponement of any discussion on the elections and the Municipality.

From 1940 to the Divided City

The crises of the 1930s having effectively paralyzed the Municipality, the city was administered by British officials from the early 1940s. At first, this responsibility was shouldered by the municipal secretary, who functioned alongside the Arab mayor, Muṣṭafā al-Khālidī. After al-Khālidī's death, however, his post was filled by officials of the British government in Palestine.

A few weeks before the outbreak of World War II, a detailed memorandum on the problems of Jerusalem's Municipality, including a review of the Arab position, was drawn up in the offices of the Jerusalem district commissioner.[53] An analysis of the views of the two sides shows that there was little scope for compromise. The worldwide political circumstances froze the situation and facilitated greater British intervention in the city's administration.

A further extensive survey of the Arab position appears in Ḥusayn al-Khālidī's memorandum submitted as testimony before Judge Fitzgerald in 1945.[54] Al-Khālidī returned to Palestine in 1943, having spent several years in Lebanon (his exile in the Seychelles lasted only one year). But he was not restored to his post as mayor of Jerusalem, even though there was no formal decree dismissing him. At any rate, his relative, Muṣṭafā al-Khālidī, whose activities as mayor were of a most limited nature, also engaged in Arab nationalist activities.[55] In May 1944, he attended a conference of Arab mayors held in Jaffa and was severely criticized for doing so by his deputy, Daniel Auster. The Arab reactions to Auster's criticisms reiterate the fundamental Arab view regarding the post of mayor.[56]

Shortly afterward, in August 1944, a severe crisis erupted upon the death of the Muslim mayor, Muṣṭafā al-Khālidī. The city's Jewish majority demanded the appointment of a Jewish mayor. The British authorities received hundreds of appeals regarding the future of the post representing Arab views on the subject, including the submission of individual candidacies for the post, like that of ʿAbd al-Fattāḥ Nusayba from Ramleh, and objections to the candidacy of ʿĀrif al-ʿĀrif because of his assistance in the sale of land to Jews in Beersheba.[57] The rest of the letters are demands for the appointment of a Muslim Arab as mayor, on the basis of the usual arguments, most of them featuring the demand for the reappointment of Ḥusayn al-Khālidī, dismissed seven years earlier.

The Arab contentions appearing in these documents can be summarized as follows: Jerusalem's Municipality must be headed by a Muslim Arab, as an expression of the will of most of the country's inhabitants regarding their capital city. A Muslim mayor of Jerusalem is an expression of the Arab character of the city, as of the country as a whole. Muslim-Arab control of the city had been accepted for hundreds of years by Christians and Jews, whose prerogatives had been safeguarded. Any change in this status would lead to unrest among the Christians and Muslims, who owned most of the city's Holy Places.[58]

Among these petitions, one of particular interest came from members of the Khālidī family, who called on the high commissioner to assuage their grief at the death of their relative by appointing another leading member of their family, Ḥusayn al-Khālidī, mayor of Jerusalem. The British did not appoint a new mayor of Jerusalem from either the Arabs or the Jews. To the end of the Mandate the post was filled by three British officials.

The Partition Resolution and the 1948 War

Following the November 1947 Partition Resolution and the onset of hostilities early in 1948, Jerusalem's municipal administration, which had been headed by a committee of British officials, progressively disintegrated. In keeping with the general Arab position, the Arab Higher Committee rejected the partition resolution, including those sections referring to the internationalization of Jerusalem and its environs. At the same time, within certain limits, the Arabs cooperated with British and international attempts to keep the peace in the city (by means of a cease-fire), even consenting to the appointment of a special municipal commissioner for Jerusalem, who was to preserve the city's united municipal administration.[59] Throughout most of 1948, opposition to internationalization was general and vigorous throughout the Arab world. In the course of the fighting during the winter and spring of 1948, the city's administration was effectively divided between Jews and Arabs, and two separate municipalities emerged. Municipal administration in the Arab sector was taken over by Anton Ṣāfiya, formerly treasurer of the united Municipality, who established his offices in the Arab orphanage in the Old City.[60] Beginning in May 1948, affairs in the Arab sector of the city were controlled by King ᶜAbdallāh and his army; and on May 18, 1948, ᶜAbdallāh al-Tall was appointed commander of the Arab forces in the city (on October 1, 1948 he was given the title of military governor of Jerusalem).[61]

From 1948 it was the de facto cooperation between Jordan and Israel that succeeded in defeating international, and, in particular, Arab, attempts to impose an international regime on the city. This de facto cooperation required many and prolonged discussions between Israel and Jordan over the demarcation lines in Jerusalem and the administration of the divided city. Contacts at the end of 1948 and early in 1949 produced the Rhodes agreement and Article 8 regarding the establishment of a special committee.[62]

Both sides displayed a readiness for mutual concessions because failure to arrive at an agreement between them was likely to remove both parts of Jerusalem from their control and deliver them over to international supervision. The sources for studying the Jordanian position in these contacts are incomplete (and, to a large extent, classified), but the following general picture emerges. Both sides understood that only direct negotiations would resolve the problem, because any kind of mediation, by the United Nations or any other body, would immediately raise the issue of internationalization. King ᶜAbdallāh and the Israeli government agreed to take as their point of departure the Status Quo created after the fighting in the city. From the Jordanian viewpoint, this involved relinquishing some Arab quarters and even more far-reaching concessions, such as permission for Jews to visit the Western Wall.[63]

Such flexibility stemmed from the fact that late in 1948 and early 1949, other Arab armies were still present on the West Bank; and ᶜAbdallāh, who wanted to be free of them, was obliged to guarantee the success of his contacts with Israel. (The other Arab forces included the Egyptians in Bethlehem and the Hebron region, up to the southern outskirts of Jerusalem; the Jihād al-

Muqaddas, who were supporters of the Mufti's Palestinian nationalism and rivals of King ᶜAbdallāh; and the Iraqi army in Samaria.) However, in April 1949, when the special Israeli-Jordanian committee instituted its direct contacts in Jerusalem, ᶜAbdallāh had already succeeded in having these forces removed from the West Bank, and his status in the West Bank and Jerusalem, in the wake of the December 1948 Jericho Congress, allowed for his position in the negotiations with Israel to become much more rigid. (At the Jericho Congress a group of Palestinian-Arab notables called for unification of Palestine with Jordan and declared ᶜAbdallāh king of Palestine.)

In addition, ᶜAbdallāh was sensitive to the constant pressure of the Jerusalem refugees, who were aware of the negotiations and urged the Jordanian government to demand the return of the Arab quarters on the Israeli side of the city. In both the special committee and the general peace negotiations, the Jordanian delegates were prepared to grant the Israeli demands (the Laṭrūn road, transit to Mount Scopus, the Western Wall, the Mount of Olives cemetery, the water pipeline to Jerusalem, and so on). In exchange, they demanded alterations in the demarcation line within the city and the restoration of the Arab quarters. (The Jordanians also consented to return the Jewish Quarter of the Old City, but this, too, was linked to the restoration of the Arab quarters.)

In the end, the situation in Jerusalem remained as it had been determined at Rhodes and earlier, and temporary arrangements—such as the Mount Scopus convoys, the demilitarized zones, the Mandelbaum Gate transit point, the Mixed Armistice Commission, and so on—became permanent. No further progress was made after the spring of 1949. The difficulties encountered in the peace negotiations between the two sides in 1950 and ᶜAbdallāh's assassination in July 1951 left the border through the city sealed until 1967, and an entirely separate municipal administration gradually emerged in East Jerusalem.

THE DIVIDED CITY: THE JORDANIAN MUNICIPALITY

The difficulties encountered by Jerusalem's municipal administration of the Jordanian sector (1948–67) were primarily political, stemming from the political structure of the Hashemite Kingdom. Among these difficulties were relations between the two banks of the Jordan, the status of the Palestinians and their integration into the kingdom, and the knotty problems linked with the Arab states and the Arab League. As a result, the archival material (found in the state archives and those of the Jerusalem Municipality) prominently features discussions of municipal problems in relation to political issues.[64]

The most important topics—development of the city, its municipal boundaries, the offices of official and public institutions to be housed in the city, and the official status of the Municipality—were weighed not against the municipal needs of the Jordanian sector of the city but, principally, against political considerations of the Jordanian government. It is clear that, as a matter of principle, the Jordanian government was afraid of any enhancement of Jerusalem's status and feared separatist trends on the West Bank, in view of the antagonism between the Palestinian national movement (headed first by the Mufti and later by Aḥmad Shuqayrī) and the Hashemite establishment.

The operations of Jerusalem's municipal authority under Jordanian rule began, in effect, with the appointment of a Municipal Committee headed by Anwar al-Khaṭib early in 1948.[65] The Municipal Archives contain documents about the activities of the Municipal Committee only from 1949 onward. The documents indicate that right from the start there were disagreements and uncertainty concerning the committee's status. Was it a municipal council or not?[66] The members of the committee and its chairman objected to the discrimination against the city displayed by the central government. In July 1950, the committee decided to resign[67] in protest to the Arab Legion's decision to evacuate a number of houses in the Sheikh Jarrāḥ section and hand them over to Israel.[68]

Until the first elections to the Municipal Council in July 1951, the Municipal Committee was chaired by Ḥannā ʿAṭāllāh and ʿĀrif al-ʿĀrif. Prior to the elections, the activities of the committee were marked by a prolonged campaign to prevent the transfer of government offices and other public institutions from Jerusalem.[69] Rumors of the transfer of offices began toward the end of 1950. At first, the members of the Municipal Committee thought that their pleas to King ʿAbdallāh had succeeded in voiding the decision; the Jordanian government denied any intention of transferring important offices from Jerusalem to eastern Jordan, and the Jordanian minister of the interior echoed the denial.[70] Yet these reassurances from the central authorities did not dislodge the fears of members of the Municipal Committee and others in Jerusalem, who kept up vigorous activity against the government's steps.[71]

Late in March 1951, the minister of interior wrote to the governor of the Jerusalem district that he had been instructed by highly placed figures to notify the members of Jerusalem's Municipal Committee that their intervention regarding the transfer of officials of the central ministries out of Jerusalem exceeded the bounds of their authority, and that the king rejected their request for a meeting on the subject.[72] The contents of the letter were brought to the attention of the members of the Municipal Committee and led to unrest among all the leaders of Jerusalem's Arab community.[73] At that time (the beginning of April 1951), the decision was already final, but the Jordanian government tried to soften the blow.[74] It was to this matter that Anwar Nusayba apparently referred in his memorandum,[75] which, as the member of Parliament for the Jerusalem region, he addressed to the prime minister, complaining that discrimination was weakening the city, in contrast to the development of the Israeli section of the city.

As this move indicates, no sooner was Jerusalem's local government formed at the end of 1950 and early 1951 than the central Jordanian government initiated efforts to diminish the status of Jerusalem as the former administrative capital of Palestine, leaving no real opportunity for repairing the damage the city had sustained during the war. At the height of the struggle over the transfer of offices, ʿAbdallāh was murdered at the entrance to the al-Aqsā Mosque (July 20, 1951). The Hashemite government responded furiously and vindictively. The questions of Jerusalem's status and the discriminatory policies that affected the city were subsequently removed from the agenda for many years.[76]

On July 31, 1951, a few days after the assassination of ʿAbdallāh, the first municipal elections were held in Jordanian Jerusalem, in accordance with the Municipalities Law published on March 3, 1951, which resembled the 1934 mandatory law.[77] The communal distribution that characterized the Municipal Committee was maintained—eight Muslim councillors (one of whom was to be appointed mayor) and four Christians (two Orthodox, one Catholic, and one from another Christian denomination)—although there were difficulties over the Christian representatives in view of the Catholics' claim that they were entitled to two councillors after the Protestants were allocated one place in the elections.[78] The largest number of votes were given to ʿĀrif al-ʿĀrif (who had served as head of the nominated Municipal Committee after the resignation of Anwar al-Khaṭīb), and he was appointed mayor.

ʿĀrif al-ʿĀrif served as mayor for six weeks before being dismissed by King Ṭalāl at the beginning of December.[79] During his brief term of office, deliberations began concerning the boundaries of Jerusalem's municipal area of jurisdiction. Without going into details, the proposal stated that the northern boundary would be the Ḥabā'il al-Ṭanṭūr lands; to the east, new al-Ṭūr and Rās al-ʿAmūd; to the south, Jabal al-Rās, so that the whole of Deir abū Ṭōr lay within the city limits.[80]

The dismissal of ʿĀrif al-ʿĀrif further illustrates the complexity of the relationships between the central government in Amman and the Jerusalem Municipality and the fact that the whole issue was of a political, and to some extent personal, nature. The elected Municipal Council remained in office, and ʿUmar al-Waʿrī was appointed mayor (on March 12, 1952, after the post was filled for three months by the Christian deputy mayor Ḥannā ʿAṭāllāh).

Even after ʿĀrif al-ʿĀrif's dismissal as mayor (he remained a member of the council), the status of Jerusalem remained a central topic in the council's deliberations. During the brief period that Ḥannā ʿAṭāllāh served as acting mayor (early in 1952), discussions were held on the Municipality's demand that the offices of UNRWA (United Nations Relief and Works Agency), transferred from Lebanon to Jordan and housed in Amman, be moved to

Jerusalem.[81] After ꜥUmar al-Waꜥrī was appointed mayor in March 1952, the status of Jerusalem was raised as a special item on the agenda of the council (at the first meeting headed by al-Waꜥrī), and a special public committee was formed to deal with the matter. Councillors were concerned about Jerusalem's humiliation at the hands of the Jordanian government.

After the organization of Jordanian Jerusalem's Municipality in the early 1950s, the question of the city's municipal boundaries became its key issue. Delineating the limits of its jurisdiction was of great significance, both political and administrative. In fact, the Municipal Council, the district governor, and the ministry of the interior continued their deliberations on the matter right up to 1967. In all these discussions, the Municipality attempted to extend its area of jurisdiction as far as it could, in face of the opposition of the central government and some of the inhabitants of the areas to be annexed to the urban zone. As indicated in later documents, the Municipality enjoyed only partial success, and the municipal area was extended very little in comparison to the plans and aspirations of the council. One of the earliest documents on this issue is a petition by the inhabitants of Arḍ al-Samār (extending from Sheikh Jarrāḥ to French Hill), presented in September 1952, objecting to the area being annexed to the municipal zone.[82]

The plan that first defined the boundaries of the Jordanian Municipality was approved by the various authorities on April 1, 1952, after the constitution of the new council and the dismissal of ꜥĀrif al-ꜥĀrif. Under this plan, the following areas were attached to Jerusalem: the village of Silwān, Rās al-ꜥĀmūd, ꜥAqabat al-Ṣuwwāna, Arḍ al-Samār, and the southern portion of Shuꜥfāṭ. The Municipality demanded that the whole of Shuꜥfāṭ be annexed, but the matter was postponed.[83]

Villagers, particularly in a place like the village of Silwān, opposed having their villages annexed to Jerusalem. The basis to this opposition appears to be the rural character of most of the annexed areas. The Municipality would be empowered to collect taxes from these areas, while finding it difficult to provide any services. No political arguments appear to have been raised. Documents contain details of Silwān's inhabitants' demand for a tax release and a legal brief submitted by the mukhtars of Silwān against the minister of the interior.[84] The inhabitants of Silwān conducted a prolonged and consistent campaign against the annexation of their village to Jerusalem. Yaḥyā Hammūda, the lawyer who acted on their behalf, argued that inasmuch as inhabitants of Silwān had not participated in the 1951 municipal elections and lacked a representative on the Municipal Council, annexation would constitute a deprivation of their rights.[85] The lawyer contended that Silwān be represented in the Municipal Council, or that a local council be established in Silwān subject to the Municipality.

Throughout the early 1950s, leading personalities in the city and its Municipality often remonstrated against the Jordanian government's discrimination against Jerusalem.[86] Episodes such as the appointment of a deputy minister of the interior to be located in Jerusalem, the question of nominating a deputy minister of education for Jerusalem, and a renewed dispute over the removal of the UNRWA offices from Jerusalem to Rāmallāh exacerbated feelings of discrimination in the city.[87] Jerusalem's Municipality kept up constant pressure to endow the city with a special administrative status because of its exceptional character, but with little success.[88] The municipal executive was aware that the city's difficulties stemmed not only from its particular relationships with the central government but also from objective difficulties such as tax collection. In the course of 1954, during the preparations to publish the new Jordanian Municipalities Law, Jerusalem's Municipal Council was active, as were other West Bank municipalities.[89] The West Bank municipalities operated in concert with the aim of strengthening their position vis-a-vis the central government.[90]

While the new law was being prepared, and in anticipation of the elections to be held after its publication, Jerusalem's municipal boundary was precisely defined. The distribution of city councillors was again approved with eight Muslims and four Christians. As in previous years, there were renewed difficulties with the inhabitants of the areas annexed to the city, especially Silwān.[91] In addition, the central administration's role within the city continued to provoke agitated reactions in the Municipal Council.[92] Issues included delays in the construction of the Jerusalem court and, after the elections, the transfer of the UNRWA offices from Jerusalem to Amman and fears concerning the transfer of the education department and other bodies to Amman.[93]

Jerusalem's municipal elections were held in September 1955 under the new law, one of whose innovations empowered the central government to appoint two additional members to the council (out of twelve). Because it was the government that appointed the mayor, the new law made it possible to nominate a mayor who had not even been a candidate in the elections.[94] The first mayor elected (and appointed) was ᶜĀrif al-ᶜĀrif, but as he was about to join the Amman cabinet, he left his post, which was filled by ᶜUmar al-Waᶜrī (for a short period) and Amīn al-Majjāj.[95] For over a year, the Jerusalem Municipality was, in effect, headed by acting mayors; and despite the fact that ᶜĀrif al-ᶜĀrif left the cabinet and returned to Jerusalem, he was not reappointed mayor. The municipal councillors demanded that one of their rank be appointed mayor, and at the end of January 1957, the government conceded to this demand and appointed Councillor Rūḥi al-Khaṭib, who served as mayor until the reunification of the city in 1967.[96]

As in the past, one of the central issues facing the new mayor was the question of extending Jerusalem's municipal boundaries, particularly to the north along the road to Rāmallāh (Shuᶜfāt), where construction of an urban nature was on the increase. A municipal committee that examined the issue (in view of past failures in annexing rural areas, such as the village of Silwān and Rās al-ᶜĀmūd), recommended that the city boundaries be extended to include an area of 500 meters on either side of the main road to Rāmallāh as far as the Qalandiya airfield.[97] The mayor intended to prepare a master plan for annexing the whole of the northern area, and the entire subject was rediscussed in principle in the council on the basis of the February 1957 decision, but in practice nothing came of it.[98] Consequently, the boundaries of Jerusalem remained more or less those that had been set after the 1948 war, together with parts of Arḍ al-Samār, Silwān, and Rās al-ᶜĀmūd. Despite all the resolutions, discussions, and plans, virtually no action was taken on the matter of boundaries throughout the 19 years of the Jordanian Municipality's existence.

Prior to the 1959 municipal elections, Jerusalem's municipal status was altered from a "municipality" (*baladiyya*) to an *amāna* (a status equal to that of the Jordanian capital). The documents do not show that this change in title was of any real significance. The change was actually instigated by Anwar al-Khaṭib, who proposed it during meetings with the prime minister and minister of the interior in Amman and then reported on it to the mayor.[99] The mayor notified the councillors, at least one of whom (Salīm Maᶜtūq) did not comprehend the distinction between *baladiyya* and *amāna*, and it was necessary for Rūḥi al-Khaṭib to explain it to him. Apparently as part of its preparations for the municipal elections, the Jordanian government decided to devote particular attention to Jerusalem, where it held a festive session in August 1959 and then published its decisions to elevate the Municipality to an *amāna* and build a royal palace in Jerusalem, "the second capital." On the eve of the elections, the *Official Gazette* published the change of status.[100]

There can be no doubt that this was an unusual gesture, considering the relationship between Jerusalem and Amman during this period—even though it was no more than a token one. Perhaps the move should be considered in light of the acute crises that overtook Jordanian policy during the period between the attempted coup in 1957 and the assassination of Premier Hazzāᶜ al-Majālī in 1960. In any case, the period during which the *amāna* was established marked the height of Jordan's political isolation following the formation of the United Arab Republic (UAR) and the revolution in Iraq. It may thus be assumed that the Jordanian government wished to conciliate its internal opponents in order to block subversion by the UAR; and one of the steps in this direction was the elevation of Jerusalem to an *amāna*. At the end of September, after the elections, the *amāna* held its first festive meeting, and Mayor Rūḥi al-Khaṭib, who had been reelected, was named "Amīn al-Quds."[101] The Jordanian government's difficulties in Jerusalem can be gauged from the fact that the newly elected (September 1959) municipal councillors included Ṣubḥi Ghausha, a radical opponent of the government who had spent many years in Jordanian prisons.

In general, it is hard to find any distinction between the activities of the Municipality prior to September 1959 and those of the *amāna* after the change. Demands were presented to King Ḥusayn when he visited the city. Representatives decried its financial straits, resulting from an absence of government assistance. As in the past, there were constant complaints about the neglect of Jerusalem, and the council requested that its status as an *amāna* be implemented, at least formally.[102] The municipal councillors appear to have realized gradually that the change to an *amāna* was devoid of any real content, and in May 1961, they submitted their resignations.[103] Despite all these crises throughout Rūḥi al-Khaṭib's term of office, Jordanian Jerusalem's municipal administration was stabilized. A draft master plan (by H. Kendall) for the city was drawn up and discussed. The issue of the municipal boundaries came up again, with pressure once more being directed principally to the north (the Rāmallāh road, as decided upon as far back as 1957). Particular significance was attached to the Qalandiya airfield and its development within the city, whose economy was almost totally dependent upon tourism. In consequence, there was also considerable sensitivity to rumors that the airfield might be closed down.

In the mid-1960s, during the period preceding the Six-Day War, political matters maintained their prominence in the activities of the Jerusalem Municipality. This holds true of the visit by Pope Paul VI in 1964, the meeting of the Palestinian National Council in May-June 1964, and the foundation of the Palestine Liberation Organization (PLO).[104] The question of the political status of Jerusalem's municipal administration arose in the wake of Tunisian President Bourguiba's famous declarations concerning a political solution of the Arab-Israel conflict in stages (March 1965), and the *amāna* council held deliberations on the matter (March 17, 1965).

From the beginning to the end of the period covered in this section, a sense of discrimination and deprivation colors events in the municipal administration.[105] In the face of complaints by councillors like ʿĀrif al-ʿĀrif or Zakī al-Ghūl, Rūḥi al-Khaṭib adopted a moderate posture. His statements at a council meeting concerning the link between the government's attitude toward Jerusalem and its attitude toward the PLO are, perhaps more than anything else, an indication of the great political significance attached to any action undertaken in Jerusalem.[106] This political significance overshadowed any substantive considerations of municipal administration.

The 1967 war found eastern Jerusalem administered by a Municipal Council that had been elected in 1963. Shortly before the end of its term of office, the Municipal Council was dismissed when the city was reunited.[107]

NOTES

1. On the Jerusalem Municipality in the nineteenth century, see Ruth Kark, "Activities of the Jerusalem Municipality in the Ottoman Period" (in Hebrew), *Cathedra* 6 (1977): 74–94 (cited in Introduction); and Emanual Gutmann, "The Beginning of Local Government in Jerusalem" (in Hebrew), *Public Administration in Israel and Abroad* 8 (1968): 52-61.

2. Gad Frumkin, *The Way of a Judge in Jerusalem* (in Hebrew) (Tel Aviv: Dvir, 1954), p. 111.

3. Ronald Storrs, *Orientations* (London: Nicolson and Watson, 1945), p. 334; a letter from Sir Ronald Storrs, October 10, 1920, Israel State Archives (hereafter ISA) CS1297.

4. Memorandum of Dr. Husayn al-Khālidī to Chief Justice Sir William Fitzgerald, who was preparing a report on municipal affairs in 1945, Zionist Archives, 525-5877.

5. Y. Porath, *The Emergence of the Palestinian-Arab National Movement 1918-1929*, vol. 1 (London: Frank Cass, 1974), p. 37.

6. Storrs, *Orientations*, pp. 333–34; extract of a report by Storrs, November 4, 1918, ISA 65 (140); extract of a memorandum of the Committee of Jerusalem Jews (undated), ISA 65(140).

7. Letter from the president of the Jaffa Muslim-Christian Society to General Clayton, November 2, 1918, ISA 65(140).

8. Frumkin, *Way of a Judge*, p. 205; interview conducted by the Section for Oral Documentation of the Hebrew University with Avraham Franco, Tape 20(90), January 20, 1972.

9. Ibid., according to interview with Avraham Franco.

10. Porath, *Emergence*, vol. 1, p. 334, note 3.

11. This claim of the Jewish representatives is contained in *The Jews and the Municipalities in Palestine* (Hebrew pamphlet) (Jerusalem: Va'ad ha-Leumi, 1924), p. 9.

12. Ibid.

13. Ibid., p. 8.

14. A memorandum on the Jerusalem Municipality, giving the views of the Arab and Jewish sides, submitted by the District Commissioner's Office on July 24, 1939, ISA microfilm, PRO no. C.O. 733/401.

15. Porath, *Emergence*, vol. 1, p. 239. The response to Mūsā Kāzim al-Husaynī is contained in a letter to him from the chief secretary of the mandatory administration, November 26, 1926, ISA 65(391).

16. The issues are set forth in *The Jews and the Municipalities in Palestine*.

17. Ibid., p. 13.

18. See George Antonius Files, ISA 65(322).

19. Frumkin, *Way of a Judge*, pp. 285–90; Porath, *Emergence*, vol. 1, p. 239.

20. According to a suggestion of Hājj Amīn al-Husaynī to Gad Frumkin, as reported by Frumkin, *Way of a Judge*, p. 287.

21. According to the election leaflets and posters addressed to the Jews by both factions in 1927.

22. Porath, *Emergence*, vol. 1, p. 239.

23. Ibid., pp. 194-207, especially p. 205.

24. *The Jews and the Municipalities of Jerusalem*, p. 11.

25. Al-Khālidī, memorandum (see note 4).

26. Storrs, *Orientations*, pp. 311–18, describes the impressive urban improvement and cultural activities of the Pro-Jerusalem Society.

27. Al-Khālidī, memorandum (see note 4).

28. The distribution of wards prepared by the District Commissioner's Office, ISA G/5/34.

29. Extract from *Gazette* no. 431, March 29, 1934, appointment of the Electoral Committee for Jerusalem, ISA G/5/34.

30. Letter from Amīn al-Tamīmī, acting president of the Supreme Muslim Council, to the chief secretary, May 17, 1934, ISA G/5/34.

31. Al-Khālidī, memorandum, pp. 5–7 (see note 4).

32. Letter from the Mufti to the Jerusalem district commissioner objecting to the distribution of the wards, August 28, 1934, ISA G/5/34.

33. For the election campaign, see newspaper extract, "Jerusalem Council Elections," ISA G/5/34.

34. Frumkin, *Way of a Judge*, p. 290.

35. Judgment of the District Court of Jerusalem in *Rāghib al-Nashāshibī* vs. *Husayn al-Khālidī*, Civil Case no. 237/34, ISA G/5/34.

36. Telegram from Hasan Sidqi al-Dajānī to the high commissioner expressing the claims of the Arab opposition, ISA G/5/34.

37. Petitions to the district commissioner by supporters of the Husayni faction, October 24, 1934, ISA G/5/34.

38. Note of the high commissioner to Moshe Shertok and Husayn al-Khālidī regarding the status of the Jewish deputy mayor, January 17, 1935, ISA 65(324).

39. Letter from the Jerusalem district commissioner to Husayn al-Khālidī regarding the controversy over the status of Jewish deputy mayor, ISA G/5/34.

40. Letter from Daniel Auster to Husayn al-Khālidī regarding principles to be adopted in regard to the official use of languages in the Municipality, ISA 65(327).

41. Report on municipal activities submitted by Husayn al-Khālidī to the district commissioner, April 17, 1936, ISA 65(327).

42. Letter of Y. Ben-Zvi et al. to Husayn al-Khālidī summarizing complaints against the mayor, May 5, 1936, ISA 65(327).

43. Letter of Arab council members requesting postponement of a Municipal Council meeting during the 1936 general strike, ISA 65(327).

44. Letter from Husayn al-Khālidī to the Jerusalem district commissioner in reply to Jewish complaints, July 6, 1936, ISA 65(327).

45. Letter from D. Auster to al-Khālidī presenting the Jewish view on tax collection, August 27, 1936, ISA 65(327).

46. Letter from al-Khālidī to Jerusalem district commissioner replying to complaints of the Jews, August 10, 1936, ISA 65(327); letter from al-Khālidī to Jerusalem district commissioner replying to complaints of the Jews, August 10, 1936, ISA G/104/36; letter from al-Khālidī to Jewish municipal councillors replying to criticism, August 27, 1936, ISA 65(324).

47. Extract from a meeting of the Jewish Agency Executive covering a report on al-Khālidī's views on the issue of a Jewish deputy mayor, December 18, 1936; report by D. Auster regarding al-Khālidī's views on deputy mayor, December 9, 1936, Zionist Archives, S/25-5877; letter from Jewish municipal councillors to al-Khālidī on language issue, March 14, 1937, ISA 65(327).

48. Letter from al-Khālidī to *The Palestine Post*, ISA 65(327).

49. In 1945, al-Khālidī was to allege in his memorandum to Judge Fitzgerald (see note 4) that immediately after his appointment in 1935, the British pressed him to go on leave so that his Jewish deputy could officiate as acting mayor.

50. The objections of the Arab councillors to a Jew serving as mayor of Jerusalem are contained in excerpts of the discussion in the Colonial Office regarding problems of the Jerusalem Municipality after al-Khālidī's exile, File no. 75258, PRO File no. 733/337, ISA microfilm no. 433.

51. Colonial Office documents on problems of the Jerusalem Municipality, PRO File no. 733/401, 733/422.

52. See the memorandum on the Jerusalem Municipality giving the views of the Arab and Jewish sides, ISA microfilm, PRO no. C.O. 733/401.

53. The fundamental Arab position was formulated in the memorandum cited in ibid.

54. Al-Khālidī, memorandum (see note 4).

55. See the interview with Ṣalāḥ al-Dīn Jārallāh, Section for Oral Documentation of the Hebrew University of Jerusalem, Tape 20(65), March 7, 1973.

56. Protests over statements of Jewish Council members at the council meeting of May 9, 1944, ISA G/5/34.

57. A private declaration of candidacy by ʿAbd al-Fattāḥ Nusayba, September 2, 1944, ISA G/5/24; telegram from ʿAbd al-Raḥim al-Sharif to the chief secretary, objecting to the candidacy of ʿĀrif al-ʿĀrif, ISA G/5/34.

58. Arab demands for the appointment of a mayor, ISA G/5/34.

59. ʿAbdallāh al-Tall, *Kārithat Filastīn*, p. 98; M. Benvenisti, *The Torn City* (Hebrew edition) (Jerusalem: Weidenfeld and Nicolson, 1973), p. 109.

60. M. Benvenisti, *Jerusalem: The Torn City* (English edition) (Minneapolis: University of Minnesota Press, 1976), p. 41.

61. ʿAbdallāh al-Tall, *Kārithat Filastīn*, p. 107.

62. Benvenisti, *Jerusalem*, p. 71.

63. The right to have free access to the Holy Places was posited in paragraph 8 of the Armistice Agreement, but Israelis were not permitted to visit the Holy Places during the 19 years of the armistice; see Benvinisti, ibid.; and U. Benziman, this volume.

64. The archival materials used in this section from the Jordanian Municipality are found in the Israel State Archives and in the Jerusalem Municipal Archives (not catalogued unless otherwise stated).

65. Benvenisti, *Jerusalem*, p. 42.

66. The third meeting of Jerusalem's Municipal Committee, April 1, 1950.

67. The tenth meeting of Jerusalem's Municipal Committee, July 8, 1950.

68. Benvenisti, *Jerusalem*, p. 42.

69. Meetings of Jerusalem's Municipal Committee on July 8, November 28, and December 19, 1950.

70. A letter from the Municipal Committee on the transfer of government offices, March 10, 1951, ISA 2704-49; report by Mayor ʿĀrif al-ʿĀrif on his efforts on behalf of transfer of government offices to Jerusalem, March-April 1951.

71. Letter from the vice chairman of the Jerusalem Chamber of Commerce on the transfer of offices, March 26, 1951, ISA 2707-49.

72. Reply of the Jordanian minister of interior on transfer of offices, March 31, 1951, ISA 2704-49.

73. Letter to Municipal Committee relaying minister of interior's reply regarding transfer of offices, April 1, 1951, ISA 2704-49: report to the minister of interior on a meeting of members of Parliament and notables on March 29, 1951, April 2, 1951, ISA 2704-49.

74. Reply to Jerusalem Chamber of Commerce on transfer of offices, April 3, 1951, ISA 2704-49; decision of Municipal Committee on transfer of offices, April 17, 1951.

75. A letter from Anwar Nusayba to the Jordanian prime minister on Jerusalem, ISA 2703-40; E. Beʾeri, *The Palestinians Under Jordanian Rule—Three Issues* (in Hebrew) (Jerusalem: Magnes Press, 1978), p. 57, dates this letter in mid-August 1950.

76. Beʾeri, *Palestinians Under Jordanian Rule*, p. 55.

77. A memorandum by Rūḥi al-Khaṭib entitled "Jerusalem Municipal Authority as a Local Government," 1965.

78. Municipal Council meeting regarding Christian representation in Municipality, July 17, 1951.

79. An account of the dismissal appears in Benvenisti, *Jerusalem*, p. 42; and related events in the council are given in detail in the report on dissent in the Municipal Council over dismissal of ʿĀrif al-ʿĀrif, December 8, 1951, ISA 2703-17; and the report of commander of the Jerusalem district in the wake of ʿĀrif al-ʿĀrif's dismissal, December 13, 1951; ISA 2704-17.

80. Municipal Council meeting discussing proposal to expand the area of Jerusalem's jurisdiction, December 1, 1951.

81. Municipal Council meeting on transfer of offices, January 3, 1952.

82. Municipal Council meeting on extension of municipal boundaries, September 16, 1952.

83. Municipal Council meeting on extension of area of municipal jurisdiction, October 7 and 10, 1952.

84. Municipal Council meeting on suit of mukhtar of Silwān against minister of interior to cancel annexation of Silwan to Jerusalem's municipal jurisdiction, May 5, 1953; Municipal Council meeting on objections of Silwān residents to annexation of the village, May 12, 1953.

85. Municipal Council meeting on extension of municipal jurisdiction (Silwān), March 30, 1954.

86. Municipal Council meeting on retarded development of Jerusalem vis-à-vis other cities in the kingdom, March 10, 1953.

87. Municipal Council meeting on appointment of deputy minister of interior for West Bank with seat in Jerusalem, October 28, 1952; Municipal Council meeting on government decision to abolish seat of deputy minister of interior in Jerusalem, January 23, 1954; Municipal Council meeting on transfer of government offices, March 16, 1954.

88. Extract from *al-Difāᶜ* of interview with acting mayor on plans and financial difficulties, July 17, 1953.

89. Benvenisti, *Jerusalem*, p. 43.

90. Municipal Council meeting on Municipalities Law, February 23, 1954; Municipal Council meeting on changes in Municipalities Law, April 4, 1954.

91. Article from *al-Jihād* on complaints of Silwān residents regarding municipal boundaries, November 11, 1954.

92. Municipal Council meeting on the question of deputy minister of interior in Jerusalem, December 14, 1954.

93. Municipal Council's approach to the prime minister regarding the construction of a court in Jerusalem, August 9, 1955; Municipal Council meeting concerning transfer of UNRWA offices from Jerusalem to Amman, March 27, 1956; Municipal Council meeting on transfer of education department from Jerusalem to Amman, October 9, 1956.

94. Municipal Council meeting on changes in the elections law, June 7, 1956.

95. Municipal Council meeting concerning ᶜArif al-ᶜArif's losing his position in the council with his appointment to a government position, December 21, 1955.

96. Municipal Council's demand that a mayor be appointed after a substantial period in which only an acting mayor functioned, December 26, 1956; Municipal Council meeting on the government's response to appoint a mayor, January 22, 1957.

97. Municipal Council meeting on recommendations regarding expansion of the municipal boundaries, February 12, 1957; proposal to extend the city's northern boundary, June 23, 1958.

98. Municipal Council meeting on contacts with UN experts over master plan for city, December 12, 1958; Municipal Council meeting on extension of municipal boundaries, November 5, 1959; Municipal Council meeting on extending municipal boundaries, December 23, 1958.

99. Municipal Council meeting on proposal to turn Jerusalem into an amāna, June 30, 1959.

100. Report on special cabinet session in Jerusalem in *al-Difāᶜ* on conversion of city to an amāna, August 23, 1959; *Official Gazette* report on conversion of Jerusalem into an amāna, September 1, 1959.

101. First Municipal Council meeting of Jerusalem in its status as an amāna, September 29, 1959.

102. Municipal Council meeting on use of Qalandiya airfield and status of Jerusalem, November 8, 1960; Municipal Council meeting on ties between council and Ministry of Interior, December 6, 1960.

103. Memorandum following a meeting with the prime minister, ties between the amāna and the district, January 31, 1961; the resignation of the Municipality and its rejection by the minister of interior, May 16, 1961.

104. Interesting material on the difficulties involved in convening the Palestinian National Council in Jerusalem can be found in Y. Harkabi, ed., *The Arabs and Israel* (Hebrew), vols. 3–4 (Jerusalem: Truman Institute, 1975), pp. 24–25. The Jordanian authorities' hostile and suspicious attitude toward the entire matter probably did not pass unnoticed by the municipal authorities, who took part in preparing the convention. Along with King Husayn and the secretary of the Arab League, ʿAbd al-Khāliq Ḥassūna, Mayor Rūḥi al-Khaṭib greeted the council at its opening session.

105. Municipal Council meeting on the demands of the amāna regarding discrimination against Jerusalem, October 6, 1965; Municipal Council meeting on the budget and status of Jerusalem, October 20, 1965.

106. Municipal Council meeting on the 1965–66 budget and government discrimination against Jerusalem, October 20, 1965.

107. Benvenisti, *Jerusalem*, p. 103.

4

ISRAELI POLICY IN
EAST JERUSALEM AFTER
REUNIFICATION

Uzi Benziman

This chapter surveys the means by which the Israeli authorities dealt with the problems stemming from the annexation to the State of Israel of an Arab minority in Jerusalem as a result of the resolution adopted on June 28, 1967 to reunify the city. The chapter, which is descriptive and factual, rests upon both published and classified documentation and two basic published works.[1]

The pertinent official decisions from June 1967 to December 1978 are considered in view of the policy formulated to deal with the Arab residents of Jerusalem. The solutions adopted by the Israeli authorities imposed their sovereignty upon the eastern portion of the city, while making continuous efforts to reduce to a minimum friction with the Arab minority. This chapter does not deal, however, with the ethnic aspect of the conflict (that is, majority-minority relationships) or specifically with the relationships between the administration and Christian ecclesiastical bodies.

LEGAL STATUS

Immediately after reunification of the city, the principal aim of the Israeli authorities was the rapid and total imposition of Israeli sovereignty upon East Jerusalem. This objective was only partly realized because of the Arab population of Jerusalem's opposition to annexation. The authorities quickly learned to adapt their decisions to the presence, interests, and aspirations of the Arab minority.

The annexation of East Jerusalem by a unilateral act of the Knesset and the minister of interior created legal anomalies. The Arab inhabitants of the annexed area automatically became inhabitants of the State of Israel while remaining Jordanian citizens. They simultaneously held Israeli identity cards and Jordanian passports. The Israeli authorities established special administrative arrangements to overcome the legal anomaly created by annexation.

The Legal Framework

The legislative path chosen by the Israeli authorities in imposing Israeli law, jurisdiction, and administration on East Jerusalem reflected a deviation from the laws then prevailing. The government—and, in its turn, the Knesset—chose to amend the Legal and Administrative Affairs (Regulation) Law in order to cast the legal framework for the annexation of East Jerusalem. The amendment stated: "The law, jurisdiction, and administration of the state shall apply in any area of the Land of Israel which the government has defined by decree."[2] At the same time, a bill was submitted to the Knesset to amend the Municipalities Ordinance so that the minister of interior could extend the jurisdiction of a municipality at his own discretion. A second amendment to the Municipalities Ordinance introduced at the same time stated that the minister of interior is empowered to appoint, by decree, members to the Municipal Council from among the inhabitants of the annexed area.[3]

The law was adapted to the specific needs arising from the annexation of East Jerusalem in subsequent years. For example, the Absentees Property Law (1950) stated that any absentee's property was to be transferred to the general custodian and that any rights to the property held by the absentee automatically passed to the custodian at the time of the property's transfer. Section 6A of the law stated that any person in possession of absentee property was required to hand it over to the custodian.[4] The East Jerusalem residents could not fulfill the requirements of this law; they held the status of absentees with regard to their property and of enemies by virtue of their Jordanian citizenship, according to the definition of "enemy" under the Penal Amendment Law (State Security, Foreign Relations, and Official Secrets) (1957).[5]

Practitioners of professions requiring licenses, owners of businesses requiring licenses, companies, partnerships, and cooperative societies—all continued their activities even though they did not possess licenses, thereby transgressing the Businesses Licensing Law of 1968.[6] The law states that a request for a license is to be submitted to the licensing authority, and the licensing authority, if it does not decide to reject it, is to forward it to whoever is empowered to approve the issue of the license.[7] Registration is also required for partnerships, cooperative societies, and companies.[8] However, companies, cooperative societies, partnerships, and businesses in East Jerusalem operated without licenses and did not meet the requirements of the laws, which instructed them to submit legal applications for registration. The same held true for practitioners of licensed professions: lawyers, doctors, pharmacists, contractors, and the like, and all ignored the requirement to submit applications for licenses.

In the absence of licenses, it was theoretically possible to annul action undertaken by practitioners of these professions and the companies, partnerships, and cooperative societies in East Jerusalem. In practice, however, the Israeli administration overlooked the legal entanglement arising from the refusal to fulfill the requirements of the law and permitted the practitioners of licensed professions, partnerships, companies, businesses, and cooperative societies to continue their operations. At the same time, the Israeli administration sought legislative means to resolve the legal anomaly.[9]

The solution was found in the Law of Legal and Administrative Regulations (1968), which declared unilaterally that East Jerusalem residents were neither absentees with regard to their property in East Jerusalem nor enemies.[10] Furthermore, the law stated that lawyers in the annexed territory would become members of the Israeli bar even without submitting applications. Concerning registration of the East Jerusalem cooperative societies, the law stated that the labor minister was empowered to register them by decree. Companies, partnerships, and practitioners of licensed professions (other than lawyers) were given an extension to register in accordance with Israeli law.

When the half year stipulated in the law had passed, it became clear that this period of grace to register was not being utilized. The authorities proclaimed a further three-month extension. In this period, the problem of registering businesses was resolved by having the Municipality, which is the licensing authority, automatically renew the licenses of those businesses in existence prior to 1967.[11] Companies and practitioners of licensed professions were registered by the authorities for a limited period under the emergency regulations. During this time, published decrees resulted in the legal registration of companies, partnerships, and practitioners of licensed professions by means of unilateral acts on the part of the authorities.[12] The registration was carried out in accordance with the Law of Legal and Administrative Affairs, which foresaw the possible necessity for registration en masse as a result of the refusal of the East Jerusalem inhabitants to register with the Israeli authorities.

Clearly, the Law of Legal and Administrative Affairs was designed to establish legal facilities for resolving these legislative irregularities, but it was unable to overcome all the problems that had arisen. Consequently, it left various legislative irregularities intact. For example, East Jerusalem residents continued to be considered absentees with regard to property within the bounds of the State of Israel other than Jerusalem; inhabitants of the occupied territories were considered absentees with regard to property in East

Jerusalem; and inhabitants of East Jerusalem who had moved to Amman, leaving behind persons with powers of attorney, were considered absentees. These problems were resolved by the Justice Ministry issuing administrative instructions to refrain from applying the Absentees Property Law to these situations.

In a series of judgments, the Israeli courts adopted the laws enacted by the Knesset to extend Israeli jurisdiction, law, and administration to East Jerusalem, and to permit the inhabitants of the annexed territory to maintain a normal way of life under the new regime. Thus the Supreme Court pronounced Israeli law to be in force in East Jerusalem from the day of publication of the annexation decree.[13] The court decided that reunified Jerusalem is an integral part of the State of Israel and that one single law (in this case, the law of inheritance) prevailed therein.[14]

The Israeli juridical system is territorially separate from the juridical system in Judea and Samaria (the West Bank). Juridical authority stems from political sovereignty, and the principle of territorial sovereignty of necessity gives rise to the principle of territorial jurisdiction. A court convened on Israeli soil is not empowered to adjudicate by virtue of a foreign law, unless it has been so empowered by Israeli law. In one case, the Supreme Court pronounced the Israeli government to be the executive authority in power in East Jerusalem.[15] Furthermore, the Supreme Court pronounced East Jerusalem to be part of Israeli territory and, consequently, "abroad" with respect to Hebron (in the case of the Jordanian Antiquities Law).[16]

Suffrage

The Israeli government refrained from imposing Israeli citizenship on Jerusalem's Arabs when East Jerusalem was annexed (though the idea did engage the attention of the special ministerial committee that dealt with preparations for the reunification of Jerusalem throughout June 1967). At the same time, the Arab population of the annexed territory was resident within Israel, and as such, was entitled to participate in the municipal elections.

According to Israeli law (Local Authorities Law—Elections), a resident who is not a citizen and who wishes to take part in elections to the local authority is required to submit an application for inclusion in the electoral roll. The Israeli authorities decided to depart from these legal requirements in order to make it easier for Jerusalem's Arabs to participate in the electoral process and thus improve the prospects of the latter taking part in the elections. The law was amended to release the city's Arabs from the necessity of submitting an application for registration in the electoral roll.[17] The Interior Ministry considered them as having submitted an application, and they were consequently regarded as eligible to vote. This was a one-time arrangement, because of the law's formulation. In preparation for the 1973 and 1978 elections, the wording of the law was again changed to include all the inhabitants of the annexed territory (the 1969 amendment applied only to those entitled to vote that year).

The Status of Government Employees

The Government Service Law (Appointments) (1959) states, in Section 16: "No person shall be appointed a government employee if he is not a citizen of Israel; if a government employee ceases to be an Israeli citizen, he will be considered as having resigned from government service."[18]

Jerusalem's Arabs did not become citizens of Israel at the time of the annexation, but some of them worked for the Israeli government (135 administrative employees and some 500 teachers.) Their employment by the government, despite their being foreign nationals, was made possible by Section 40 of the law, which states: "Nothing stated in this law shall prevent the government from drawing up a special contract with a person employed in the government service . . . and the requirements of this law shall not apply to a person employed under special contract, other than to the extent defined in that contract."

Applying this section to the employment of East Jerusalem inhabitants in government service meant that, for the purposes of the Government Service Law (Appointments), the state regarded them as foreign nationals, while the framework laws that led to the reunification of Jerusalem regarded the city's Arab citizens as residents of the State of Israel. The Government Service Regulations (Appointments) (Special Contract) (1960) states that the maximum period for the government service to employ a person who is not an Israeli citizen is six years, unless the government service commissioner believes that such a person's services are essential to the state or that the employee will receive Israeli citizenship during the period of his employment. In other cases, the maximum period of employment is only three years. In practice, however, the government service employs East Jerusalem inhabitants over and above the period laid down in the regulations.

This was made possible by a decree published by the finance minister ordering that the Government Service Regulations (Appointments) (Special Contract) shall state that the maximum permissible period for the government service to employ a person who is not an Israeli citizen shall be ten years, starting on June 1, 1974. This means that until June 1, 1984, it will be legally possible to employ Arab inhabitants of Jerusalem in government service by means of special contracts.[19]

Because they were, prima facie, employed by contracts, Jerusalem Arabs working in government service were deprived of the seniority and pension rights enjoyed by tenured workers. They demanded to be recognized as tenured employees—to ensure eligibility for social benefits—and that the calculation of their social benefits take into account their period of service under the Jordanian government. After deliberations, the Ministerial Committee for Jerusalem adopted the view of the finance minister (who is responsible for the government service), according to which the seniority rights of East Jerusalem Arab employees would be recognized in the following manner: Their rights (for the purpose of pension, severance, or seniority) would be calculated according to the financial yardsticks prevailing in Jerusalem prior to June 1, 1967. From that date onward, the reckoning would be made according to the Israeli pension law. For other purposes (sick benefits and vacations), the financial conditions prevailing in Israel would be calculated retroactively for their period of service under the Jordanian administration. Jerusalem Arabs would continue to be employed in government service by special contract but would, in fact, enjoy the status of tenured employees. However, being employed under special contracts, they would be released from the obligatory oath of allegiance to the state.

A similar problem—resolved in a similar manner—arose concerning municipal employees from East Jerusalem. After the city's reunification, 485 Arab employees were engaged by the Municipality. The Ministerial Committee for Jerusalem decided to extend to them the rules of eligibility stipulated for government employees from East Jerusalem.[20] The Municipal Council adopted three resolutions concerning the pension rights of its Arab employees. One stated that the Municipality recognized the pension rights arising from their period of service under the Jordanian regime, in accordance with the pay rates prevailing during the aforementioned period; from the beginning of Israeli rule onward, seniority and pension rights would be reckoned according to the rates prevailing in Israel.[21] In a further resolution, the Municipal Council agreed to extend the eligibility rates prevailing in Israel to their period of service under the mandatory government.[22] A third resolution applied Israeli eligibility rules to their period of service under the Jordanian regime and placed the Arab employees on an equal footing with the Jewish employees (under Jordanian law, this small group was entitled to severance pay, but not to pension rights).[23]

With respect to the rights of its Arab employees, the Municipality was guided by basically humanitarian intentions. It endeavored to grant fully equal rights to its employees, Arabs and Jews, and to solve the human and social problems its Arab employees faced as a result of the annexation. These intentions were successfully implemented by means of the constant adaptation of Israeli laws and practices to the special circumstances of East Jerusalem. From the viewpoint of Israeli law, such flexibility was "beyond the strict letter of the law," as pointed out in an internal memorandum by the municipal service manager.[24]

Representation

Although the law empowered the Israeli government unilaterally to co-opt prominent Jerusalem Arabs onto the Municipal Council, not only did it refrain from doing so, in practice, but it even tolerated the activities of unofficial shadow representatives acting on behalf of the city's Arabs. These representatives functioned as successors to the Arab Municipal Council that had been dispersed on June 29, 1967. They possessed neither official authority nor any real power; and symbolically, at least, their activities ran counter to the Israeli administration's decision to unify the city and establish a single Municipal Council. To top it all, every year this Arab shadow council published "the budget of the Jordanian Municipality," discussed the municipal problems of the eastern sections, and elected a mayor. [25]

Various attempts by numerous Israeli bodies to persuade prominent Arabs to join the Israeli Municipal Council failed. In practice, the authorities were faced with a situation without parallel in Israel: A well-defined local community was left without representation. The authorities therefore agreed to a further compromise: the creation of a committee of mukhtars to act as intermediaries between the Jerusalem Municipality and the Arab community, principally on the city periphery. [26] The mukhtars are traditionally empowered to act as registrars of births and deaths, to register land ownership where there is no land settlement, to maintain ownership registers, and to verify documents. Even after June 1967, these functions, which are performed in Israel by state bodies, were left to the Jerusalem mukhtars.

Property Compensation

The Knesset enacted the Absentees Property Law (Compensation) (1973) in order to grant compensation to Jerusalem Arabs for property left within the State of Israel in 1948. [27] The enactment of this law reflected a special effort on the part of the Israeli authorities to adapt the legal system to the circumstances existing in East Jerusalem. The Absentees Property Law (1950), promulgated with regard to Israeli Arabs to give them the right to compensation for property abandoned as a result of the 1948 war, restricted the possibility of declaring persons "present absentees" and left to the exclusive prerogative of the custodian general the granting of such a status to certain persons. The custodian was also entrusted with the possibility of compensating present absentees for their property (on the recommendation of an official committee) [28].

On the face of it, the Israeli authorities were entitled to refer to the 1950 law and its requirements in granting Jerusalem Arabs compensation for their property in Israel. However, the authorities preferred to initiate special legislation for this purpose. The special law of 1973 permitting the payment of compensation to Jerusalem Arabs (and to those Israeli Arabs who had not demanded compensation under the Absentees Property Law, 1950) for property declared "absentee" was intended to encourage them to claim compensation. Since the reunification of Jerusalem, its Arab inhabitants had been eligible to demand compensation under the 1950 law, but they refrained from doing so for political reasons (they were reluctant to take any step that implied renunciation of their property within the State of Israel), as well as for practical reasons (the rate of compensation under the aforementioned law was determined by a decision of the committee of officials and the custodian general, not in accordance with clearly defined criteria).

The requirements set out in the new law were quite different from those in the 1950 Absentees Property Law, even though both laws refer to the same matter.[29] The new law laid down well-defined yardsticks for calculating compensation payments; under it both the occupants (lessees) and the owners of the property were entitled to compensation, and the value of the property on which compensation was to be paid would be determined in a manner entirely different from that determined under the earlier law. Furthermore, compensation would be granted to whole families, not just to parts of families, even if some of the claimants were not inhabitants of Israel.

RELIGIOUS AUTONOMY

The Sharī^{c}a Court

On July 11, 1967, the minister of religious affairs notified the Muslim leadership of East Jerusalem that the unified city came under the Islamic laws in effect in Israel. However, this pronouncement did not go into legal effect. In East Jerusalem, a *sharī^{c}a* court is the supreme religious authority for the Muslims of the city and of the West Bank. This court operates in accordance with the Islamic laws in effect in the Kingdom of Jordan, which conflict with the requirements of Israeli law in important respects. The *qāḍīs* (judges) of this court practice by virtue of their appointment by Jordan, not Israel, and the functioning of this court contravenes the Israeli Qāḍīs' Law.

The Qāḍīs' Law (1961) set out a number of conditions for the appointment of a *qāḍī*, who would act as judge in the religious affairs of Israeli Muslims.[30] These conditions include the requirements that a *qāḍī* be an Israeli citizen, undergo a process of selection by an appointments committee, declare his allegiance to the State of Israel, that his appointment must be published in the *Official Gazette*, and that he receive his appointment from the president of Israel. The members of the *sharī^{c}a* court in East Jerusalem obviously do not meet these conditions. They function without receiving their authority from the officially designated bodies as laid down in Israeli law, and they accord validity to Islamic laws that do not rule in Israel, such as polygamy, child marriages, and certain rules of inheritance.

The Israeli authorities tried to resolve this anomaly by placing a series of proposals before the Muslim establishment in East Jerusalem. These attempts failed; the Muslim leadership refused to accept them, attaching political significance to any settlement reached with the occupation authorities.

An examination of the compromise proposals advanced by the Israeli authorities testifies to their readiness to depart considerably from the legal requirements prevailing in Israel in order to adapt Israeli practices to the Muslims in East Jerusalem.

On February 20, 1968, the following proposal was formulated in the defense minister's Knesset office: The government would publish a decree granting recognition to the religious courts of East Jerusalem; the prime minister would grant the judges a letter of recognition; the *shari'a* court would adjudicate in accordance with the religious law in force in East Jerusalem prior to the Six-Day War; the president of the *shari'a* court would continue to function as president of the High Court of Appeal for the West Bank, for which he would receive the approval of the military governor of the area; likewise, the other *qāḍis* would gain confirmation of their appointment to the Jerusalem religious court, which functions as the religious-judicial authority for the city's Muslim inhabitants and as a court of appeal for the population of the West Bank.[31] This proposal was designed to release the *qāḍis* from the conditions of appointment laid down in Israeli law. Another proposal expressed the authorities' readiness to drop the idea of a letter of appointment from any Israeli entity whatsoever.

In February 1973, a third proposal was formulated: The Qāḍis Law would be amended with the aim of favoring the East Jerusalem *shari'a* court; the *qāḍis* would be appointed by the Muslim Council, which would pay their salaries; they would be released from the oath of allegiance to the Israeli government; they would not be required to receive their appointment from any Israeli entity; they would be released from supervision by the Israeli Ministry for Religious Affairs; *qāḍis* would take up their duties by virtue of notification from the Muslim Council to the Prime Minister's Office; and Israel would recognize the verdicts of the *shari'a* court.

Retroactively, the Israeli administration agreed to permit the *shari'a* court to function in the manner to which it had been accustomed during the Jordanian regime. The government turned down a proposal by the minister for religious affairs to establish a parallel *shari'a* court in East Jerusalem and to subject the Muslim community in Jerusalem to the laws of matrimony in force in Israel.[32]

The authorities tried to apply pressure on the Muslim establishment in response to the latter's refusal to accept their proposals for settling the problem of the *shari'a* court's status. Instructions were issued to the Bailiff's Office not to enforce verdicts of the *shari'a* courts; the Interior Ministry did not recognize marriage certificates issued by the court; and other authorities did not recognize the inheritance orders it issued.[33] For its part, the *shariᶜa* court did not recognize the annexation of East Jerusalem, did not permit Israeli attorneys to appear before it, and refused to initiate any approaches to Israeli authorities.

In practice, Jerusalem's Muslims solved the problems arising from this mutual nonrecognition by approaching the marriage registrate in the nearby Israeli Arab village of Abū Ghōsh to set his seal upon the documents relating to marriages performed by the Jerusalem *qāḍi*. In the same way, the Jaffa *shariᶜa* court would give formal validation to decisions of the Jerusalem court.[34]

Mutual nonrecognition also affected the activities of the *waqf* (which administers the Muslim Holy Places), as well as the financial affairs of the Muslim Council. The Israeli government did not pay the salaries of the East Jerusalem *qāḍis* and *waqf* officials. The Jordanian government pays these salaries to this day.

The Muslim Council

On July 24, 1967, the Supreme Muslim Council was established in Jerusalem, proclaiming itself to be the authority that would "deal with all Muslim affairs on the West Bank, including Jerusalem, until the termination of the occupation."[35] The council appointed one of its members to be the chief judge (*qāḍi l-quḍāt*) for the West Bank, according to Jordanian law; it "invested the *shariᶜa* court in Jerusalem with all the authority of the Council of the Waqf and Muslim affairs and the Committee for the Restoration of the al-Aqṣā Mosque and the Dome of the Rock in the West Bank, as laid down in Jordanian law, as well as with all the authority invested in the director-general of the *waqf*." In addition, it decided on a number of personal appointments to the *shariᶜa* court and the Waqf Council and resolved that these bodies would "deal with those matters concerning them, and which are within their jurisdiction according to Jordanian law, in the West Bank, including Jerusalem, until the termination of the occupation."

The Supreme Muslim Council had been founded in 1921 by virtue of a British mandatory decree. Its purpose was to supervise and conduct the Muslim *waqf* institutions and the *shariᶜa* courts within the bounds of Palestine. According to Islamic law, only under non-Muslim rule is it necessary to establish an autonomous Muslim authority to supervise Muslim religious affairs. Prior to British rule, there was no need for such a body, because the religious affairs of the Muslim community were conducted under the Islamic juridical system of the Ottoman Empire. In 1937, the British stripped the Muslim Council of its jurisdiction over *waqf* affairs, in view of the militantly political character the council displayed under the influence of the Mufti of

Jerusalem, Ḥājj Amīn al-Ḥusaynī. A government committee was established to conduct *waqf* affairs, while the Muslim Council continued to supervise the *sharīᶜa* courts.

In 1951, the Jordanian government dissolved the Muslim Council, and authority to appoint *qāḍis* was transferred to the Ministry for the Waqf and Muslim Affairs in Amman. Department heads, subject to the ministry in Amman, functioned on the West Bank and in Jerusalem. All *waqf* income was forwarded to Amman.[36]

With the Israeli government's annexation of East Jerusalem, its Muslim community once again came under non-Muslim rule and, consequently, the Supreme Muslim Council was reestablished. The Israeli authorities did not formally recognize the council, but in practice they established contact with it, regarding it as a representative body possessing great influence over the inhabitants of East Jerusalem. The Muslim Council's decisions concerning the appointment of a new chief judge and the election of a *qāḍī* to the Court of Appeals were transmitted to the Israeli authorities. However, the Ministry for Religious Affairs announced that it did not consider these appointments as legally binding. In practice, the Israeli authorities tolerated the existence of the Muslim Council, even though they did not recognize it. A de facto agreement was reached whereby the council restricted its activities to those matters and to that form of expression considered reasonable by the authorities, while the latter refrained from taking drastic steps to terminate the council's existence.

The Temple Mount

On July 17, 1967, the scope of Muslim supervision over the Temple Mount (Ḥaram al-Sharīf) was defined. In the course of a visit to the Temple Mount that day, the defense minister notified the Muslim leadership that it would remain responsible for arrangements there, while the Israeli security forces would be in charge of the approaches to the site.[37] As a result, the Muslim leadership retained its sphere of responsibility and authority, with one exception: The defense minister served notice on the Muslim leaders that Jews had the right to unrestricted visits to the Mount, as long as they respected traditional customs and practices. To give practical expression to this decision, the key to the Mughrabi Gate (one of the entrances to the Mount, above the Western Wall) was removed from the *waqf* office by Israeli soldiers. This Israeli takeover of one of the Temple Mount gates weakened the Muslim leadership's control there. On the other hand, the Israeli government endeavored to permit the Muslims to exercise control on the Temple Mount. With this aim in mind, it decided to prevent Jews from worshipping there.

The Law for the Preservation of Holy Places states that the Holy Places shall be "protected from desecration, or any other harm, or from anything liable to prejudice the freedom of access of members of the religion to their

Holy Places, or their feelings towards those places.''[38] The Supreme Court decided that freedom of access to the Holy Places includes the freedom to worship there.[39] At the same time, the Supreme Court approved the government's decision, instructing the police to prevent Jews from worshipping on the Temple Mount. The judges explained this ruling by declaring that it is within the prerogative of the executive branch to make the arrangements for visits and prayers at places that are holy to two religions.[40]

The Chief Rabbinate decided that because of the sacredness of the Temple Mount, Jews should refrain from visiting the site and praying there. However, this opinion did not influence the government's position. Instead, by means of the Religious Ministry, the government supervised the Mughrabi Gate with the single aim of guaranteeing access by Jews to the Temple Mount. The government also proclaimed that Jews have the right to pray there, and the minister of religious affairs announced this position publicly in the Knesset. The Supreme Court adopted this approach and took note of the right of Jews to pray on the Temple Mount on the condition of government approval.

Despite the Israeli government's decision, in principle, to permit the Muslim leadership to maintain Temple Mount arrangements as it saw fit (providing Jews be permitted to visit) and to prevent Jews from worshipping there, the authorities did in fact take a number of steps that constituted intervention in the sphere apparently entrusted to the Muslims. For a time the authorities intervened to supervise the contents of the weekly sermons delivered by the preachers at the Ḥaram al-Sharīf mosques. (Government censorship of mosque sermons is a usual practice in Arab countries.) The authorities prevented the waqf from opening a ticket-sales office beside the Mughrabi Gate.[41] They pressed Muslim leaders to reopen the site to visits after the al-Aqṣā Mosque fire.[42]

On August 21, 1969, a fire broke out in the al-Aqṣā Mosque, destroying a valuable pulpit, the *minbar* Ṣalāh al-Dīn, and part of a prayer niche (*miḥrāb*) and causing slight damage to part of the roof of the southeast corner and the cupola. The incident alarmed the Arabs of Jerusalem and the West Bank, who regarded it as a deliberate act of the Israeli government. The fire embarrassed the Israeli authorities, as it jeopardized its claim to be competent in safeguarding the Holy Places. The next day, Michael Dennis Rohan, an Australian tourist, was arrested. In his trial he ascribed the deed to a divine command. He was found non compos mentis and committed to an asylum for the mentally disturbed. As a result, the Israeli authorities urged the Muslim leadership to implement safety recommendations to safeguard the mosques.

To sum up, it should be stressed that Muslim control over the Temple Mount was basically preserved. Israeli intervention was regarded as trifling compared to the government's decision to leave the supervision of the site to the Muslim leadership and, consequently, pay a price that was, from a Jewish standpoint, very high: the ban on Jews worshipping on the Temple Mount, in defiance of the spirit of the law.

The Israeli attitude toward the Muslim and Christian Holy Places in Jerusalem was in marked contrast to the conduct of the Jordanian government when it controlled East Jerusalem. Jordan did not abide by the 1949 Armistice Agreement, which recognized the right of Israelis to have free access to the Holy Places in East Jerusalem. Jewish and Muslim citizens of Israel were not permitted to visit East Jerusalem or their Holy Places. Christian citizens of Israel were permitted to visit the Holy Places in East Jerusalem once a year at Christmas. And Christians of dual nationality (Israeli and other) were permitted to visit the eastern part of the city on Easter. Jews who were citizens of other countries were not permitted to visit the Western Wall.

From the time East Jerusalem was annexed to Israel, Muslims and Christians of all nationalities, including citizens of Arab states, have been permitted to visit the Holy Places in Jerusalem (and in all of Israel). In accordance with the ''open bridges'' policy, allowing free passage (along with a security check) from Jordan to the West Bank (and from there to Israel, as there are no borders, transit stations, or barriers between the West Bank and Israel), citizens of Arab states are permitted to visit the Holy Places in Jerusalem and other cities in Israel. Every summer there are mass visits of citizens of Arab countries to the West Bank, Jerusalem, and all of Israel. From 1968 to December 1978, 1,514,482 visitors from Arab countries crossed the bridges from Jordan to the West Bank (according to statistics of the Israel Ministry of Defense).

THE EDUCATIONAL SYSTEM

On August 7, 1967, the government adopted decisions concerning educational problems in East Jerusalem and on the West Bank.[43] The decisions stated that the schools were to reopen and that the Jordanian curriculum, previously in use in East Jerusalem, would be abandoned, to be replaced by the curriculum in use in the Arab schools in Israel. This decision was not implemented, however, as there was opposition to the government's decree on the West Bank and in East Jerusalem. Pupils demonstrated and teachers served notice that they would not return to work. In the end, this opposition induced the government to reconsider. Regarding the West Bank, it resolved to leave the Jordanian educational system in force, together with its textbooks (with the exception of two), while in East Jerusalem it decided that the Israeli Arab curriculum would apply solely to government schools (not UNRWA [United Nations Relief and Works Agency] schools nor private educational establishments).[44]

This new decision did not withstand the test of practice. Arab high school pupils preferred private schools to the government schools because of the recently instituted Israeli curriculum. Studying under the Israeli Arab curriculum would deprive the Arab students of the chance of being accepted at Arab universities because it prepared them to meet the requirements of the Israeli matriculation examinations, not those prevailing in Jordan. Compared to 1,317 pupils attending government high schools in 1967, the number declined 50 percent in 1968 (684) and continued to drop, falling to 116 in 1970.[45]

Under pressure from the Jerusalem Municipality, the policy was modified. In 1970, it was decided that, together with the Israeli curriculum, the government high schools would institute supplementary lessons adapted to the Jordanian curriculum in order to prepare their pupils for the Jordanian matriculation examinations. Yet this change did not have far-reaching results. A majority of the pupils still refrained from attending government schools. On the other hand, the private schools continued to expand, further attracting pupils by instituting a series of reductions and rebates on tuition fees.

Following the recommendation of a public commission appointed by the minister of education, a new study program was instituted in 1972.[46] The new curriculum combined both the Israeli Arab and Jordanian curricula. Now the Jordanian component of the curriculum was not taught in supplementary lessons but became an integral part of the official study program. This curriculum applied to preparatory schools as well as high schools.

In August 1975, a three-person committee presented its recommendations concerning the desired curriculum in East Jerusalem to the minister of education and the Jerusalem Municipality. The committee found that the integrated curriculum introduced in 1972 had not succeeded in halting the flow of pupils into private schools. Admittedly, in the course of the first two years following the introduction of the integrated curriculum, the number of pupils attending government schools had increased. However, the Jordanian government erected a new obstacle by declaring that any pupil sitting for a matriculation examination under the Jordanian system would be required to produce an affidavit that he or she had previously completed the ninth grade of school in accordance with the Jordanian curriculum. Accordingly, many pupils transferred to private schools while still at preparatory school age. The committee recommended the institution of two parallel study courses in East Jerusalem, commencing in the seventh grade. One course would follow the Jordanian curriculum and the other would follow the curriculum in use by Arabs in Israel. In either case, the curriculum should include lessons in Hebrew and civics. These recommendations were applied in the 1976 school year.

The departures from educational practices prevailing in Israel found expression beyond the modification of the curriculum to meet the wishes of the East Jerusalem population. The education system and its methods, as applied in East Jerusalem, diverged considerably from those customary in Israel.

Unlike the Israeli system (as of 1967, which has since been changed), the East Jerusalem educational system possessed the following structure: primary school (six grades), preparatory school (three grades), and high school (three grades). Likewise, East Jerusalem has been served by three educational networks: government, UNRWA, and private. Pupils in governmental high schools in East Jerusalem were not required to pay tuition fees, in contrast to what had been Israeli practice until 1978. Pupils in private schools do pay tuition fees, even at primary school age, also in contrast to Israeli practice.

The Ministry of Education has no control over a considerable portion of East Jerusalem schools (those of the UNRWA network and private establishments); and since the reunification of the city, the Muslim private schools have continued to follow the Jordanian curriculum, using Jordanian textbooks (unlike the textbooks in the West Bank, which have undergone revision). The Christian private schools have abandoned the Jordanian curriculum and now follow European study programs.[47] The private schools, together with those of UNRWA, embrace nearly half of the pupils in East Jerusalem (private schools serve 30.6 percent of the pupils, the UNRWA schools another 11.7 percent). As a result, the requirements of Israeli education laws have not been applied to a large number of pupils in East Jerusalem.[48]

As for the other half of the East Jerusalem pupils (those attending government educational establishments), the Arab Israeli syllabus has been applied to the primary schools alone. In the seventh to twelfth grades of government schools, the curriculum has been progressively adapted to the requirements of the Jordanian Ministry of Education (as described above). This trend was developed further in 1976, when it was formally decided to institute two study courses—one Jordanian, the other Israeli—in government schools, commencing in the seventh grade. The official committee that decided on this step and the educational authorities that enforced its decisions clearly foresaw that East Jerusalem pupils would choose the Jordanian course.

It is generally supposed that, in the future, this decision will also be extended to the primary schools (first to sixth grades). This trend is anchored in the 1953 State Education Law, Section 4, which states: "The Minister shall lay down the curriculum of every official educational establishment; in non-Jewish educational institutions, the curriculum shall be adapted to the special conditions thereof."[49] On the basis of this wording, it is apparently possible to make a distinction between the "special conditions" of the Arab population in other parts of the State of Israel and the "special conditions" affecting the Arabs of Jerusalem and, consequently, to institute a different curriculum in each case.

THE ECONOMIC SYSTEM

Since 1967, East Jerusalem's economic activity has been conducted on the basis of extensive consideration for the Arab community's reluctance to obey regulations and laws it views as running counter to its national aspirations. On the practical side, the economic structures of both parts of the city have interlocked; however, exceptional procedures have been left in effect in East Jerusalem on the legal, structural, and formal planes.

Tax Laws

Immediately after the reunification of the city, the National Revenue Administration adopted a cardinal decision: For taxation purposes, East Jerusalem would be on the same footing as the city's western sections. However, this decision has not been enforced. In contrast to the position adopted by the tax authorities, various interministerial committees practiced a policy designed to moderate the attitude of the National Revenue Administration, in consideration of the views and feelings of Jerusalem's Arab inhabitants. The decisions of the interministerial committees, which foiled the intentions of the National Revenue Administration, affected every form of taxation imposed upon Jerusalem's Arab population.

Income Tax

While the income tax authorities' East Jerusalem representative intended to require the Arab inhabitants to pay their taxes in full, the Committee of Directors-General for East Jerusalem decided that the tax authorities were to act with restraint and not apply the full letter of the law to those required to pay taxes.[50] A similar instruction was issued by the interministerial committee responsible for directing policy in the city.[51] The taxes that the city's Arabs were required to pay included the following: income tax, absorption loan, and defense levy. In April 1970, these were followed by the defense and savings loans. The East Jerusalem Arabs objected to both the size of the assessments and the payment of taxes designed to underwrite Israel's defense requirements (the defense loan). Their objection took the form of a commercial strike.

The interministerial committee adopted a series of decisions in consideration for the feelings of the city's Arabs, in opposition to the views of the National Revenue Administration's representatives. The committee resolved to instruct the tax authorities to reexamine the tax assessments sent out to the city's Arabs, to refrain from collecting arrears, and to set up public committees (in an advisory capacity to the tax authorities), which would function as boards of appeal for the Arab assessees.[52] Subsequently, the committee decided to release the Arab bus company from charging defense levies and to instruct the Revenue Administration to consider the hotel owners' applications for tax rebates, on the ground that they were operating in a "development area."[53]

From 1970, assessments were sent to independently employed taxpayers without charging tax on their income from previous years. In 1971, assessments were sent out in accordance with the previous year's income, in spite of the economic prosperity prevailing in the city that year. The committee decided that only in special cases would there be any increase in tax demands (to be no more than 10 percent), and even then, only after prior consultation with the assessee. At the same time, excess taxes would be repaid to certain assessees. The committee instructed the tax authorities that, in drawing up the tax forms, they were to refrain from detailing the constituent components of the taxes (defense levy and defense loans) but were to calculate the taxes with the inclusion of these components.[54]

Subsequently, advisory committees were chosen from among the city's Arabs to function as boards of appeal on the size of assessments.[55] A similar policy was pursued in subsequent years. In 1974, the Interministerial Committee on Security decided that tax collection was to be at a moderate rate, with the aim of attaining a level of revenue equal to that of the previous year.[56] Final assessments would be made so as to ensure that the correct tax was paid. Notifications of advance tax payments would include the sums payable as defense taxes, but without them being entered separately. In 1978, the rate of collection of income tax in East Jerusalem reached the usual level of West Jerusalem (statistics of the Ministry of Finance).

Property Tax

The tax authorities refrained from collecting property tax and compensation fund payments from Jerusalem Arabs. This policy, introduced immediately after the city's reunification, was maintained by decision of an interministerial team meeting at the Attorney General's Office.[57] In October 1975 a decision was adopted at the Finance Minister's Office whereby property tax would be collected from East Jerusalem inhabitants residing outside the Old City walls (this referred to Jews); inhabitants who had resided outside the walls in the period prior to the city's reunification (Arabs) would be required to pay property tax in full, but only in stages; property tax would not be collected from inhabitants (Jews or Arabs) residing within the walls—following Ottoman and mandatory legislation, which released residents of the Old City from property tax.[58]

In practice, the Arab inhabitants of East Jerusalem, both inside and outside the walls, did not pay property tax, other than in cases of transactions. The situation began to change in 1977 when the tax authorities started to collect property tax also from the Arab residents of the city. This decision was implemented gradually. In 1977, the Arab residents were required to pay 20 percent of the assessments of the tax authorities and 40 percent in 1978 (statistics of the Ministry of Finance).

Betterment Tax

Until 1972, betterment tax was not collected from the non-Jewish inhabitants of East Jerusalem. From that year onward, the tax was collected from Arab inhabitants whenever property transactions were concluded.[59] Even after this date, tax was not collected from churches.[60]

Value Added Tax

On July 1, 1976, a value added tax (VAT) was instituted in Israel. Officially, the same rate of VAT applies to East Jerusalem as to Israel in general, but in practice, the degree of collection of this tax was lower than anticipated.

National Insurance Payments

The National Insurance Law was extended to East Jerusalem shortly after the reunification of the city; but while its benefits came into effect, the obligatory payments it imposes were not rendered in full.

National Insurance representatives protested to the interministerial committee dealing with security matters in Jerusalem that its decision to refrain from sending income tax assessments to independently employed inhabitants of East Jerusalem for the period between 1967 and 1970 prevented the National Insurance Institute from collecting arrears from these assessees.[61] At the same time, the National Insurance Institute paid allowances for the children of independently employed assessees.

The National Insurance Institute was instructed not to collect premiums from ecclesiastical bodies.[62] On the other hand, the Ministerial Committee for Jerusalem decided to extend National Insurance benefits to those Jerusalem Arabs who held identity cards and who had kept up their payments to the National Insurance Institute, even if they had moved to places of residence beyond the city bounds.[63]

Municipal Taxes

By a Municipal Council decision, inhabitants of East Jerusalem were completely exempt from municipal taxes during FY 1968-69.[64] In subsequent years, the Municipal Council decided to impose taxes by stages: 35 percent in 1968-69, 60 percent in 1969-70, and 80 percent in 1970-71 and 1971-72. Only in the fifth year of the city's reunification would the full tax be imposed. In practice, the collection rate was lower than foreseen, beginning at a rate of 27 percent in 1968-69 and going up to 65 percent in 1975-76.[65] This rate remained constant in following years. The collection rate for the western sections is about 85 percent.

Banking

At the outbreak of the Six-Day War, the six Jordanian and two British banks operating on the West Bank and in Jerusalem closed their doors. On the eve of the war, all the cash in the vaults of the East Jerusalem banks had been transferred to the Central Bank in Amman.[66] In spite of protracted negotiations between Israel and Jordan, the Jordanian and British banks were not reopened.

The effort at negotiations of the two governments can be explained by their common interest. Israel wished to achieve normalization in banking, while Jordan wished to appease those inhabitants of East Jerusalem and the West Bank whose deposits had been transferred to Amman. At the same time, the failure of the negotiations is further evidence that the two countries were unable to reach agreement in formal matters. The principal stumbling block was the character of the links that the local branches in East Jerusalem and the West Bank were to have with their central office in Amman.

In place of the British and Arab banks, branches of five Israeli banks began to operate in East Jerusalem. The scope of their operations was very limited, and in practice they were utilized solely by Israeli bodies.

The overall financial situation in East Jerusalem was also affected by an unofficial flow of money, in considerable sums, from Jordan. Israel knew of these transfers but ignored them, as these Jordanian funds were essentially sent to underwrite opposition to Israeli rule (*ṣumūd* money) and to pay the salaries of those employees who refused to work for the Israeli administration. The Arab nationalist organizations also sent in money, often to finance terrorist acts. Possession of Jordanian money constituted an infringement of Israeli currency regulations and reflected contact, of a political and military nature, with the enemy (according to Israeli legal definitions).

Financial activity in East Jerusalem was also affected by the Israeli government's decision to establish a IL 10 million fund to grant loans for operating capital to the inhabitants of the West Bank. Under pressure from the Jerusalem Municipality, more than IL 3 million were allocated to grant government-guaranteed loans to owners of businesses in East Jerusalem. Funds were also established to issue mortgage loans to finance independent building by the city's Arabs. The size of the funds did not meet the demand for loans.[67]

Money changers remained a fixture in East Jerusalem, reflecting a further example of the Israeli authorities' toleration of a situation peculiar to the annexed territory. Within the State of Israel, there is no official recognition of money changers, and they are not considered "authorized dealers" as defined by the Defense Regulations (Money) (1941).[68] At the same time, the Ministerial Committee for Jerusalem decided to permit the activities of the money changers of East Jerusalem.[69]

The Law of Legal and Administrative Affairs permits the pursuit of money changing by whoever engaged in it prior to the annexation. Consequently, a decree was issued authorizing the East Jerusalem money changers to change foreign currency into Israeli pounds, providing they carried out the transaction according to the official exchange rate and sold the foreign currency in their possession to an authorized dealer (a bank) within seven days.[70] In practice, the money changers did not obey these instructions, a circumstance the authorities generally overlooked.

Chamber of Commerce

This body was subject to Israeli law but was elected in accordance with Jordanian law. In addition to its activities in East Jerusalem (within the State of Israel), the Jerusalem branch headed the Committee of Chambers of Commerce on the West Bank, elected and functioning under Jordanian law. In practice, the East Jerusalem Chamber of Commerce functioned as a consulate of the Kingdom of Jordan, issuing para-notarial affidavits for all purposes. It authenticated signatures on checks, powers of attorney, bills of sale for cars, matriculation certificates for pupils wishing to study at Arab universities, and declarations that goods to be exported to Arab states had been manufactured in "Arab Jerusalem." It also approved bills of sales for land registration in Jordan and approved declarations of inhabitants applying for Jordanian identity cards or passports.

All these documents, when issued by the Chamber of Commerce, were recognized by the Jordanian government.[71] However, this para-notarial activity of the East Jerusalem Chamber of Commerce was illegal from the viewpoint of Israeli law.[72] The chamber's links with the Jordanian government were also illegal, as was its function in making secret allocations of money to inhabitants of East Jerusalem.

THE STATUS OF FOREIGN INSTITUTIONS

United Nations

The UN Observers Headquarters, whose task was to supervise the 1949 armistice between Israel and Jordan, continues to function in Jerusalem, despite the termination of the circumstances that led to its constitution. The United Nations continues to maintain its institutions, procedures, and arrangements as though the Six-Day War had not taken place.

On June 27, 1967, the Israeli government resolved to restore to the United Nations the High Commissioner's Residence, which had fallen to Israeli forces during the war.[73] However, the return of the building was made subject to a number of conditions: The United Nations would receive only rights of occupancy to the building; the headquarters would deal exclusively with the cease-fire instituted subsequent to the Six-Day War, and not with matters pertaining to the 1949 armistice; the area returned would be reduced to include only the area of the residence and its gardens.

The United Nations rejected the Israeli government's conditions on the grounds that the armistice had not come to an end, and consequently the arrangement concerning "the area between the lines" (which had permitted the United Nations to occupy an area of about 700 acres around the High Commissioner's Residence) had not been terminated. The United Nations could not consider the restoration of the High Commissioner's Residence as a sovereign Israeli act because such an interpretation would run counter to UN General Assembly Resolution 2253 invalidating the annexation of East Jerusalem. Thus the United Nations refused to sign a lease agreement with the Israeli government.

After negotiations, it was agreed that the area restored should include 179 acres only; Israel promised not to utilize the remaining area for military purposes; and Israel gave written notification that it was handing the area and the building over to the United Nations with the intention that the latter supervise the cease-fire, and this transfer was "a sovereign Israeli act." UN Secretary-General U Thant consented to the agreement solely on practical grounds, stating that his consent had no bearing on UN rights to the residence, to the UN's position vis-à-vis the area as a whole, or to the matter of defining the tasks of the truce supervision staff. The UN position implied rejection of all the conditions advanced by Israel, with the exception of the reduction in the area restored to the United Nations (although here, too, the United Nations did not relinquish its claims to the area as a whole).

At the end of 1970, Israel began land clearance beside the High Commissioner's Residence. The UN secretary-general asked the government to halt these operations and restore the area to the United Nations. U Thant threatened to appeal to the Security Council and to the Hague International Court, citing the Convention of Immunity of UN buildings, to which Israel is a signatory. In response, the government announced that work would be halted, but at the same time it rejected the demand to restore the rest of the area around the residence to the United Nations.

The United Nations continued to occupy a building near the Mandelbaum Gate. This property never belonged to the United Nations but was leased from its Armenian owners. Rooms in the building were allocated to the chairman of the Mixed Armistice Commission and his observers. The cost of upkeep was financed equally by Israel and Jordan. After the Six-Day War, the chairman of the Mixed Armistice Commission remained in the building; but Israel tried to get the UN personnel out, claiming that the armistice had been terminated, and, with it, the functions of the Israeli-Jordanian Mixed

Armistice Commission. The United Nations rejected the Israeli demands, and to this day its flag continues to fly above the building.

Consulates

The Vienna Convention defines the duties of consuls acting on behalf of their states in foreign countries in the following manner: to further economic, commercial, cultural, and scientific ties between the states they represent and the local inhabitants; to engage in any other task imposed upon them by the state they represent and to which the host state does not object. It is doubtful whether the status of the consuls in Jerusalem meets the convention's definitions. The representatives of ten states serve as consuls in Jerusalem without their respective states recognizing the rule of Israel (and, previously, of Jordan) over the city that serves as their base. These are the representatives of the United States, Britain, Italy, Belgium, Turkey, France, Sweden, Greece, Holland, and Spain (Britain having been the only one of these states to recognize Jordanian rule in East Jerusalem). These states adhere to the UN General Assembly resolution of November 1947, under which Jerusalem was to acquire the status of a corpus separatum.

The consuls in Jerusalem of these states do not present a consular letter of authorization to the Foreign Ministry, and, unlike other consuls serving in Israel, they do not receive the signature of the President of Israel, which authorizes them to operate within the State of Israel. They are issued consular identity cards and Israeli residence permits, and they enjoy the usual diplomatic privileges. Unlike other consuls operating in Israel, these ten consuls conduct their contacts with the Israeli authorities by way of the district commissioner, not the Israeli Foreign Ministry.

After the reunification of the city, the ten states refused to recognize Israeli rule over East Jerusalem, even de facto. (The activity of the ten consuls in both sections of Jerusalem prior to the Six-Day War constituted de facto recognition of the rule of Israel and Jordan over the two sections of the city.) Several consuls engaged in political activity among the Arab population in East Jerusalem and the West Bank.[74]

The Jerusalem Municipality considered imposing municipal taxes on the buildings the ten consuls owned in East Jerusalem. Action was initiated in this direction, but in the end the Municipality refrained from charging taxes on the consular buildings in question.[75] It contented itself with collecting a service fee from the consulates. For their part, the consuls made it clear that the separate consular branches each country maintained in the eastern and western sections of the city were, in each case, operating as a single unit.[76] The Foreign Ministry was of the opinion that it would be better to refrain from tackling the subject of the consuls' status, as it was not a priority Israeli interest.[77]

SYMBOLS

As symbols, by their very nature, can provoke great sensitivities, the Israeli authorities generally endeavored to avoid sharp confrontations with the Arab population in this area. As a result, government decisions were modified in response to the views of officials (principally from the Jerusalem Municipality) who reported the views of the Arab community.

Language

One of the first instructions issued in the Jerusalem Municipality after reunification stated that any official letter addressed to an Arab employee or inhabitant was to be written in both Hebrew and Arabic.

The Arabic broadcasts of Israel radio referred to Jerusalem as "Ūrushalīm," while East Jerusalem residents were accustomed to the name "al-Quds." At the instigation of Jerusalem municipal officials and the Arab department of the Israel Broadcasting Authority, the terminology was altered, and on the morning of August 20, 1967, Jerusalem was referred to as "al-Quds." This change provoked objections in Israel, and the subject was brought up at a meeting of the cabinet, where it was decided that the city would be called "Ūrushalīm—al-Quds."[78]

By a decision of the Jerusalem Municipal Council, street names at the junction between the city's two sections were changed. Allenby Square was renamed Ẓahal (an acronym for Israel Defense Forces) Square; part of Süleyman the Magnificent Street was renamed Paratroopers' Street; and the names of military units (Jerusalem District, Har'el Brigade, Central Command) were given to streets west of the old demarcation line. Hebrew names were added to 90 streets in the Old City.

In the Jewish Quarter the former Hebrew names were restored; in a number of cases the Hebrew name of an Old City street differed from its Arabic name. In two cases, street names were split. For example, in one street, the first section was called "ʿUmar ibn al-Khaṭṭāb Street," the middle section was "Armenians' Street," and the end section was named "Hostels' Street." The western section of the main street running outside the northern section of the Old City wall was called "Paratroopers' Street," while its eastern section remained "Süleyman the Magnificent Street." Non-Arabic names of streets were rendered upon street signs in Arabic transcription.[79]

Commemorative Events and Monuments

In spite of international protests, the parade of the Israeli army in honor of the state's twenty-fifth anniversary followed a route from East Jerusalem to the city's western sections. In other instances, the Israeli authorities did con-

sider the feelings of Jerusalem's Arabs: On the occasion of the annual Israeli
mass (civilian) march, the route was changed and the marchers were directed
to the eastern edges of West Jerusalem; the annual events in honor of
Jerusalem's reunification were held in West Jerusalem, and a particular effort
was made to avoid giving them an ostentatiously national character.[80]

Eleven monuments were erected in memory of 181 Israeli soldiers who
died in Jerusalem during the Six-Day War. (The monuments were consecrated on the first anniversary of the war.) They were erected on the sites
where spontaneously improvised memorials, usually mounds of rocks, were
set up immediately after the end of the fighting. Most of the monuments were
along the old demarcation line, but some were in the eastern section, in the
heart of Arab neighborhoods. One monument was erected on *waqf* land, near
a mosque. (The *waqf* management did not object to the erection of the monument and refused to accept financial compensation for the use of the ground.)
In general, these monuments were not damaged.

In the early morning of June 4, 1968, a monument to the Arab victims of
the Six-Day War was erected in the garden of the Nusayba family's home in
East Jerusalem. It was followed by a dozen additional monuments, which
sprang up in various places in the city; and the Security Committee decided to
take action to reduce the number of monuments. (The Arab victims of the Six-
Day War were, in part, buried on the sites of the battles. After the war, at the
suggestion of the Municipality, they were transferred to the Muslim cemetery
by the waqf.) Negotiations were initiated with the waqf, and on November 17,
1968, it was agreed that six monuments would be erected. When the agreement was made public, it aroused a storm of protest among Jerusalem's
Jewish inhabitants. In the meantime, waqf employees erected one monument
beside the Muslim cemetery. The Israeli authorities decided not to object to
this monument, but demanded that the waqf submit plans of two further
monuments for approval. In the end, only that single monument was erected
because the waqf management refrained from submitting plans for the erection of two further monuments.[81]

Press

In November 1968, the first edition of the newspaper *al-Quds*, edited by
Maḥmūd Abū Zuluf, appeared. The permit to publish the paper was issued
through the mediation of Mayor Teddy Kollek, who also guaranteed a IL
100,000 loan taken out by the publisher to buy printing presses. The publication of an Arabic newspaper placed both its editors and the Israeli authorities
in a situation calling for mutual tolerance and caution. The administration
was careful to avoid vigorous intervention regarding the views expressed by
the paper, while its editors endeavored to express moderate views and adopted
a restrained manner so as to avoid provoking the authorities. In one case, after

publishing a statement of protest by the Muslim Council on land expropriations, the editor was called in for a talk with an official representative.

The authorities displayed a different attitude, however, toward two additional newspapers, al-Fajr and al-Shaᶜb. The tone adopted by these two papers was more extreme, and the Interministerial Security Committee devoted considerable deliberation to the question of shutting them down. In April 1973, the editors of al-Fajr were arrested for censorship offenses and released on bail. In November 1974, the editor of al-Fajr appealed to the Supreme Court against the official refusal to grant him a publication license. The Interior Ministry later abandoned its refusal to issue the license. On November 4, 1974, the Security Committee instructed the Communications Ministry to turn down a request by the publisher of al-Fajr to install a Telex terminal in the editorial offices.[82] In August 1975, a team consisting of the police minister, the attorney general, and the mayor of Jerusalem decided to close al-Shaᶜb, but prior publication of the decision forestalled its implementation. In 1977, a Communist weekly called al-Ṭalīᶜa began to appear in East Jerusalem. Its distribution was prohibited in the West Bank by order of the military government. According to unofficial statistics, the distribution of al-Fajr and al-Shaᶜb is lower than 10,000, whereas al-Quds reaches about 15,000. Less than 1,000 copies of al-Ṭalīᶜa are printed.

The authorities, in the last resort, permitted the organs of East Jerusalem's inhabitants to give vent to their opinions and refrained from taking drastic steps to cease their publication. In the absence of official representatives for Jerusalem's Arabs, the newspapers became their principal means of expression, thereby acquiring considerable political significance.

Culture

The cultural life in East Jerusalem is concentrated mainly in some 30 clubs, 20 under communal and 10 under municipal patronage. The communal clubs are run by religious groups (Muslim, Catholic, Greek Orthodox, and so on) or have a national or ethnic character (Armenian, Assyrian, and so on). The municipal clubs are organized on a neighborhood basis. The functions of the communal clubs include social gatherings, celebrations of religious and national holidays, musical activity in the form of choirs, orchestras, and dance, and libraries. In the municipal clubs sports are the main attraction. Occasionally, intellectual pursuits are carried on. A small number of Arab youths in East Jerusalem belong to the scout movement.

The activities in all the clubs include about 6,000 people, according to statistics of the Jerusalem Municipality. In the eastern part of the city, there are also two prestigious social clubs whose members are of the economically elite classes. These two clubs offer their members varied social and cultural activities. The Jerusalem Municipality organizes for the Arab population study sessions, lectures, and tours, and some 1,500 people participate per month. There is a theater group in East Jerusalem, and occasionally smaller groups are organized on a temporary basis. Two groups exist that promote Arab-Jewish social contact—one founded by a Jewish academician and the other under the patronage of the Histadrut (Israel Labor Federation). Participation is limited.

SUMMARY

The very manner in which East Jerusalem was annexed created the framework for the city's development and symbolized the relationships between the Israeli authorities and the Arab population. The annexation was a unilateral act, and this fact dictated the way in which the Israeli administration dealt with the practical problems arising from the reunification of the city. In order to maintain a normal way of life in the annexed territory, the Israeli administration was obliged to take further unilateral steps, for the Arab population, which considered itself to be under occupation, was not expected to cooperate.

Consequently, the attitude of the Israeli administration toward the Arab minority in Jerusalem can be gauged from a series of unilateral decisions that gradually merged into a policy. This policy clearly inclined toward releasing the Arab population from many of the obligations imposed upon inhabitants of the State of Israel. This policy differentiated between the laws pertaining to Arab citizens of Israel and laws applying to the Arab residents of the annexed area of Jerusalem. At the same time, it expressed the intention of granting a considerable part of the social benefits enjoyed by inhabitants of Israel to the population of the annexed area. The result is a situation whereby Israel tolerates the preservation of the way of life that prevailed in East Jerusalem before the onset of Israeli control.

These governmental decisions, which in retrospect crystallized into a policy, found formal expression in the three types of solutions adopted by the Israeli government to overcome the legal problems arising from the refusal of Jerusalem's Arabs to follow the modes of behavior customary in Israel.

The first solution was Israeli legislation designed to legalize the modes of behavior peculiar to East Jerusalem. This category covers such matters as the status of present absentees; permission to practice licensed professions and to operate cooperative societies, companies, and partnerships; the inclusion of East Jerusalem's inhabitants in the municipal electoral roll; permission for Arab inhabitants to work as government employees under special contract—well beyond the customary time; permission for Jerusalem Arabs to receive compensation for their ''absentee'' property; and sanction for the activities of East Jerusalem money changers.

The second solution was to solve legal entanglements by means of administrative regulations. Business licenses were renewed; the social benefits of Arab state and municipal employees in Jerusalem were regulated; the bounds of sanctioned Jewish behavior on the Temple Mount were laid down; government schools were permitted to adhere to the Jordanian curriculum; income tax was collected by stages and in moderation; the city's Arabs were not required to pay property tax; and betterment tax was only collected to a limited extent.

Furthermore, the authorities refrained from pressing claims against Arab residents who held the status of "absentees" regarding property in parts of Israel outside East Jerusalem, inhabitants of the occupied territories who held the status of "absentees" regarding their property in East Jerusalem, and East Jerusalem inhabitants who had moved to the Arab states and left behind trustees. These administrative regulations gave rise to a special attitude toward the Arab inhabitants that generally, if not totally, ran counter to the law exercised in other parts of Israel.

The third solution was to overlook legal infringements. This category includes the activities of the East Jerusalem $shari^{\bar{i}c}a$ court and the Muslim Council; the authorities' toleration of the illegal flow of money into East Jerusalem and of the notarial activities of the Chamber of Commerce; permission for private schools to function in East Jerusalem without supervision by the Israeli Ministry of Education; and official tolerance of practices differing from those customary in the Israeli educational system.

Despite the fact that East Jerusalem has been annexed to the State of Israel, it is doubtful whether the attitude of its population toward Israel differs in any practical way from that of the West Bank population. In the economic field, there is no significant difference between the residents of East Jerusalem and the West Bank population in the degree of dependence upon the Israeli economy. Furthermore, the attitude adopted by the Israeli authorities toward the population of East Jerusalem does not differ markedly from the approach they have taken to the West Bank population. Both populations maintain their previous way of life in the religious, educational, political, and social spheres. And the ties of both Arab populations with Israeli society were affected by the same factors. The effect of annexation on the inhabitants of East Jerusalem was therefore marginal in this respect.

Thus the annexation of East Jerusalem has not generated a way of life or mode of behavior different from what prevails in the occupied territories. Annexation found its expression largely on the formal and symbolic plane, that is, laws and regulations were designed to give expression to Israel's desire to regard East Jerusalem as an integral part of the state. Once these framework laws were translated into practical laws and regulations, however, the Israeli authorities preferred to leave the Arab population to its own devices and permit it to function according to its political and social traditions and maintain its links to the forms of government that existed in the past.

In addition to formal acts, however, an extremely practical expression of the Israeli government's intention of absorbing East Jerusalem into Israel relates to immovable property. In contrast to the consideration the Israeli authorities displayed toward the wishes of the annexed population in all matters related to the conduct of its own affairs, they ignored its desires in formulating their policy to build up and populate the city. This aspect of government policy was expressed in the introduction of Jewish control over the Western Wall and the Jewish Quarter and, particularly, in the attempt to establish a Jewish presence in the unpopulated expanses of land in the northeast of the city. The government's population and building policy, which involved confiscation of Arab lands, clashed with the interests of the Arab population. This is, therefore, one of the most salient practical expressions of the Israeli authorities' aim of making East Jerusalem an integral part of the State of Israel. In addition, the government adopted important decisions, such as the elimination of the demarcation line (even at difficult moments, when there was a danger of direct confrontation between Jews and Arabs), safeguarding order and control in East Jerusalem, and the unification of municipal and government services in both parts of the city.

NOTES

1. M. Benvenisti, *Jerusalem: The Torn City* (Minneapolis: University of Minnesota Press, 1976); U. Benziman, *Jerusalem: A City Without Walls* (Hebrew) (Jerusalem and Tel Aviv: Schocken, 1973).

2. *Laws*, vol. 19, p. 8684.

3. Section 8 of the Municipalities Ordinance states: "If the minister considers that it is desirable to alter the jurisdiction of a certain municipality . . . he is empowered to order a commission of inquiry to hold an inquiry concerning the jurisdiction of the municipality . . . and, after studying the commission's report, he is empowered, according to his discretion, and by proclamation, to alter the area of jurisdiction, extending or reducing it" (*Laws of the State of Israel*, no. 8, p. 197). The amendment reads: "The minister is empowered, by his discretion, and without conducting an inquiry, to extend—by proclamation—the jurisdiction of a certain municipality, by inducing an area defined by decree, according to Section 11B of the Legal and Administrative Affairs (Regulation) Order 1948."

4. An absentee is defined by the law as "any person who— at any time during the period between November 29, 1947, and the day of publication of the proclamation . . . that the state of emergency declared by the Provisional State Council on May 19, 1948, was no longer in existence—was the legal owner of any property in Israeli territory, or enjoyed its proceeds, or possessed it, himself or by means of another, and at any time during the aforementioned period was a citizen or subject of Lebanon, Egypt, Syria, Saudi Arabia, Transjordan, Iraq or Yemen. . . ." An absentee's property is defined by the law as ". . . property whose legal owner, or he who enjoyed it, or who possessed it himself or by means of another, was absent . . . at any time during the period between November 29, 1947, and the day of publication of the proclama-

tion . . . that the state of emergency proclaimed by the Provisional State Council on May 19, 1948, is no longer in existence . . .'' (*Book of Laws*, no. 37, 1950, p. 86).

5. ''An enemy—one who is a combatant or maintains a state of war against Israel, or declares himself to be one of these, whether or not war has been declared and whether or not there are acts of hostility'' (*Laws*, vol. 5, p. 2155).

6. *Book of Laws*, no. 537, August 16, 1968, p. 204.

7. The penalty clause in the law reads as follows: ''A person without a license who engages in a business requiring a license, or who does not fulfill any of the conditions of the license . . . is liable to a fine of IL 5,000 or six months' imprisonment.''

8. Partnerships' Order (*Laws*, vol. 25, p. 11357); Cooperative Societies' Order (*Laws*, vol. 1, p. 17); Companies' Order (*Laws*, vol. 8, p. 3275).

9. Benvenisti, *Jerusalem*, pp. 149–50.

10. *Book of Laws*, 1968, p. 247.

11. Benvenisti, *Jerusalem*, p. 151.

12. *Book of Laws*, 1969, p. 254.

13. Civil appeal 687/69, *Judgments*, vol. 24, pt. 2, 1970, p. 464.

14. High Court of Justice, 171/68, *Judgments*, vol. 23, pt. 1, 1969, pp. 261 ff.

15. High Court of Justice, 222/68, *Judgments,* vol. 24, pt. 2, p. 141; and High Court of Justice, 109/70, *Judgments*, vol. 25, pt. 1, pp. 226 ff.

16. High Court of Justice, 283/69, *Judgments*, vol. 24, pt. 2, 1970, pp. 420 ff.

17. The amendment states: ''A person registered in the Population Registry as a resident of an area designated by an order under Section 11B of the Law and Administration Ordinance 5708/1948 shall be deemed to have submitted in due time an application for inclusion in the supplementary list of that area for the register year following the order coming into effect or this Law coming into effect, whichever is the later event'' (*Book of Laws*, 549, 1969, p. 36).

18. *Book of Laws*, 279, April 15, 1959, p. 86. Section 34 of the law states: ''A government employee is required, before receiving his appointment . . . to deliver the following declaration: 'I undertake to be loyal to the State of Israel and its laws, and to fulfill, honestly and faithfully, every duty imposed upon me as a government employee.' This declaration shall be delivered in the presence of the minister or a state employee so empowered by regulation.''

19. Regulation 3343, dated May 25, 1975.

20. Decision of the Ministerial Committee, January 21, 1969.

21. Municipal Council decision, April 20, 1970.

22. Municipal Council decision, August 23, 1970.

23. Municipal Council decision, August 31, 1975.

24. Memorandum dated February 2, 1975, signed by Y. Danenberg.

25. Benvenisti, *Jerusalem*, pp. 141–42.

26. Ibid., p. 140.

27. *Book of Laws*, 701, 1973, p. 164.

28. *Book of Laws*, 37, 1950, p. 86.

29. The Absentees Property Law (Compensation) 1973 stated: ''A person entitled to demand compensation for property is someone who was an inhabitant of Israel on the day this law came into effect or was an inhabitant of Israel after its coming into effect and before the property was transferred to the custodian-general, and was one of the following: (1) the owner of the property, including his heir; (2) an absentee who is only a tenant of an urban property, including his wife, who resides with him at that time; (3) the lessee of the property; (4) a person possessing the rights to benefit from the property. The finance minister shall appoint advisory committees to clarify the claimant's rights to the property for which he demands compensation, or the rate of compensation, and also to determine the annual value of the property. . . . The Advisory Committee shall have the authority of a committee of inquiry . . . the compensation to the claimant who was the owner of the property shall be calculated in accordance with the contents of the Ap-

pendix [which laid down well-defined yardsticks for the calculation]; any disagreement concerning the verdict of the appointed official with regard to the right to compensation, or concerning its rate, shall be settled in accordance with a petition presented on behalf of the claimant, or of the attorney-general, in the Jerusalem District Court or in the District Court within whose area of jurisdiction the property is to be found'' (*Book of Laws*, 701, 1973, p. 164).

30. *Book of Laws*, 1961, p. 118.

31. Memorandum signed by Col. Shlomo Gazit, February 20, 1968.

32. Files of the Ministerial Committee on Jerusalem, May 1, 1970.

33. Benvenisti, *Jerusalem*, p. 296.

34. Ibid., p. 297.

35. Proclamation dated July 24, 1967.

36. Benvenisti, *Jerusalem*, pp. 280–83.

37. Ibid., pp. 277–78.

38. *Book of Laws*, 499, 1967, p. 75.

39. *Judgments*, 24(2), p. 141.

40. *Judgments*, 24(2), pp. 141 ff.

41. Decision of the Interministerial Committee, March 28, 1974.

42. Ibid., October 13, 1969.

43. Benvenisti, *Jerusalem*, p. 195.

44. Ibid., pp. 196–97.

45. Jerusalem Municipality, ''Survey of State and Municipal Education Establishments,'' 1973.

46. Benvenisti, *Jerusalem*, p. 200.

47. Ibid., p. 201.

48. These requirements state, inter alia, that both parents of a child of compulsory-education age have a duty to ensure that their child regularly attends a recognized educational establishment that the minister of education has declared—in a proclamation published in the *Official Gazette*—to be a recognized educational establishment for the purpose of this law. The minister of education has not declared the private schools in East Jerusalem to be recognized establishments. (Compulsory Education Law, 1949, *Book of Laws*, 26, p. 287.)

49. *Book of Laws*, 131, 1953, p. 137.

50. September 23, 1969.

51. Minutes of the Interministerial Committee, May 25, 1970.

52. Minutes of the Security Committee, May 30, 1970.

53. Ibid., June 11, 1970.

54. Benvenisti, *Jerusalem*, p. 169.

55. Digest of Publications, no. 1882, February 2, 1972.

56. Minutes of the Security Committee, April 25, 1975.

57. Memorandum, June 11, 1970.

58. Memorandum, October 19, 1975.

59. Information from the spokesman for the Ministry of Finance.

60. Memorandum from Teddy Kollek, October 14, 1975.

61. Memorandum from the Institute for National Insurance to the Security Committee, 1970.

62. Ibid., 1975.

63. Minutes of the Ministerial Committee, February 13, 1973.

64. Benvenisti, *Jerusalem*, p. 169.

65. Data from the Municipal spokesman.

66. Benvenisti, *Jerusalem*, p. 97.

67. Ibid., p. 190.

68. The Defense Regulations (Money) (1941) state: "A person who is not an authorized dealer shall not buy, borrow, or receive into his possession in any other manner foreign currency or gold, other than from a dealer, and shall not sell, lend, or transfer from his possession in any other manner foreign currency or gold, other than to an authorized dealer, unless he received permission from the finance minister or from someone appointed by him; the term 'authorized dealer' in this regulation means, in connection with any transaction connected with foreign currency, a person who has been authorized by the finance minister, or on his behalf, to deal in foreign currency" (*Laws*, 2/9, p. 13217).

69. Decision dated December 9, 1970.

70. Regulation 2712, 1971, June 22, 1971.

71. Benvenisti, *Jerusalem*, p. 166.

72. The Law of Notaries for Documents for Foreign Use (1950) (*Laws*, 17, p. 7785).

73. Benvenisti, *Jerusalem* (Hebrew edition), pp. 157-59.

74. The political activity of the consulates is discussed by Benvenisti, *Jerusalem* (Hebrew edition), pp. 156-57; and Benziman, *Jerusalem*, pp. 212-13. See also Benvenisti, *Jerusalem* (English edition), pp. 14-15.

75. Municipal Archives, documents from August 3, 5, and 16, 1969.

76. Letter from the U.S. consul to Teddy Kollek, August 29, 1969.

77. Knesset *Proceedings*, vol. 53, pp. 380 ff.

78. Benvenisti, *Jerusalem*, pp. 323-25.

79. Ibid., pp. 325-27.

80. Ibid., p. 328.

81. Ibid., pp. 328-36.

82. Minutes of the Security Committee, November 4, 1974.

5

DEMOGRAPHIC AND ECONOMIC DEVELOPMENTS IN JERUSALEM SINCE 1967

Israel Kimhi and Benjamin Hyman

Since Jerusalem was reunited as the capital of Israel in June 1967, far-reaching changes have taken place in all areas of the city's life. The population has increased, and the city has been transformed from a small border town into the largest city in the State of Israel. Its economic situation has been strengthened, and it has absorbed thousands of new Jewish immigrants, as well as Arabs from other parts of the country.

Jerusalem has regained its traditional position as a focal point for tourism and as a spiritual center with powerful attraction for people all over the world. The city has established itself as the national administrative center with the transfer to it of most of the government ministries. Jerusalem has also become an important center of employment in the building and services fields, relying on daily commutation of thousands of workers from outside the city.

Special efforts have been made to beautify the city by constructing public gardens, parks, and boulevards. Entire neighborhoods have been restored and improved using architectural and environmental principles that combine traditional building styles with the modern environmental values of contemporary life. The quality of life in the city has greatly improved and along with it the living conditions and income levels of its inhabitants. Dozens of youth clubs have been built, and schools and other public institutions have been erected. Many national and international institutions have been added and

This chapter is an updated and revised summary of I. Kimhi and B. Hyman, *A Socio-Economic Survey of Jerusalem, 1967–1975* (Jerusalem: The Jerusalem Committee, 1978).

expanded in keeping with the character of the city as a spiritual and religious center. These include reestablishment of the Hebrew University and Hadassah Hospital on Mount Scopus, the Ecumenical Research Institute, the Municipal Theater, and the Van Leer Institute, among many others.

The aim of this chapter is to survey the development of Jerusalem since the city's reunification, focusing on the differential development of the two main ethnic groups—Jewish and Arab—living in the city.

DEMOGRAPHIC DEVELOPMENT

Since 1967, Jerusalem has been transformed from a dormant, provincial town into a dynamic, expanding city. The accelerated rate of development of population, construction, and economic activities is rapidly changing Jerusalem's traditional character. At the end of 1978, Jerusalem's population numbered 389,200, of whom 280,900 were Jews and 108,300 non-Jews. Since the city's reunification, its population has grown by 43 percent (see Table 5.1).

TABLE 5.1: Changes in the Size of Jerusalem's Population, 1967-78

| | | | | Percent of Total | |
Year	Total	Jews	Non-Jews	Jews	Non-Jews
1967	267,800	196,500	71,300	73.4	26.6
1970	291,700	215,500	76,200	73.9	26.1
1973	333,000	244,900	88,100	73.5	26.5
1977	376,000	272,300	103,700	72.4	27.6
1978	389,200	280,900	108,300	72.2	27.8

Source: Central Bureau of Statistics, *Statistical Yearbooks*, 1968–78.

Jews

The Jews have constituted the largest religious community in Jerusalem since the 1870s and the majority of the city's population since around 1880, that is, before the onset of waves of immigration stimulated by the modern Zionist movement.[1] The present ratio of Jews to non-Jews (about 70 to 30) was established soon after 1948 with the influx of Jewish immigrants to Israel in the years 1948–51 and the decline of the Arab population as a result of the 1948 war and the Jordanian government's neglect of East Jerusalem.

In the decade preceding the Six-Day War (1956–66), the population of Israeli Jerusalem increased by 31 percent—from 149,400 to 195,700—representing an average annual growth rate of 2.7 percent. In the decade following the Six-Day War (1967–77), the Jewish population of Jerusalem increased by 38 percent, an average annual growth rate of 3.2 percent (from 197,700 to 272,300).

There are three main reasons for the accelerated growth of the Jewish population was only 6.4 in Tel Aviv, 8.8 in Haifa, but 22.9 in Jerusalem. This to be a dead-end at the terminus of a narrow corridor and regained its geographical centrality. The city's economic position was reinforced by the addition of 70,000 inhabitants (of East Jerusalem) plus a substantial hinterland. Jerusalem rapidly became the center of tourism in Israel. The increased attractiveness of Jerusalem transformed a negative balance of internal migration, which had prevailed from 1948 to 1967, into a positive net balance of 900 per year (annual average for 1968–78).

Second, the government of Israel promoted the development of Jerusalem and undertook an ambitious program of residential construction. The government also adopted a policy of directing a higher proportion of new immigrants to the city. (Despite this policy, however, the number of new immigrants actually settling in Jerusalem was not significantly larger than in previous years. An annual average of 3,020 new immigrants settled in Jerusalem in the years 1969 to 1978, making up hardly 8 percent of the national total.)

And third, the factor that has contributed most to the increase in the Jewish population of Jerusalem is the high rate of natural increase (that is, births over deaths). While considerably lower than that of the Arab rate of natural increase in Jerusalem, the Jewish rate is higher than that of most other urban settlements of Israel and much higher than that of Israel's two other major cities. In 1976, for example, the rate of natural increase per 1,000 population was only 6.4 in Tel Aviv, 8.8 in Haifa, but 22.9 in Jerusalem. This is probably the result of a combination of factors present in Jerusalem, such as a higher proportion of Jews from Oriental communities (from Middle Eastern and North African countries), a higher proportion of religious Jews, and a younger population (see Table 5.2).

TABLE 5.2: Jewish Population of Jerusalem, Sources of Increase, 1968–75 (in thousands)

	Total	Natural Increase	New Immigrants	Net Migration
Total	61.6	38.6	15.1	7.9
Annual average	7.7	4.8	1.9	1.0
Percentage	100	63	24	13

Source: B. Hyman and G. Eizenreich, *Population of Jerusalem and Region* (Jerusalem: Municipality of Jerusalem Policy Planning Department, 1977).

Non-Jews

Jerusalem's Arab population has been increasing at a faster rate than its Jewish population. There has been a small but steady decline in the proportion of Jews in the city—from under 74 percent in 1969 to under 72.3 percent in 1978.

The data on the dynamics of the non-Jewish population in Jerusalem have certain limitations. The published figures do not include Arabs living in Jerusalem who are unregistered migrants from the West Bank hinterland. The extent of this phenomenon is unknown. And the figures include only people residing within the municipal boundaries of Jerusalem. In many instances, this boundary, drawn in 1967, does not reflect close functional linkages with, or even the extent of, the continuous urban area of the city.

Some Arab villages are divided by the boundary; others are just beyond it, even though they are essentially an extension of the city. For these areas there are no data (apart from the initial 1967 census); and their ties with the Arab population within the boundaries of Jerusalem are unclear and certainly not quantifiable. It is obvious that in the past decade great changes have occurred in these areas, particularly in Abū Dīs, al-ᶜEizariyya (Bethany), al-Rām, Beit Ḥanīnā, ᶜArab al-Sawāḥira, and ᶜAnātā, as well as in the neighboring urban areas of Rāmallāh and El-Bīra to the north and Bethlehem, Beit Jālā, and Beit Sāḥūr to the south.

The September 1967 census showed that there were 68,600 inhabitants in East Jerusalem.[2] With the addition of the non-Jews residing in West Jerusalem, the total non-Jewish population of Jerusalem in September 1967 was 71,300. In 1961, there had been 76,500 non-Jews in the same area. These statistics indicate a negative balance of migration during the years of Jordanian occupation, as well as an accelerated emigration immediately following the June 1967 War.

East Jerusalem must be viewed during the period from 1948 to 1967 in its geopolitical setting within the West Bank of the Hashemite Kingdom of Jordan. Jordanian policy favored development of the East Bank of Jordan and restricted development of the West Bank.[3] This situation created economic difficulties for residents of the West Bank and resulted in large-scale emigration. In East Jerusalem, there was a conspicuous tendency to emigrate to the East Bank of Jordan or abroad. The number of newcomers did not compensate for emigrants, thus producing an overall negative migratory balance.[4] In addition, a trend toward the suburbs (which came to be included in post-1967 Jerusalem) also reduced the number of residents within the municipal boundaries of Jordanian Jerusalem.

After September 1967, Jerusalem's non-Jewish population actually decreased for a period of a few months. From 1969 on, however, it has increased rapidly. At the end of 1978, the non-Jewish population was 107,200 compared to 71,800 at the end of 1968. This is an increase of 45 percent in only nine years, representing an annual average increase of 4.1 percent. There have been fluctuations in the annual rate of increase. According to one interpretation, these fluctuations constitute an adjustment to the Jewish rate of increase, presumably reflecting years of greater economic well-being in the city as a whole, as well as an accelerated rate of housing construction (and more employment opportunities).[5] However, on a multiannual average, this interpretation of the data does not hold, as Table 5.3 illustrates.

TABLE 5.3: Average Annual Increase for Four-Year Periods, 1969–76, Jerusalem, Jews, and Non-Jews (percent)

| | Population | |
Years	Non-Jews	Jews
1969–72	4.2	3.7
1973–76	4.2	3.0

Source: Central Bureau of Statistics, *Statistical Yearbooks*, 1970–78.

A significant trend among non-Jews has been the decrease (absolute and relative) in the Christian population of Jerusalem. The Muslims have become the overwhelming majority (over 85 percent) in the non-Jewish sector (compared to 50 percent in 1946). The decline of the Christian population in Jerusalem has been especially pronounced since the termination of the British Mandate.[6] This decline is the result of the departure of thousands of non-Arab Christians (of the various religious orders and mandatory officials), the propensity of Arab Christians to emigrate to Western countries, and the lower birth rate of Arab Christians compared to that of Muslims. In 1946, Christians made up 19 percent of the population of Jerusalem, and in 1972 under 4 percent (see Tables 5.4 and 5.5).

Natural Increase

Most of the rapid increase of the Arab population of Jerusalem is a result of a high rate of natural increase. It may be said that East Jerusalem now enjoys an Oriental birth rate with an Occidental death rate, engendering one of the highest rates of natural increase in Israel.

The birth rate is about 44 per 1,000 annually, an increase over that prior to 1967, resulting from the inclusion of villages whose birth rate is generally higher, as well as the continued dwindling of the Christian population, whose birth rate is lower. While the birth rate has been constant since 1967, there has been a notable reduction in the death rate, thanks to improved medical care, from 14 per 1,000 in 1961, 11.3 in 1970, to under 7 in 1977.

TABLE 5.4: Population in Jerusalem by Religion, 1922–78 (within 1978 boundaries)

Year	Total	Number Jews	Number Non-Jews	Percent Total	Percent Jews	Percent Non-Jews
1922	72,564	34,124	38,440	100	47.0	53.0
1931	108,472	54,033	54,398	100	49.8	50.2
1946	186,470	99,640	86,830	100	53.4	46.6
1952	196,600	140,000	56,600	100	71.2	28.8
1961	243,900	165,022	78,900	100	67.7	32.2
1967	267,800	196,500	71,300	100	73.4	26.6
1977	376,000	272,300	103,700	100	72.4	27.6
1978	387,600	279,400	107,200	100	72.3	27.7

Note: Municipal boundaries as established in June 1967.
Source: U. O. Schmelz, "A United Jerusalem; Demographic Characteristics in Judea and Samaria," in *Studies in Settlement Geography*, ed. A. Shmueli, D. Grossman, and R. Zeevy (Jerusalem: Canaan Publishing House, 1977), pt. 2, p. 468

TABLE 5.5: Population in Jerusalem by Religion, 1922–72 (within contemporary boundaries)

Year	Total*	Number Jews	Muslims	Christians	Percent Total	Jews	Muslims	Percent Christians
1922	62,731	34,124	13,413	14,699	100	54.4	21.4	23.4
1931	93,101	53,820	19,894	19,335	100	57.8	21.4	20.8
1946	164,440	99,320	33,680	31,330	100	60.4	20.5	19.1
1961	227,923	165,022	50,296	12,385	100	72.4	22.1	5.4
1967	267,800	196,500	58,100	13,000	100	73.3	21.7	4.9
1972	313,861	230,325	71,770	11,704	100	73.3	22.8	3.8

Note: Table based on the most recent census. Within the municipal boundary as defined in each of the years specified.

*The columns add up to a few hundreds less than the totals. The difference may be itemized as "others."

Source: U. O. Schmelz, "A United Jerusalem; Demographic Characteristics in Judea and Samaria," in *Studies in Settlement Geography*, ed. A. Shmueli, D. Grossman, and R. Zeevy (Jerusalem: Canaan Publishing House, 1977), pt. 2, p. 468.

Internal Migration

Little is known about the migration of non-Jews. The period preceding reunification witnessed an emigration of non-Jews owing to poor economic conditions. Since the city's reunification, these factors have been alleviated, and the exit of families that was still in progress in 1968 has been arrested. Concurrently, the reunion of families also reversed the emigration trend. In addition, there is a positive balance of migration between Jerusalem and the West Bank, mainly from the Hebron district. The economic boom and the drawing power of family ties initiated a process of migration (often beginning with commuting) whose extent is often difficult to assess. Nevertheless, it is possible to estimate migration by deducting the natural increase from the total. Table 5.6 summarizes the components of natural increases and migration for the non-Jewish population during three periods.

TABLE 5.6: Estimate of the Components of Changes in the Non-Jewish Population Size in Jerusalem, 1967–77
(rate per 1,000 inhabitants)

Components	*1967–72*	*1972–74*	*1975–77*
Total increase	33.5	42.0	35.6
Natural increase	30.0	35.0	37.0
Migration	3.5	7.0	-1.4

Source: U. O. Schmelz, "A United Jerusalem; Demographic Characterisitcs in Judea and Samaria," in *Studies in Settlement Geography*, ed. A. Shmueli, D. Grossman, and R. Zeevy (Jerusalem: Canaan Publishing House, 1977), pt. 2, p. 470.

AGE STRUCTURE

The Jewish population in Jerusalem is considerably younger than that of Haifa and Tel Aviv. People under the age of 35 make up 51 percent of the population of Tel Aviv and 54 percent in Haifa, while in Jerusalem they are 67 percent of the total. In fact, while Tel Aviv has more Jews (331,900 compared to Jerusalem's 279,400), Jerusalem has more children under 14 (84,600 as opposed to 71,100) as of the end of 1978. The younger age structure of Jews in Jerusalem is related to Jerusalem's ethnic and religious composition. A relatively high proportion of Jerusalem Jews are of Oriental origin (47 percent compared to 35 percent in Tel Aviv and 23 percent in Haifa; the figure for the entire country is 48 percent). Jerusalem also has a larger representation of Orthodox Jews. Both of these groups tend to produce large families.

The Jewish population of Jerusalem is young in relation to other Jewish settlements in Israel but not when compared to the Arab population in general and to that of Jerusalem in particular. In the Arab sector there is a high proportion of children. More than half of Jerusalem's non-Jewish population are under 18, reflecting a high birth rate and a higher number of children per Arab family than are found in the Jewish sector (see Table 5.7).

TABLE 5.7: Age Structure, Jews and Non-Jews, 1976

	Absolute Numbers (in thousands)		*Percent*	
	Jews	*Non-Jews*	*Jews*	*Non-Jews*
0-17	98.7	53.5	37	53
18-34	80.0	24.7	30	25
35-54	48.8	13.8	18	14
55 +	38.6	8.2	15	8
Total	266.1	100.3	100	100

Source: Central Bureau of Statistics, *Statistical Yearbook*, 1978.

PHYSICAL DEVELOPMENT

The geographical extent of Jerusalem, including the spread of both the built-up area and the administrative municipal boundaries, has changed considerably since 1967. A hundred years ago, the city began growing beyond the Old City walls, mainly westward and northward. This direction of expansion was determined by topographical considerations—the existence of a continuous plateau relative to the surrounding hilly, steep, and dissected terrain.[7] Moreover, the direction has been toward the country's economic center. After 1948, Israeli Jerusalem was circumscribed by borders to the north, east, and south, and thus urban development was restricted to the western side of the city and filled in most of the clear space left by earlier development. In Jordanian Jerusalem a new business and commercial center developed just north of the Old City, and the old neighborhoods surrounding it were considerably reinforced.

The most rapid development spread northward in a ribbon pattern along the road to Rāmallāh—conforming both to the line of the watershed (building in Jerusalem has always tended to be located on the hilltops and higher slopes rather than the valleys), as well as to the tendency of local Arab building to develop haphazardly in ribbon development along main roads.

From the city's reunification in 1967, the Arab sector has experienced an unprecedented building boom, generating a large expansion of the urban area and bringing about the inclusion of several villages within the urban sphere.

This building activity tends to be widespread, largely uncontrolled, and geographically extensive.[8]

Jewish development, on the other hand, has been, by and large, centrally controlled and intensive. First to be built after 1967 were neighborhoods linking the northern suburbs to Mount Scopus, where the Hebrew University campus and the Hadassah Hospital remained an enclave within Jordanian territory during the 1948–67 period, namely, Ramat Eshkol, Ma'alot Daphna, Giv'at Hamivtar, and Giv'at Shapira (French Hill). Following this first spurt, the Ministry of Housing proceeded with an ambitious program of building on sites overlooking the city: Ramot and Newe Ya'aqov to the north and east and Talpiyyot and Giloh to the south. Notable also has been the rebuilding of the Jewish Quarter in the Old City. Private building tended to concentrate upon further development of existing neighborhoods in the western part of the city (see Table 5.8).

TABLE 5.8: Progress in Construction of Dwelling Units in the New Jewish Quarters, May 1979

Quarter	Number of Planned Dwelling Units	Populated Units	Under Construction	Percent of Occupancy
Jewish Quarter	650	480	150	73
Newe Ya'qov	4,200	3,040	900	72
Ramot	8,000	2,020	1,250	25
Giloh	9,000	1,650	3,400	18
East Talpiyyot	4,500	2,000	930	44
Giv'at Shapira	2,300	1,700	100	74
Ramat Eshkol	2,200	2,120	80	96
Sanhedria	1,270	680	100	53
Ma'alot Daphna	1,320	840	200	63
Total	33,440	14,530	7,110	43

Source: Ministry of Housing.

The municipal boundary was significantly extended in June 1967. The combined area of the two municipalities (Israeli and Jordanian) had been 13,000 acres, while the new extension created a municipal area of 28,000 acres, the largest municipality in Israel. This extension had more than local significance, as the new area was included under Israeli jurisdiction.

CONSTRUCTION

Non-Jewish Sector

In East Jerusalem there has been a process of displacement from the center to the outskirts. The contribution of the Old City to the overall population of the area fell most noticeably by some 50 percent in the decade preceding 1972. This contrasted with a rise in population in the northern and southern areas, which for the most part were not within the municipal boundaries before 1967. The areas of growth to the east (Abū Dīs, ᶜEizariyya) are beyond the municipal border, and no reliable data are available concerning their growth rate.

It is possible to make a detailed comparison between 1967 and 1972, years when the most recent full population census were carried out.[9] The districts that grew most in population during this period were Abū Ṭōr, Silwān, and Rās al-ᶜĀmūd, on the hills immediately southeast of the Old City—a rise of over 40 percent. Ṣūr Bāhir and ᶜArab al-Sawāḥira, two villages on the southeastern fringes, gained about 40 percent. Beit Ḥanīnā, a northern suburb, gained some 30 percent. Analyses of building activities between 1967 and 1977 from aerial photographs indicate an addition of some 2,000 new buildings in the Arab or eastern part of the city and many additions to existing houses. This process is continuous and has even accelerated recently.

Attempts have been made by the government to encourage local contractors to build apartment houses for Arab young couples. A few hundred of these have been built with government support. However, the overwhelming preference of the local Arab population is to build single-family dwellings on privately owned land, even if located at a distance from urban services and community facilities.

East Jerusalem is heterogeneous in its structure. It includes modern, middle-class suburbs spread along the road to Rāmallāh (Beit Ḥanīnā and Shuᶜfāṭ); villages with a distinct social identity but relying on Jerusalem economically (ᶜĪsāwiyya, Ṣūr Bāhir, and Beit Ṣafāfā); a semiurban Bedouin settlement (ᶜArab al-Sawāḥira); the Armenian, Muslim, and Christian quarters of the Old City; and the area north of the Damascus Gate, developed mainly between the 1930s and the 1960s (Bāb al-Sāhira, the American Colony, and Wādī al-Jōz).

Jewish Sector

Jerusalem in the past dozen years has undergone an unprecedented period of expansion and construction.[10] There have been large fluctuations in the building activity in Jerusalem, affected mainly by two factors: the general economic situation in the country and the specific efforts directed by the Israeli government for developing Jerusalem. These efforts are mainly in the form of a higher proportion of construction undertaken directly by the government or its agencies, as well as in the encouragement of building activity by indirect methods, such as loans, tax concessions, and making land available.

As Table 5.9 shows, prior to 1972, construction activity increased every year, up to a record of more than 1 million square meters of commenced building in 1972. From 1973 there has been a definite slowdown. New buildings commenced in 1976 made up merely a third of the floor area of 1972. This was a result of a general slowdown in the country, resulting in a reduction in the amount of investment, as well as a government freeze on all new public buildings, which applied also to Jerusalem. In 1978 there was renewed interest, especially in construction of housing, hotels, and offices.

TABLE 5.9: Construction Commencements in Jerusalem by Type of Building, 1967–78

(in thousands of square meters)

Year	Total	Housing	Public Buildings	Hotels and Offices	Industry and Crafts
1968	485.2	293.8	73.9	97.6	19.9
	100%	60.4	15.3	20.2	4.1
1971	934.4	643.9	110.0	94.3	86.2
	100%	68.9	11.8	10.1	9.2
1974	602.0	437.0	61.7	42.7	60.6
	100%	72.6	10.2	7.1	10.1
1976	354.0	260.0	54.0	9.7	3.3
	100%	73.4	15.3	2.7	8.6
1978	445.0	29.4	32.4	34.6	24.0
	100%	6.6	20.7	7.8	5.5
1967–76	5,886.1	850.6	1,026.9	520.3	488.3
	100%	65.4	17.5	8.8	8.3

Sources: Central Bureau of Statistics, *Building in Israel*, special series of publications nos. 332, 439, 467, 499, 585, 620.

Most of the construction effort has gone into housing. Housing in Jerusalem, on a multiyear average, splits 50-50 between private housing put up by contractors and public housing directly controlled and financed by the Ministry of Construction and Housing. (This is in terms of number of dwelling units. In terms of floor space, apartments built in the private sector are larger than the public ones.) The overwhelming majority of new buildings, both private and public, are multidwelling apartment blocks.

Following the reunification of the city, there was a great upswing in the volume of residential building in Jerusalem. In 1965, a peak year in the prewar period, there were over 3,000 commencements of housing units. In 1966 and 1967, this figure dropped to 1,000 to 900 units a year, mainly because of the economic recession. From 1968 to 1971, however, there was an extremely steep increase in commencement for dwellings, from 3,200 in 1968 to 7,200 in 1971. This situation was the result partly of the recovery in the city's building market but chiefly of the major momentum of public housing, which expressed the government's policy of rapidly populating Jerusalem and building new housing developments on the city's outskirts. From 1972 onward, the construction volume for residential building has diminished steadily, reaching a low point in the three-year period 1976–78.

A multiannual perspective shows that the declared government policy of encouraging the development of Jerusalem has not been easy to achieve (save 1970 and 1971). From 1968 to 1976, public housing in Jerusalem accounted for only 10 percent of the total public housing effort in Israel, hardly more than the existing proportion of Jews in Jerusalem to Jews in Israel as a whole. In the six-year period from 1972 to 1977, Jerusalem received only 8 percent of the new public housing effort. It is apparent, therefore, that in the two areas where the government has direct influence—the construction of housing and the settlement of new immigrants—the declared policy of giving Jerusalem first priority has not been satisfactorily implemented.

TABLE 5.10: Construction Commencements of Dwelling Units in Jerusalem, 1968–78

| | | *No. of Units* | | | *Percent* | |
Year	Total	Private	Public	Total	Private	Public
1968	3,200	1,240	1,960	100	39	61
1971	7,202	3,345	3,857	100	45	54
1974	4,400	1,740	2,660	100	40	60
1977	2,060	940	1,120	100	46	54
1978	2,550	1,650	900	100	64	36
1968–78	43,750	21,601	22,149	100	49.4	50.6

Sources: Central Bureau of Statistics, *Building in Israel*, special series of publications nos. 332, 434, 467, 499, 585.

An analysis of the size of apartments in new buildings (as measured by the number of rooms in the apartment) indicates that between 1967 and 1974 there was a change of emphasis relative to the previous period—more apartments of three to four rooms than smaller ones of two to three rooms. This trend reflects a rise in housing standards and in economic means. However, there seems to have been a regression in the years 1974–75, when there was a large increase in the proportion of new two-room apartments (from 4 percent of all apartments in 1972 to 25 percent in 1975). This apparently resulted from a new Ministry of Housing policy whereby young couples without children did not require more than two rooms, as well as to an increasing awareness of the special needs of elderly people (especially immigrants) and single persons. As this measure did not prove popular, a surplus of two-room apartments in government housing projects accumulated, and the previous trend of large apartments has been resumed (see Tables 5.9 and 5.10).

EMPLOYMENT STRUCTURE

Jews

The employment structure of Jewish Jerusalem reflects the city's special strengths and weaknesses. The city is principally based on tertiary employment, reflecting Jerusalem's role as the capital city of Israel and a center of culture and education. The city has no natural resources and is not situated in an advantageous geographical position vis-à-vis the country at large. It has no special access to markets and is not part of the economic center of the country on the Mediterranean coast. On the other hand, because Jerusalem is the capital of Israel, the government has espoused a declared policy of locating its main offices there, as well as those of the Jewish Agency. Jerusalem is a main center of education and culture; national, academic, and religious institutions; and health services. Jerusalem also enjoys a special position in the tourist trade; but from the viewpoint of employment, this has chiefly benefited the Arab sector as tourism employs a large proportion of non-Jews.

The trends in the employment structure of Jerusalem since 1967 may be summarized as follows: an almost constantly rising trend in public services, finance, and business activities; a general equilibrium of the number of employees in electricity and water supply sections; and a diminishing trend in industry, trade, transportation, building, and personal services.

The predominant feature in the Jewish employment sector is the over-representation of those employed in the public services. In 1968, 42.6 percent of the city's Jews were employed in public services, rising steadily to 52 percent in 1978. Thus public and communal services now employ half of Jewish Jerusalem's working population. A comparison with Tel Aviv (22.5 percent) and Haifa (29 percent)—and 28 percent in the country as a whole—highlights the lopsided employment structure of Jews in Jerusalem. The remaining sectors are decidedly of secondary importance. In 1977, only 11 percent were employed in the industrial sector, 10 percent in the commerce and tourist service sector, and 8 percent in financial and business services. All other sectors had even a lower proportion of the city's Jewish employees.

Non-Jews

The non-Jewish residents of Jerusalem are far less conspicuous in the economic than in the demographic sphere. In 1977, for instance, Jerusalem non-Jews made up 27.5 percent of the population, and 23.5 percent of these were 14 years and over (composing the potential work force), but only 16 percent were actually employed or sought work. There are several reasons for this. For instance, the high proportion of children and low percentage of adults and the low number of Arab working women all contribute to the low rate of participation in the labor force. There was an inexplicable decline in the rate of participation from 40 percent in 1971 to 31.5 percent in 1977. (The rate of participation refers to those actively seeking work of all those aged 14 and over.)

Between 1973 and 1977, the resident Arab labor force of Jerusalem remained constant at 18,000, even though the number of non-Jews over 14 increased by more than 9,000. It is probable that the lack of increase in the number of Arab workers in Jerusalem reflects the opportunities for work in Jordan and the oil-rich Gulf Emirates. Workers who go there usually do not change their basic place of residence and often leave their families in Jerusalem. Jordan traditionally employs Palestinians in positions requiring higher education and has a growing demand for skilled workers in construction.

The slack in the resident Jerusalemite non-Jewish labor force has been compensated for by commuters from the West Bank.[11] The estimated number of these commuters has been declining—no doubt owing to the slowdown in economic activity and especially construction work—from nearly 14,000 in 1973 to just over 11,000 in 1977.

The general census of Jordan in 1961 may provide some basis of comparison for post-1967 developments.[12] According to that census, 33 percent of East Jerusalem residents were employed in services, 19 percent in industry, 16 percent in commerce, and 7.5 percent in construction. As M. Roman stated in 1972:

> The sudden amalgamation of two separate distinct economic systems called for an adjustment in the economic structure of both sections of the city, though the main changes were felt in East Jerusalem. . . . The main beneficiaries of the city reunification were the blue-collar workers—formerly at the bottom of the income scale—while the income of many officials and professionals hardly rose at all, and in some cases actually dropped in real value, since they had to assimilate a fraction of the rise in prices consequent on the city's reunification.[13]

The structure of non-Jewish employment in Jerusalem, as of 1977, is not radically different from that of the period before 1967, though there was apparently an initial reduction in public services. This is still the largest mode of employment—around 27 percent of all employees. Commerce (including tourist services) employs some 18 percent, industry 17 percent, and construction 14 percent. Trends since 1967 are difficult to assess, both because of changes in the statistical definitions and relatively large annual fluctuations in the percentages reported (see Table 5.11).

TOURISM

Tourism is important in the city's economy, but its development has been irregular. Of special interest is the differing development of tourist services in the Arab and Jewish sectors of the city, a condition that is still apparent today.

After the partition of Jerusalem in 1948, tourism in each sector of the city developed in a different manner, with the possibility of crossing the frontier through the Mandelbaum Gate creating only marginal contact.

Jewish Sector

During the 1948–67 period, Israeli Jerusalem was cut off from the attractions that make a united Jerusalem a focus of international tourism—the Old City and the Holy Places of the three monotheistic faiths. West Jerusalem was located at the end of a territorial corridor, with few attractive sites in or around the city. Although most tourists who came to Israel visited Jerusalem, they generally came only for a brief excursion.

After 1967, the western part of the city took the lead in the rapid development of tourism. Existing services and new facilities suited the level of services demanded by tourists. Both foreign tourists and Israelis demonstrated a clear preference for West Jerusalem hotels. And the development of tourist services enjoyed considerable government assistance.

Almost all the statistical indicators—numbers of rooms, number of bookings, occupancy rate, revenue—show great progress in tourist services in the western part of the city from 1967 to 1972, which was a record year for the number of tourists visiting Jerusalem.

A recession in the tourist trade occurred during 1973–75. The negative influence on tourism by worldwide economic problems was reinforced by the October War in 1973 and the strained security situation thereafter. The loss in tourism, which reduced hotel bookings in West Jerusalem, was compensated for somewhat by a sharp rise in the number of Israelis filling the vacancies. Nevertheless, there was a drop in the occupancy rate, as the expansion in the

TABLE 5.11: Percentage of Employees by Economic Branch, Jerusalem and Israel, 1977

Economic Branch	Jerusalem			Israel	
	Total	Jews	Non-Jews	Total	Jews	Non-Jews
Total	100.0	100.0	100.0	100.0	100.0	100.0
Public services	45.6	49.2	27.0	28.0	29.5	14.5
Industry	12.1	11.1	17.4	24.1	24.8	17.7
Commerce, hotels	11.6	10.3	18.0	12.2	12.3	12.1
Construction	7.6	6.3	14.0	7.4	5.8	22.7
Personal services	7.0	6.5	9.6	6.6	6.4	7.6
Transportation	6.7	6.6	7.3	7.0	7.1	6.0
Finance	7.5	8.3	3.4	7.2	7.8	2.0
Utilities	1.5	1.1	3.4	1.2	1.2	0.7
Agriculture	0.5	0.7	—	6.3	5.2	16.8

Source: Central Bureau of Statistics, Survey of Manpower, 1977.

number of hotel rooms undertaken in the boom years came into effect in the stagnant years of 1974 and 1975. This resulted in arresting almost all hotel development in the city and caused a shortage of hotel space once the tourist trade picked up after 1976. The revival started a scramble to build new hotels and enlarge existing ones, similar to the expansion of 1971–72. The time lag in matching physical facilities to the number of tourists is one of the problems of the tourist trade in Jerusalem.

Non-Jewish Sector

It was the tourist trade which can be considered as the main economic base of East Jerusalem [prior to 1967]. Most of Jordan's large tourist flow made its way to Jerusalem, where the bulk of the kingdom's tourist facilities were concentrated. Jerusalem boasted a large share of Jordan's hotels, travel agencies and other tourist services. . . . All in all, roughly one-quarter of all employed persons in East Jerusalem were estimated to be in tourist-oriented occupations.[14]

In 1966, more than 600,000 tourists visited Jordanian Jerusalem, more than twice as many as visited Israel. Over 70 percent of Jordan's tourists came from Arab and other Muslim countries. After 1967, Jerusalem lost its standing as a center of Muslim tourism. A wave of tourists from Western countries preferred the facilities of West Jerusalem.

Thus the Six-Day War and the reunification of the city had contrary effects on tourist services in the eastern and western parts of the city. The relatively lower standards of tourist services in East Jerusalem did not, on the whole, attract Western tourists. Israeli tourists also were not attracted to stay in the eastern sector; in 1972, only some 3 percent of bookings were by Israelis, as against 11 percent of those in the western part of the city. Not until 1977 did bookings in East Jerusalem surpass the bookings of 1972.

It is clear that hotel services in East Jerusalem have lagged behind the general development of tourism in Jerusalem. The number of hotel rooms has hardly increased. They now make up less than 40 percent of Jerusalem's hotel rooms, while in 1968 the proportion was 60 percent. More than half these rooms are graded 3 stars and lower. East Jerusalem commanded only 36 percent of the bookings as of 1977 (see Tables 5.12 and 5.13).

INDUSTRY

Jewish Sector

Industry in Jerusalem has always been inferior in size and organization to that of the rest of Israel. Industry in Israel employed (as of 1977) fully 25 per-

TABLE 5.12:   Rooms in Hotels, Jerusalem, 1966–79

Year	1966	1968	1970	1972	1974	1976	1979
Total	2,941	2,939	3,293	3,967	4,596	5,297	5,666
East Jerusalem	1,891	1,746	1,720	1,803	1,996	2,065	2,087
West Jerusalem	1,050	1,193	1,573	2,164	2,600	3,232	3,579
Percent West Jerusalem of Total	36	41	48	55	57	61	63

Note: Rooms in hotels recommended by the Ministry of Tourism. Add 400 to 500 nonrecommended hotel rooms.

Sources: Hashemite Kingdom of Jordan, Department of Statistics, *Statistical Guide to Jordan*, 1966; Ministry of Tourism, *Survey of Hotels in East Jerusalem*, July 1967; Central Bureau of Statistics, *Tourism in Israel*, special series of publications, nos. 291, 428, and 464; *Statistical Quarterly for Tourism and Hotel Services*; nos. 500, 501.

TABLE 5.13:   Bookings in Recommended Jerusalem Hotels, 1969–77 (in thousands)

Year	Total	West Jerusalem	East Jerusalem
1969	989.7	57.0	442.7
1971	1,450.3	796.3	654.0
1973	1,445.7	834.0	611.7
1975	1,445.3	895.2	550.1
1977	2,322.6	1,496.4	856.2

Sources: Central Bureau of Statistics, *Tourism in Israel*, 1968, special series of publications, no. 428; *Statistical Quarterly for Tourism and Hotel Services*, vol. 3, no. 4, 1976; nos. 500, 501.

cent of the Jewish workers, as against 11 percent in Jerusalem. Jerusalem's share of total industrial employment in Israel has been steadily declining from 7.5 percent in 1952, 6 percent in 1961, 5.5 percent in 1967, to only 5 percent in 1977.[15] The city's contribution to the country's industrial output is even lower than its share of industrial employment, indicating indirectly the fragmented and relatively inefficient nature of the city's industrial enterprises.

In fact, reunification has caused little overall change in Jerusalem's industrial status vis-à-vis the country as a whole, though no doubt Jerusalem's new position quickened modernization tendencies. The number of Jewish industrial employees has hardly changed in the past few years and remains around 10,000. There are some 3,500 industrial and craft enterprises in Jerusalem, most of them small workshops. Only a third of these enterprises employ more than five persons, of which perhaps 130 have more than 20 employees. Only a few factories employ more than 100 workers.[16]

However, the number of employees might be misleading. Since 1968, there has, in fact, been a large increase in the floor space available to industrial enterprises. In 1968, Jerusalem had an estimated 270,000 square meters of industrial floor space, to which 300,000 have since been added.[17] There is obviously a drive toward modernization and expansion, reflected in more floor space per worker and greater capital investment.

Since the city was reunited, three new industrial areas have been developed. One area is located in the vicinity of Qalandiya airport, in the northern part of the city, and is developing rapidly. Another is designated for science-based industries. Special efforts are being made to exploit the scientific potential of Jerusalem's research institutions and to encourage industries that need not depend upon Arab employees from outside of Jerusalem (the West Bank). A third industrial area (Talpiyyot) is developing in the southern part of the city. Many of the enterprises in these new industrial areas have moved from former premises in older areas of the city.

The existing industrial areas within the municipal boundaries are rapidly reaching saturation. Moreover, there are limitations on development of certain types of industry in Jerusalem. The decision to preserve an environment suitable to Jerusalem and to prevent ecological pollution in the city and its environs creates restrictions regarding pollution-intensive industries.

The government of Israel has recently commenced development of a large new industrial area in Ma'ale Adummim, to the east of the city, on the road to Jericho. The industry diverted to this area receives government support as a preferred development area. The prominent branches in Jerusalem industries (in the Jewish sector) are textiles, clothing, footwear, printing and publishing, metal products, and foodstuffs.

Non-Jewish Sector

In East Jerusalem, industry remained at a low level of development until 1967, partly because of a deliberate policy of the Jordanian government. Government support and assistance, essential for extensive industrial development, were allotted mainly to industrial enterprises in the East Bank. Until 1967 there were less than ten big industrial concerns in the whole of the West Bank. Of these, not a single one was within the present boundaries of Jerusalem.

In 1973, a peak year, some 3,400 non-Jews were employed in industry in Jerusalem. The non-Jewish industrial concerns are small workshops and on a strictly local scale. There is hardly a basis of comparison even with the weak Jewish industrial sector. Of East Jerusalem's workshops 50 percent employ one to two persons, 37 percent have three to five employees, 11 percent have six to fifteen, and just 2 percent employ more than sixteen persons.[18]

CONCLUSIONS

During the 19 years that the city was divided, the eastern and western parts developed along different economic, political, and social lines. The division harmed both sides of the city; but the eastern part, despite its severance from the western half, maintained its regional position as a successor to the Arab sector of mandatory Jerusalem, providing certain services to the whole area of the West Bank. East Jerusalem was the largest city in that area and was situated in the heart of its most populous section. Other large urban settlements were linked to its economy, including Rāmallāh and Bethlehem. This metropolitan area contained more than 150,000 inhabitants, or nearly half of the West Bank's total urban population.[19] Israeli Jerusalem after 1948 became a "regionless city." The establishment of new settlements in the "Jerusalem Corridor" did not compensate the Israeli sector for the loss of the hinterland's population. Thus Jerusalem's constant decline was indicated by its diminishing share of the country's population, from 9.6 percent in 1948 to 7.4 percent on the eve of reunification.

Since reunification, Jerusalem's relative location has shifted from peripheral to central, with full access both to the coastal plain and to Judea and Samaria (the West Bank). This situation stimulated its growth in unprecedented fashion and enhanced its value as a city-region to Israel as a whole.

NOTES

1. Y. Ben-Arieh, *A City Reflected in Its Times: Jerusalem in the Nineteenth Century, The Old City* (Hebrew) (Jerusalem: Yad Izhak Ben-Zvi Publications, 1977), p. 403. See also U. O. Schmelz, "Development of the Jewish Population of Jerusalem During the Last Hundred Years," *Jewish Journal of Sociology* 2 (1960): 56–73

2. State of Israel, Central Bureau of Statistics, *East Jerusalem Census of Population and Housing*, 1967.

3. M. Benvenisti, *Jerusalem: The Torn City* (Minneapolis: University of Minnesota Press, 1976), Ch. 4; and D. Rubinstein, this volume.

4. U. O. Schmelz, "Population Changes in Judea and Samaria," *Jerusalem Quarterly* 4 (1977): 100–5.

5. Economic Consulting and Planning, Ltd., "Developing Jerusalem 1979–1983" (Hebrew, unpublished), 1979, p. 5.

6. U. O. Schmelz, "The Evolution of Jerusalem's Population," in *Urban Geography of Jerusalem*, eds. D. H. K. Amiran, A. Shachar, and I. Kimhi, a companion volume to the *Atlas of Jerusalem* (Jerusalem: Massada Press, 1973), p. 69.

7. D. H. K. Amiran, "The Development of Jerusalem 1860–1970," ibid., pp. 20–52.

8. Municipality of Jerusalem, Policy Planning Section, *The Volume of Construction in East Jerusalem 1968–1977* (Hebrew).

9. State of Israel, Central Bureau of Statistics, *East Jerusalem Census of Population and Housing* 1967; *Population and Housing Census*, 1972.

10. State of Israel, Ministry of Housing, *Israel Builds*, 1977, pp. 161–224.

11. Hebrew University, Department of Geography, "Commuting to Jerusalem" (Hebrew, unpublished), 1975; Central Bureau of Statistics, *Statistical Quarterly for the Occupied Territories*, no. 2, 1978.

12. Hashemite Kingdom of Jordan, Department of Statistics, *First Census of Population and Housing*, 1961.

13. M. Roman, "The Economic Development of Jerusalem 1860–1970," in *Urban Geography of Jerusalem*, ed. D. H. K. Amiran, A. Shachar, and I. Kimhi (Jerusalem: Massada Press, 1973), p. 105. See also I. Amir, *An Assessment of the Changes in the Economic Situation of Jerusalem's Arab Population, 1967–1969* (Hebrew) (Jerusalem: Israel Society for Economic Services, 1969).

14. Roman, "The Economic Development of Jerusalem," p. 105. See also M. Roman, *A Socio-Economic Survey of Reunited Jerusalem* (Hebrew) (Jerusalem: Maurice Falk Institute for Economic Research, 1967).

15. State of Israel, Central Bureau of Statistics, *Statistical Yearbooks* (for the relevant years).

16. Municipality of Jerusalem, Business Tax Files, 1976/77.

17. Municipality of Jerusalem, *Survey of Industry and Crafts, 1973*, part B, 1974.

18. See note 16.

19. Roman, "The Economic Development of Jerusalem," p. 105.

6

THE CHRISTIAN ESTABLISHMENT IN JERUSALEM

S. P. Colbi

An unmistakable link between Jewish and Christian views of Jerusalem's sanctity is to be sought in the Jewish roots of Christianity. Because Jewish spiritual and ceremonial life was intensely bound up with Jerusalem, it was natural that the final crucial events in Jesus' life should take place there. Consequently, Christians sought to provide tangible evidence of the events relating to Jesus' life. Thus originated the marking of Christian Holy Places, the object of such deep veneration on the part of Christian faithful and the cause of such bitter interconfessional conflicts over their exclusive possession.

This chapter is concerned with the Christian establishment in Jerusalem. It surveys the denominations represented in the city by their churches and religious institutions, as well as the issue of the Christian Holy Places, the jurisdictional struggles over their possession, and the evolution of the Status Quo determining the rights and privileges of the various confessions.[1]

The earliest church was in Jerusalem. A record of the beginnings of the Mother Church with its center on Mount Zion is to be found in the Acts of the Apostles (Chapter 15). Its first leader, according to Christian tradition, was James the Less, remembered as the first Bishop of Jerusalem. On the presumed site of his martyrdom stands the Armenian Cathedral of St. James. In the year 49 or 50, as recorded in Acts, a local council, meeting in Jerusalem, made fateful decisions for the young church. It was decided that Gentiles could be admitted to the Christian fellowship and that upon conversion they would not be required to uphold the precepts of Judaism.

In the first half of the fourth century, under the reign of Constantine the

153

Great, Jerusalem was turned into a Christian city, a lodestone for Christian believers from the world over. It was during this age that many Holy Places were located and churches erected to mark sacred events. By the emperor's direction, the holy sites of Calvary and the Holy Sepulchre were located. The Temple of Venus, erected by the Romans in Aelia Capitolina, was razed, and three sacred monuments erected on its site (A.D. 326)—the Anastasis (the Resurrection) on the site of the empty sepulchre, a large basilica (the Martyrion), and a votive cross upon the Rock of Calvary marking the site of the Crucifixion. (During the Crusader period the sites of the sepulchre and the Crucifixion were brought under one roof.)

Tradition has it that Constantine's mother, the Empress Helena, supervised construction of the buildings. And, allegedly by her initiative, the Church of Eleona on the Mount of Olives was founded. The remains exist today in the precincts of the Pater Noster Convent. Pomoenia, a wealthy Roman woman, built the Rotunda of the Ascension, the site where, according to tradition, Jesus ascended to heaven. Empress Eudocia, wife of Theodosios II, who made a pilgrimage in 438 and spent her last years in the Holy Land founding churches and other religious institutions, is also credited with the erection of churches—St. George in the Valley of Hinnom, the Church of St. John, the Church of St. Sophia adjacent to the Praetorium of Pilate, the Church of St. Peter near the House of Caiaphas, the Church near the Pool of Siloam, and the Church of St. Stephen. In the same period of tracing and marking holy sites were built St. Peter in Gallicantu, the Church of the Tomb of Mary, the Church of Gethsemane, and Hagia Sion.

During the period of Justinian, the pious emperor erected (A.D. 543) a monumental church in Jerusalem, the Sancta Maria Nea, in honor of the Virgin Mary ("Theotokos"). The remains of the Nea Church were discovered during the excavations in the Jewish Quarter of the Old City (conducted by N. Avigad); the debris of centuries was removed and the original structure is now visible. During the Byzantine period pilgrimages and veneration of holy relics were popular.

THE THREE PATRIARCHATES

The Patriarchate of Jerusalem was established in 451, when the Bishop of Jerusalem was elevated to the rank of patriarch at the Council of Chalcedon.[2] In the great schism of the Christian Church (1054), the Jerusalem Patriarch, who followed the Eastern tradition, aligned with the Patriarch of Constantinople. When the Crusaders founded the Latin Kingdom of Jerusalem in 1099, they appointed a Latin Patriarch for the city.

The Greek Orthodox Church claims that its patriarchs resumed residence in Jerusalem after the city was conquered by Saladin in 1187. But between the sixteenth and nineteenth centuries, several patriarchs of Jerusalem preferred to reside in Istanbul because of the need to maintain direct links with the central Ottoman authorities. The last patriarch to reside there died in 1845. From 1187 to 1291, the Latin patriarchs resided in Acre. After the fall of the Crusader Kingdom (1291), there were only titular patriarchs of Jerusalem. In 1847, the Latin Patriarchal See of Jerusalem was reestablished.

The Armenian community has had a patriarch in Jerusalem since the beginning of the fourteenth century, though the Armenians have lived in the city since the first centuries of the Christian era. What distinguishes the Armenian Patriarchate from the other two is the fact that its congregation is not ethnically Arab; the members of the community are Armenian by nationality as well as by religion. The size of this community in Jerusalem, as in Palestine as a whole, never exceeded 10,000. There were 8,000 Orthodox Armenians in the country in 1948, mostly residents of Jerusalem.[3] There are now 1,500 Armenians residing in the city. The patriarchate of this small community is of importance, however, because it shares control of the principal Holy Places and owns extensive properties in and around Jerusalem.

In addition to the Latin Patriarch, the Catholic Church has two important church dignitaries in Jerusalem who have no equivalent in the other churches, namely, the Apostolic Delegate and the Franciscan Custos. The first Apostolic Delegate "to Jerusalem and Palestine" was appointed in 1929, and since then an Apostolic Delegate has been in residence in Jerusalem. The duty of the Apostolic Delegate, in fact, a diplomatic official of the Holy See, is both to supervise the activities of the Catholic churches and to report to the Pope thereon (*Codex juris canonici*, canon 267). He possesses considerable influence as the Pope's spokesman to all the Catholic communities, maintains contact with the Israeli authorities, and plays a prominent role in all interdenominational activity in Jerusalem.

The Custos is the head of the Custody of the Holy Land, a body within the Franciscan Order, vested by Pope Clemens VI with the guardianship of the Holy Places (bulls of November 1342). Under an agreement signed with the Mamluk Sultan al-Nāṣir in 1335, the Cenacle (site of the Last Supper) was purchased by the King of Naples and presented to the Franciscans to serve as their headquarters. In 1552, however, they were evicted and occupied the site of today's St. Savior Monastery, the present headquarters of the Franciscan Custody.

With the restoration of the Latin Patriarchate of Jerusalem in the middle of the nineteenth century, frictions and collisions of competence developed between the Patriarch and the Custos. To overcome these difficulties the Vatican chose to appoint a Franciscan monk to the post of Latin Patriarch (1889). However, the problems engendered by the restoration of the Patriarchate were settled only in 1923, when an arrangement was worked out to delineate the areas of jurisdiction of each institution. Since then, the Vatican has not displayed consistency in its appointments: In 1947, it appointed the former Franciscan Custos as patriarch; in 1966, the former head of the Franciscan Order was nominated Apostolic Delegate; and the Latin Patriarch appointed in 1970 did not come from the ranks of the Franciscans. To this day, however, it is the Custos, not the Patriarch, who acts on behalf of the Roman Catholic Church in all matters pertaining to the Holy Places. See Table 6.1 for a listing of the heads of the various Christian churches in Jerusalem.

TABLE 6.1: Heads of the Christian Churches in Jerusalem

Church	Head
Latin Communities	
Roman Catholic (Latin)[a]	Patriarch of Jerusalem
Greek Catholic	Under patriarchal vicars subject to
Armenian Catholic	their respective patriarchs residing in
Syrian Catholic	Syria, Lebanon, or Iraq
Maronite	
Chaldean	
Coptic Catholic	Franciscan parish priest (the head of the Coptic Catholics is a patriarch residing in Cairo)
Orthodox Communities	
Greek Orthodox	Patriarch of Jerusalem[b]
Russian Orthodox	Archimandrite (subject to the Patriarch of Moscow and all Russia)
Russian Orthodox Church in Exile	Archimandrite (subject to the Metropolitan residing in New York)
Rumanian Orthodox	Archimandrite (subject to the patriarch residing in Bucharest)
Monophysite Religious Communities	
Armenian	Patriarch of Jerusalem[c]
Coptic	Archbishop (residing in Cairo and subject to the Pope)
Ethiopian	Archbishop (subject to the patriarch residing in Addis Ababa)
Syrian (Jacobites)	Archbishop (subject to the Patriarch of Antioch residing in Homs)
Protestant Churches in Israel[d]	

TABLE 6.1: Heads of the Christian Churches in Jerusalem (Continued)

Church	Head
Evangelical Episcopal (Anglicans)	Bishop, member of a synod of four bishops governing the church in the Middle East (subject to the Archbishop of Canterbury)
Lutheran	Representative (Propst of the German Lutheran Church)
Scottish Church (Presbyterian)	Representative of the Church of Scotland
Southern Baptist Convention Church of the Nazarene British Pentecostal Mission Christian Missionary Alliance Mennonite Church	

[a]All the Catholic communities owe allegiance to the Pope, the Latin community directly, the Uniate Catholic communities (that is, Eastern rite churches united with Rome) indirectly.

[b]The Patriarch of Constantinople, whose seat is in Istanbul, is "the first among equals" among the Orthodox churches. The Patriarch of Jerusalem, like the other patriarchs and heads of religious communities, regards him as no more than a spiritual mentor and is careful about maintaining his Patriarchate's independent status. As a matter of principle, the Patriarch of Jerusalem is opposed to having the Patriarch of Constantinople express any opinion about the Jerusalem Patriarchate or the Holy Places.

[c]The Armenian church is headed by the Catholicos, who resides in Etchmiadzin, in the Soviet Republic of Armenia. The Armenian Patriarch of Jerusalem is subordinate to him, both in religious matters and in the nomination of bishops; but in keeping with a centuries-old tradition, he maintains independence with regard to his Patriarchate's daily affairs, its property, and the Holy Places.

[d]Most Protestant churches and missions are members of the United Christian Council in Israel (UCCI).

Source: Compiled by author.

THE PROBLEM OF THE CHRISTIAN HOLY PLACES

The problem of the Christian Holy Places in Jerusalem is complex because of the large number of Christian communities and their historical disagreements—some dating back hundreds of years—over their respective rights in the Holy Places. Matters have been complicated even further by centuries of Muslim rule and intervention by foreign powers in the affairs of the various communities and the Holy Places.

In his memorandum on the Status Quo in the Holy Places (which has served since its composition in 1929–30 as the authoritative description of the situation regarding the Holy Places), L. G. A. Cust makes the following comment on the rivalries between the Christian churches and powers:

> The history of the Holy Places is one long story of bitter animosities and contentions, in which outside influences take part in an increasing degree, until the scenes of Our Lord's life on earth become a political shuttlecock, and eventually the cause of international conflict. If the Holy Places and the rights pertaining thereto are an "expression of man's feelings about Him whose story hallowed those sites," they are also an index of the corruptions and intrigues of despots and chancelleries during eight hundred years. The logical results have been the distrust and suspicion, and the attitude of intractability in all matters, even those of only the most trivial importance, concerning the Holy Places.[4]

The Christian world attaches importance to all places in Palestine associated with events in the earthly life of Jesus, Mary, Joseph, the Apostles, and saintly men and women. From a Christian viewpoint, it is difficult to define degrees of importance or sanctity, especially as various places are regarded differently by individual churches and communities. There is no disagreement, however, over the preeminence of the Church of the Holy Sepulchre, the site of Jesus' ascent to Heaven, the tomb of the Virgin at Gethsemane, the Church of the Nativity in Bethlehem, and the Deir al-Sulṭān (which is holy to the Ethiopian and Coptic churches). These places are under the regulation of the Status Quo because of the disagreements over their possession and rights to worship among the various churches.

From the Muslim Conquest to the Ottoman Period (638-1517)

The Muslim Conquest

In 634 the Muslims invaded Syria and Palestine. Jerusalem surrendered in 638. The capitulation of the Holy City was allegedly negotiated between Caliph ᶜUmar I and Patriarch Sophronios. Many fictitious incidents embellish the event. It is related, for example, that the caliph came personally to the Mount of Olives to accept the city's surrender from the patriarch, after which the two proceeded to the Church of the Holy Sepulchre. The caliph, however, did not enter the church so as not to give his followers a pretext to transform the basilica into a Muslim shrine.

The ᶜUmariyya Mosque was erected on the spot where, according to legend, the caliph stood. According to Greek sources, ᶜUmar gave Sophronios an *ᶜahdnāme*, or edict, having the legal force of a warrant of protection. This edict is regarded by the Greeks as their "Magna Carta of Rights," which they claim confers upon them a privileged position in the Holy Places. The authenticity of the document is challenged by many historians and is denied by the Latins, the principal contenders of the Greeks for possession of the Christian shrines since the Crusaders' conquest and the establishment of the Kingdom of Jerusalem.

On the eve of the Muslim conquest, the Christians in Jerusalem belonged to various national churches and sects. There can be no doubt, however, that they all conducted prayers at the Holy Places and had concluded agreements regulating the times of their respective ceremonies. There was only one patriarch in the city at the time. Memoranda and statements by the Roman Catholic Church, including the memorandum presented to the Paris Peace Conference (1919) and the Franciscan memorandum of 1922, make no mention of any claim by the Roman Catholic Church to rights in the Holy Places prior to the period of the Crusades.[5] On the other hand, there is no historical justification for the Greek Orthodox claim that the Caliph ʿUmor placed the Holy Places under the exclusive jurisdiction of the Patriarch of Jerusalem.

The Period of the Crusades (1099–1291)

A fundamental change came about during the Crusader period, when a Latin Patriarch was appointed over Jerusalem.[6] The patriarchal dignity had been exercised until then by the Greek Orthodox Patriarch Simeon. According to Greek sources, Simeon had fled to Cyprus before the Crusaders besieged Jerusalem; according to the Latin version, he had died. The validity of the appointment of the Latin Patriarch rests upon acceptance of the Latin version. The Latin Patriarch was the sole patriarch to reside in the city until it was reconquered by the Muslims in 1187. The new establishment was intended to latinize the local church totally. To that end 20 Latin canons were installed in the Church of the Holy Sepulchre to conduct religious services. Moreover, the Orthodox and the Eastern church clergy, expelled by the Muslims when the siege started, were not reinstalled by the Crusaders. Orthodox monks were also evicted from the other monasteries of the city and its vicinity.

Yet it would be erroneous to assume that the Greek Orthodox and other Eastern Christian churches were entirely dispossessed from the Holy Places during the period of the Crusades. There is evidence that in 1106-07, the Holy Fire ceremony in the Basilica of the Church of the Holy Sepulchre, held on Easter Saturday, was conducted by the head of the Greek Orthodox monastery of St. Sabba in the presence of the Latin King Baldwin I and the Latin priests. In 1172, the Roman Catholic pilgrim Theoderich wrote that other confessions that were different in language and in the way they conducted religious ceremonies were functioning under the roof of the Church of the Holy Sepulchre.[7]

Under the Crusaders, Jerusalem experienced a period of intensive building activity. The Dome of the Rock became the Templum Domini and a monastery for the canons of the Temple was added to it. The al-Aqṣā Mosque became the Templum Solomonis, the headquarters of the Order of the Templars, and its basement was used for stables. Special attention was paid to the Basilica of the Holy Sepulchre, which was greatly enlarged and altered in shape. The main achievement of the Crusader architects was to bring the site of the Crucifixion and the empty tomb under one roof. From that period dates also the present-day façade of the Basilica with its double portal. In the vicinity of the Basilica were built the churches of St. Mary of the Latins and St. Mary the Great. Their remains are partially preserved within the precincts of the Lutheran Church of the Redeemer and its annexes. The finest example of a Romanesque church of the Crusader period is the Church of St. Anne near St. Stephen's Gate. Another building that goes back to the time of the Crusader Kingdom is the one on Mount Zion, where, according to Christian tradition, the Room of the Last Supper is located.

In July 1187, Saladin, ruler of Egypt, inflicted a crushing defeat on the Crusader army at the Horns of Ḥaṭṭin. In September, he laid siege to Jerusalem and conquered the city a month later. Saladin permitted the Eastern Christians to remain but forced the Latins to leave the city. This discriminatory action betokened Saladin's awareness of the divergent attitudes of the two Christian persuasions toward the Muslim reconquest. Saladin's humane behavior toward non-Muslims was in striking contrast with the sanguinary onslaught of the Crusaders who had a century earlier massacred the city's Muslim and Jewish population. On the other hand, Saladin converted most of Jerusalem's churches into mosques. The Dome of the Rock and the al-Aqṣā Mosque were naturally restored to Muslim worship. Saladin did not follow the advice of Muslim leaders who counseled him to destroy the Church of the Holy Sepulchre. He was convinced that Christians would venerate the site even if no edifice stood there. The Basilica remained closed for only three days, and when it was reopened Christians had to pay an entrance fee. A Muslim attendant, belonging to the Nusayba family, was appointed by order of Saladin to guard the entrance, a duty performed until the present by the descendants of the same family.

In the Third Crusade, mounted after the fall of Jerusalem, the Christians reconquered part of the country, failing however to recapture Jerusalem. On September 2, 1192, a treaty was concluded between Saladin and King Richard the Lion-Hearted of England, allowing pilgrims to visit the Holy Places freely. The sultan also permitted a limited number of Latin priests to officiate in the Church of the Holy Sepulchre. This concession was resented by the Greeks. After the defeat of the Crusaders, the Byzantine Emperor Isaac Angelos had sent a delegation to Saladin, congratulating him on his victory and requesting that the Holy Places that had been under Greek Orthodox control at the time of the Fāṭimids should be restored to the Greeks. Saladin did not, however, accede to the request, preferring to retain the power of arbiter between the Latins and Greeks. This policy was to be followed later by the Ottoman sultans throughout their 400-year rule over Jerusalem.[8]

The Third Crusade succeeded in reconstituting the Kingdom of Jerusalem which did not, however, include Jerusalem itself, a situation the Christians could hardly tolerate. A new crusade, aimed at reconquering the Holy City, was fought mainly in Egypt. Sultan al-Malik al-Kāmil offered to cede Jerusalem in return for the Crusaders' evacuation of Egypt. The barons were willing to accept the proposal, but it was refused by the papal envoy Pelagius and by the military orders, who demanded further concessions. Thus, during the following years Jerusalem continued under Muslim domination.

Christian sovereignty was finally restored by a treaty signed on February 18, 1229 between the Sultan al-Malik al-Kāmil and Frederick II of Hohenstaufen, emperor of Germany and king of Sicily. The treaty stipulated that the city had to be unfortified and that the Dome of the Rock and the al-Aqṣā Mosque were to be left in Muslim hands. The treaty drew upon Frederick the wrath of the Pope, who claimed that Jerusalem had to be retaken by force of arms and not through negotiations.

Through a treaty with the Syrian Ayyūbids, the Crusaders succeeded in getting back the Dome of the Rock and the al-Aqṣā Mosque and evicted the Muslims from the precinct of the Temple Mount. In the war that broke out in 1244 between Egypt and Syria, the Crusaders allied themselves with the latter. In retaliation, an army of Khwārazmians, in Egypt's pay, invaded the Holy Land and conquered Jerusalem. Several thousand Christians were killed. Great damage was caused to the Basilica of the Church of the Holy Sepulchre, and many churches in Jerusalem were destroyed. From the year 1244, Jerusalem was to remain under Muslim control for seven centuries.

The Mamluk Period (1260–1517)

The Mamluks, of Turkish or Circassian stock, were slaves who established a military caste that succeeded in rising to power in Egypt and conquered the area of Syria and Palestine.[9] The Mamluk rulers were most rigorous in enforcing a Muslim religious policy, and life for the Christian inhabitants of Jerusalem became increasingly intolerable. The numbers of pilgrims dwindled, and bribes had to be paid to local officials to gain access to the Christian shrines. No new churches were permitted to be built, and if one were erected it was demolished. Several existing churches were converted into mosques by the Mamluk rulers, who considered themselves the legal owners of the Christian shrines by right of conquest. Thus they regarded the reversion of the shrines to Christian believers a concession revocable at will.

Though the treatment of the Latins was particularly harsh, the Mamluk rulers, for political reasons based on strategic considerations, granted special rights to the Georgians and the Ethiopians. The former were then in possession of the Monastery of the Cross and of the St. James Cathedral and enjoyed extended rights in the Basilica of the Holy Sepulchre and in the Church of the Tomb of Mary. The Ethiopians also enjoyed a special status in the Christian shrines. The Greeks, according to their own sources, were reinvested with some of their former rights by intervention of the Byzantine emperors, who bestowed magnificent gifts upon the Mamluk sultans of Egypt.

The Latins were no less anxious to recover a standing in the Holy Places from which they had been ejected after the Crusaders' defeat. Their struggle was waged mainly by the Franciscan friars. St. Francis of Assisi, founder of the Order, had personally visited the Holy Land, and in his steps several friars had established themselves in the country. In 1342, Pope Clemens VI vested the Franciscans with guardianship over the Holy Places. Seven years earlier, the friars had installed themselves on Mount Zion, according to Christian tradition the site of the Room of the Last Supper. The shrine had been acquired by Robert of Anjou, King of Naples, and ceded to the Franciscans. The friars were then also installed in the Church of the Holy Sepulchre and in the Church of the Tomb of Mary. Although the Christian clergy had succeeded in renewing its presence in the Holy Places, the general situation of the Christian residents of the holy city was disconcerting. By the end of the Mamluk period they numbered barely 1,000.

The Struggle over the Holy Places and the Status Quo in the Ottoman Period (1517–1917)

In 1517, during the reign of Sultan Selim I, Jerusalem came under Ottoman rule.[10] For the next 400 years the history of Christianity in the Holy City was to be mainly a chronicle of disputes over possession of the Holy Places. The patriarchates of Constantinople, Alexandria, Antioch, and Jerusalem were under the sway of the Ottoman Empire. This resulted in a considerable degree of centralization and endowed additional prestige to the ecumenical Patriarch of Constantinople, the imperial capital. He was now regarded as head of the Greek Orthodox *millet* (religious community) in the Ottoman Empire, with authority also over all non-Greek Orthodox Christians under Ottoman sovereignty. Inasmuch as the Greeks of Constantinople held important positions in the central administration of the Ottoman Empire, Orthodox Christianity had a direct influence over the affairs of the Holy Places.

In 1662, the Brotherhood of the Holy Sepulchre, the Orthodox monastic body in control of the Holy Places in Jerusalem, underwent a reorganization enhancing its authority in all matters concerning the holy shrines. It became the authorized representative of the Greek Orthodox Church in Palestine and in the Holy Places in particular. The preeminence of the Greeks could not be overlooked by the Latins. Latin interests were attended to by the Franciscan friars after 1342; and during the Middle Ages, the Franciscans could rely on the support of the Italian maritime cities, whose influence was then strongly felt in the Mediterranean. When that influence declined following the discovery of the New World, France emerged as protector of Latin interests. France could claim a rich tradition of links with the Holy Land, reaching back to the Crusades and even to the reign of the Frankish kings.

The political and commercial constellation of the sixteenth century persuaded King Francis I of France to negotiate a Capitulations treaty with Sultan Süleyman the Magnificent. The treaty was signed in 1535. Its first part deals with the commercial relations between the two countries; the second, with the status of the Europeans residing in or visiting the Ottoman Empire, who were subject to the jurisdiction of French consuls. The treaty thus proved advantageous both to pilgrims and to the Franciscan friars, the guardians of the Holy Places. A broad interpretation of the treaty would later provide France with a pretext to support the Franciscans in their claims to the Holy Places.

The Franciscans suffered a serious setback in 1552 when they were evicted from the Cenacle on Mount Zion; the shrine was converted into a mosque. Then the Franciscans occupied the site of today's St. Savior Monastery, present headquarters of the Franciscan Custody of the Holy Land. In 1555, the Franciscans succeeded in obtaining permission to repair the Edicule of the Holy Sepulchre, a concession that alarmed the Greek Orthodox, as restoration work by the Latins could be regarded as an act of possession.

A new Capitulations agreement negotiated in 1604 between France and the Sublime Porte made explicit mention of the Holy Places for the first time. It guaranteed protection for pilgrims visiting them and for the religious personnel in charge. A year later, the rights granted to the Latins in the 1604 treaty were abrogated by a firman issued by Sultan Ahmet I, granting the Greek Orthodox Patriarch Sophronios IV the northern part of Calvary (place of the Crucifixion), a site the Greeks possess until today. Further concessions were won by the Greeks in 1637 during Patriarch Theophanes' incumbency. Until 1690, the Greeks continued to enjoy a favored status in the Holy Places. A new Capitulations agreement was negotiated between France and Turkey in 1673, but it did not alter Greek primacy in the Holy Places, which was confirmed by a firman of 1675. At that time, the Greek Patriarchate also succeeded in acquiring religious properties belonging to the Armenians and the Ethiopians.

The tide again turned in favor of the Latins when a firman of April 23, 1690 accorded them a privileged status in the Holy Sepulchre and other shrines. Latin preeminence obtained full recognition in the new Capitulations agreement negotiated on May 29, 1740 between King Louis XV of France and Sultan Mehmet I. During this period, Turkey suffered a succession of serious defeats at the hands of the Austrian, and later the Russian, army. In the ensuing treaties and mainly during the negotiations that led to the peace of Belgrade (1739), France was instrumental in securing reasonable terms for Turkey. The Capitulations agreement evidently was a reward for the good offices provided by France.

The treaty of 1740, set out in 85 chapters, confirmed the far-reaching rights granted to the Latins by the firman of 1690, but it differed from previous pacts in that its stipulations were binding not only on the signatories but upon their successors as well. Furthermore, the treaty was committed to ensuring the safety of the Franciscans and implied the admission of French intervention in case of encroachment upon Latin rights in the Holy Places. Until the present, the Capitulations of 1740 are cited by the Latins as the legal basis for their rights in the Holy Places.

The situation created in 1740 favoring the Latins was reversed 17 years later to the advantage of the Orthodox. On the pretext of a quarrel that had broken out in the Church of the Holy Sepulchre during Holy Week, Sultan Osman III issued a firman in 1757 restoring to the Greeks all the rights they had enjoyed prior to 1690. Among the serious losses suffered by the Latins as a result of the firman of 1757 was their dislodgement from the Tomb of the Virgin Mary in Gethsemane. The de facto conditions created by the firman of 1757 formed the basis of all subsequent firmans and treaties of the nineteenth and twentieth centuries. After 1757, a de facto situation of joint control in the Holy Places gradually developed and came to be called the regulation of the Status Quo.

During the first half of the nineteenth century, several fierce controversies over the Status Quo brought about foreign power intervention and international complications. France traditionally backed Latin claims, while Czarist Russia emerged at the turn of the nineteenth century as protector of Orthodox interests. Russia had conducted two successful wars against the Ottoman Turks, and in the subsequent treaties of Küçük Kaynarca (1774) and Jassy (1792), had obtained the right to act on behalf of Orthodox Christian subjects of the Ottoman Empire. Russia broadly interpreted the wording of these treaties, finding in them sanction for direct interference in matters regarding the Holy Places.

A serious controversy erupted in October 1808 when a fire swept through the Basilica of the Holy Sepulchre and caused the dome to collapse, destroying the Edicule enclosing the sepulchre. Exploiting the involvement of the European powers in the Napoleonic wars, the Greeks managed to obtain a firman from Sultan Mehmet II authorizing them to carry out the Basilica's restoration. The required funds were raised by the Greek subjects of the Ottoman Empire, as is recorded in an inscription in the Edicule. The authorization granted to the Greeks drew vehement protests from the Latins and the Armenians, for under the regulations of the Status Quo the restoration of the roof of a building could lead to the transfer of the right of possession of the entire edifice to those undertaking the repairs. The Latin states pressed the Ottoman authorities to issue a declaration to the effect that the restorations carried out by the Greeks would not prejudice the rights of the other denominations. Because the repairs had been done poorly and hastily, the dome was again in danger of collapsing a few decades later. It was replaced after an agreement had been reached among France, Russia, and Turkey to share the costs equally.

The restoration of the Holy Sepulchre and the equally serious struggle caused by the theft of the silver star from the Grotto of the Nativity in Bethlehem induced the Sublime Porte to settle once and for all the question of the rights of the various denominations in the Holy Places. Moreover, the revolt of the Egyptian governor Muḥammad ʿAlī against the Ottomans and his conquest of Syria and Palestine (1831), the Greek war of independence, and intensified French activity in the Middle East had the combined effect of increasing pressure upon Turkey. The Latin Patriarchate, renewed in 1847 under French protection, began to direct and concentrate Roman Catholic influence throughout Palestine. In 1850, the French ambassador to Constantinople, General Aupick, acting on behalf of the French government and the Catholic kingdoms of Sardinia, Belgium, Spain, and Austria, presented a demand that the Ottomans restore to the Franciscans those Holy Places they controlled prior to 1757. This demand was opposed by Czarist Russia, which threatened to sever diplomatic relations with Turkey if it were so much as discussed. This dispute was, in fact, one of the causes of the Crimean War.

In February 1852, Sultan Abdülmecid I dispatched to the governor of Jerusalem a firman known as the *hatt-i şerif* (noble rescript) of 1268 (A.H.). The firman, save for minor amendments, confirmed the de facto situation that had existed since the firman of 1757. The 1852 firman constitutes the official proclamation of the Status Quo in the Christian Holy Places. It refers to a thorough investigation conducted by a government-appointed committee, rejects Latin demands for complete possession of the principal Holy Places (as detailed by General Aupick), and reaffirms the status as defined in 1757. The hatt-i şerif became a fundamental and authoritative document—a "constitution" that has regulated rights in the five principal Holy Places to this day.

Shortly after the 1852 firman, the Crimean War broke out, and the Treaty of Paris (1856) ending the war reaffirmed the provisions of the 1852 firman, favoring the Orthodox and disappointing the Latins. The Great Power signatories, including Russia, undertook to maintain the Status Quo in every sense. To satisfy the French government, however, France was given control over the Church of St. Anne, which had been converted by Saladin into a Muslim religious school. In 1868–69, subsequent firmans of Sultan Abdülmecid I reaffirmed the Status Quo; and the 1878 Treaty of Berlin, which terminated the Russo-Turkish Wars, specifically stated that there would be no changes in the Status Quo without the agreement of the signatory powers.

This was the first international agreement to employ the term "Status Quo" in connection with the Christian Holy Places.

The first half of the nineteenth century witnessed an improvement in the conditions prevailing among Jerusalem's Christian inhabitants, who by 1840 numbered 3,350 in a total population of 13,000. The change for the better began in 1831, when the city was occupied by Ibrāhīm Pasha, in the name of his father, Muḥammad ʿAlī. Interested in winning the friendship of the European powers, Ibrāhīm Pasha inaugurated a policy favorable to the Christians. He abolished the taxes levied upon pilgrims, as well as the fee that since Saladin's time was demanded of those wishing to enter the Church of the Holy Sepulchre. In 1834, as a gesture of goodwill, Ibrāhīm Pasha even attended the Greek Orthodox ceremony of the Holy Fire.

When Ibrāhīm Pasha's rule in Jerusalem ended in 1840 and Ottoman control was reestablished, demands for modernization could no longer be disregarded. Though important reforms had been promised by the Sublime Porte in the Imperial Rescript of Gülhane, issued in November 1839, it was only in February 1856 that a *hatt-i hümayun* (imperial rescript) granted the non-Muslim subjects of the empire a measure of equality regarding rights of citizenship.

With the decline of the Ottoman Empire, intervention by European powers in matters concerning Jerusalem increased. In the middle of the nineteenth century, Protestant Christianity became involved for the first time along with the traditional players in the affairs of Jerusalem.

Greek and Russian Orthodox

At the beginning of the nineteenth century, the Greek Orthodox Church was unquestionably the most important Christian communion in the Holy City in respect to numbers of its faithful and its standing in the Holy Places. Yet the growing influence of the other churches challenged Orthodox primacy; an Anglican bishop was appointed in Jerusalem and the Holy See restored the Latin Patriarchate to the city. In view of these developments, the Orthodox Church finally transferred the Greek Patriarch's residence from Istanbul to the Holy City.

Several major events marked the second half of the century: the settlement of 1852 concerning the Holy Places, favoring the Greeks; the establishment of a theological seminary in the Greek Orthodox Monastery of the Cross; and the reconstruction of the Dome of the Holy Sepulchre. Also significant was the statute that the Ottoman government granted in 1875 to the autocephalous Greek Orthodox Patriarchate of Jerusalem. The nineteenth century also witnessed a closer relationship between the Greek Patriarchate and the Russian Orthodox Church.

In the 1840s, the Russian Archimandrite, Porphyrios Ouspensky, came to Jerusalem at the invitation of the Greek Patriarchate to investigate the possibility of establishing a Pravoslav (Russian Orthodox) mission in the Holy City.[11] In January 1848, he returned as appointed head of a Russian ecclesiastical mission and installed himself temporarily in a Greek monastery that was placed at his disposal. When a second Russian ecclesiastical mission later settled in Jerusalem, it could rely on the financial support of a committee established in Moscow to deal with Holy Land affairs. Its president was Grand Duke Constantine, who visited the Holy Land in 1859 and acquired much real estate in Jerusalem. He purchased an historic site near the Church of the Holy Sepulchre and a parcel of land outside the Jaffa Gate of Jerusalem, where the Russian Compound was erected, comprising the magnificent Cathedral of the Holy Trinity, a hospital, a hostel for pilgrims, a residence for the Russian consul, and a monastery with a chapel.

In 1882, the Orthodox Palestine Society was founded. Its president, Grand Duke Sergei, had visited the country in 1881 and shown great interest in the development of the Russian religious institutions. In the 1880s, more Russian churches were built, including the Church of the Ascension on the top of the Mount of Olives, the Church of Alexander Nevsky near the Church of the Holy Sepulchre, and the Church of St. Maria Magdalena on the slopes of the Mount of Olives, inaugurated by Grand Duke Sergei himself in 1888. In a crypt in that church were later laid to rest the remains of Sergei's wife, the Grand Duchess Elisabeth, who was put to death in 1918 during the Russian Revolution.

Protestants and Anglicans

Protestant missionaries had already come to Jerusalem on exploratory visits in the first decades of the nineteenth century, but their attempts to establish themselves in the city had encountered many obstacles. It was only in 1833, during the rule of Ibrāhīm Pasha, that the Protestant minister John Nicolayson succeeded in initiating a more permanent project. He bought a piece of property near Jaffa Gate (the site of today's Christ Church hostel), but no sooner had he laid the foundations of a church than his work was halted by the Ottoman authorities. Though permitting existing churches to function, they would not permit the building of new ones.

Other Anglican and Protestant missionaries established themselves in the country. They lacked a legal status, however, and in contrast to the old established churches could not rely on the support of any European power. In order to obviate this handicap, King Frederick William IV of Prussia and Queen Victoria of England jointly agreed to establish an Anglican bishopric in Jerusalem, to which a Protestant mission might be annexed. The first incumbent was Michael S. Alexander, who settled in Jerusalem in 1841. It is noteworthy that the title he assumed was that of Anglican Bishop *in* Jerusalem and not *of* Jerusalem, so as to avoid arousing resentment among the heads of the local Eastern churches.

Upon his untimely death in 1845, Alexander was succeeded by Bishop S. Gobat, whose name is linked with the school he founded on Mount Zion. In January 1849, during his tenure, Christ Church was completed and consecrated, the first and, at that time, the sole Protestant church in the Near East. In 1874, a new Anglican church, St. Paul's, was erected in the Musrāra Quarter of Jerusalem to serve the Arab Anglican population, which consisted mainly of converts from the Eastern churches.

The second half of the century witnessed remarkable building activity by the various English missionary societies. Among the edifices erected were the English Mission Hospital, St. John's Ophthalmic Hospital, the Collegiate Church of St. George Martyr, the bishop's residence, and two schools, one for boys and the other for girls.

The German Lutheran Church, which had started its work in cooperation with the Church of England, continued its activity independently after 1886. Among the German institutions established in Jerusalem in the first period were a girls' school and a hospital, both directed by the deaconesses of Kaiserwerth; a hospice in the Via Dolorosa run by the German branch of the Knights of St. John; and the Syrian Orphanage founded by the Schneller family.

In 1869, the Sultan presented the King of Prussia with the Mūristān area near the Church of the Holy Sepulchre. On this site the Lutherans built a chapel in 1871. Following the unification of Germany, the Jerusalem Evangelical Foundation of Berlin was created; and Jerusalem witnessed the erection of such monumental buildings as the Church of the Redeemer near the Basilica of the Holy Sepulchre and the Augusta Victoria Stiftung between Mount Scopus and the Mount of Olives.

In the second half of the nineteenth century, Jerusalem attracted several large groups of devout Protestants, including the German Templars, members of a pietistic movement that had seceded from the Lutheran Church and founded the German colony in the southern part of Jerusalem. In 1881, pious Americans, led by Horatio Gates Spafford, settled in the Holy City and founded the American Colony. Prominent among the Protestant institutions founded in that period was the Jerusalem YMCA, which celebrated its centennial anniversary in 1978.

The Catholics

The year 1847 is a milestone in the history of the Roman Catholic community of Jerusalem, for it marks the reestablishment of the Latin Patriarchate in the city. From 1291, when the fugitive Patriarch Nicholas of Hanane drowned in the Bay of Acre, there had only been titular patriarchs of

Jerusalem. By the middle of the nineteenth century, however, developments favored a revival of the patriarchal dignity. The Holy See could hardly remain idle in view of the appointment of an Anglican bishop in Jerusalem, nor could it ignore the moves being made to install a Russian mission in the city.

Opposition to the appointment of a Latin Patriarch was not confined to the Greek Orthodox but extended to Catholic quarters as well. The Greek Catholic Melkite Patriarch of Antioch, who also bore the titles of Alexandria and Jerusalem, considered the appointment of a Latin Patriarch an utterly superfluous duplication in view of the few Latin congregants in the territory under his jurisdiction. The Melkite Patriarch expressed his opposition by convening a Greek Catholic synod in Jerusalem in the newly built Greek Catholic Cathedral of the Annunciation.

Nor were the Franciscans particularly happy about the appointment. Over the centuries they had been the sole representatives of Latin interests in the Holy Land. More than once the good offices of the Holy See were invoked to help clarify the respective areas of competence of the Latin Patriarch and of the Franciscan Custos.

Thus the task of Monsignor Valerga, the first Latin Patriarch, was not easy. Convinced of the necessity of creating a local clergy, Valerga established a seminary for priests in Jerusalem. He also built the Latin con-cathedral near Jaffa Gate as an auxiliary to the Church of the Holy Sepulchre, the main cathedral of Jerusalem, where the ceremonies had to be celebrated according to a rigorous schedule because it was shared by several denominations.

The expansion of the religious activities created a need for additional religious personnel. During the tenure of Valerga's successors, members of several religious orders and of many conventional congregations settled in Jerusalem and opened schools and orphanages, hospitals, clinics, and pilgrim hostels.

Among the religious orders represented were the Dominican Fathers. At the end of the nineteenth century they founded the Monastery of St. Stephen and the prestigious French Biblical and Archeological Institute. The Benedictines of Beuron settled in the Dormition Abbey in 1906. It was built on Mount Zion on a plot of land granted by the sultan to the Emperor of Germany.

In addition to the Roman Catholic Church, several Uniate Catholic churches made their presence felt in Jerusalem during the final years of Ottoman rule by the appointment of patriarchal vicars in the city. In 1901, the Syrian Catholics built a chapel and residence for their patriarchal vicar. An Armenian Catholic vicar settled in Jerusalem in 1885, a Maronite vicar in 1895, and a Chaldean vicar in 1903. The Greek Catholic Melkite Church, which had the largest following among the Uniate churches, had already built a cathedral in Jerusalem in 1849.

The Monophysite Churches

The presence in Jerusalem of Monophysite churches goes back to the beginnings of Christianity. Among them the Armenian Church ranks first in importance. At the inception of Ottoman rule in the Holy Land, the Armenian Patriarch of Jerusalem was recognized by Sultan Selim I as head of all Monophysite denominations. That situation is reflected today in the processions during the main religious feasts. Jerusalem's first Armenian Patriarch was appointed in 1311. His predecessors bore only the title of "bishop." Like other churches in the Holy City under Ottoman rule, the Armenians frequently found themselves in critical financial straits because of the heavy taxes levied upon them. They were also involved in protracted disputes with the Greeks over the Monastery of St. James.

Almost half of the present Armenian residential quarter was built during the first half of the seventeenth century. In the nineteenth century, the Armenian Patriarchate was finally able to expand its educational activities in Jerusalem. In 1833, a printing press (Jerusalem's first) was founded for producing liturgical and ritual books. In 1843, a theological seminary was opened; and in 1863, the Fraternity of St. James adopted a constitution that was ratified by the Ottoman authorities.

The Syrian Church is perhaps the oldest among the Christian churches in Jerusalem. The seat of the archbishop is the Monastery of St. Mark, which, according to Syrian tradition, is the site of the Room of the Last Supper.[12] In 1718, the Syrian Bishop of Jerusalem restored the ancient monastery and his successor improved the library, where ancient manuscripts and valuable icons are preserved.

The Coptic Church, which has its center in Egypt, maintains close ties with Jerusalem.[13] There were several Coptic churches in the Holy City in the period preceding the Crusades. The first Coptic bishop in Jerusalem was installed in the thirteenth century under the Mamluks. During the Ottoman period, the Copts succeeded in acquiring rights in the main Holy Places. In the second half of the nineteenth century, they built the Cathedral of St. Anthony near the Church of the Holy Sepulchre and opened schools for boys and girls.

The Ethiopian Church has very old ties with Jerusalem.[14] In the past it possessed important rights in the Holy Places, but it lost most of them because of its poverty and the taxes imposed by the Turkish pashas. In the nineteenth century, the Ethiopians were hard pressed by the Copts, who restricted their rights, considering them as their tolerated guests in the wretched huts that they occupied in the Deir al-Sulṭān Monastery on a roof of the Church of the Holy Sepulchre. In 1891, the Ethiopians built a monastery and a chapel in the Old City of Jerusalem, intended to serve also as the residence of their bishop.

The British Mandate Period (1917–48)

General Allenby's entrance into Jerusalem in 1917 brought 673 years of uninterrupted Muslim rule to an end. The British were confronted with the unenviable task of handling the multidenominational character of Jerusalem's population. Dealing with the Christian churches was a particularly delicate matter in view of the conflicting claims of various Christian confessions regarding the Holy Places. The British adopted a policy of maintaining the Status Quo, while accommodating changes that stemmed from the transfer of political control. For example, Christian (and Jewish) religious courts were relieved of the need to apply to Muslim religious courts in matters of religious endowments and trusts, as well as other affairs for which Ottoman law had required the approval of local courts.

The fluid situation immediately following World War I seemed to provide a unique opportunity to settle the complex problem of the Holy Places. The rival churches presented their respective memoranda to the Paris Peace Conference, with the Catholics demanding restoration of what they had forfeited in 1757, and the Greek Orthodox Church insisting on retaining possession of what it had acquired at that time. The peace treaty with Turkey, followed by the League of Nations Mandate over Palestine granted to Great Britain, contained articles requiring the establishment of a committee for the Holy Places. However, the whole matter foundered on the question of the committee's composition.

In 1922, the British government advanced certain proposals but withdrew them in the face of opposition by the Catholic powers. A year later, the British foreign secretary proposed that until a committee for the Holy Places could be established, an Ad Hoc Special Commission of Inquiry, composed of one or more British judges not resident in Palestine, should be appointed whenever a dispute arose over one of the Holy Places. This commission of inquiry would then become subject to the Committee for the Holy Places, whenever that body would be constituted. This proposal was, likewise, never implemented. As a result, the legal procedure for settling disputes was reduced to minimal proportions: Whenever a question was in dispute, the British government (that is, the high commissioner) would issue a decision. If one of the parties was dissatisfied with the decision, it could submit an official protest, which would be duly registered. Thus the decision would not constitute an official change in the Status Quo.

In 1924, the publication of the King's Order in Council (Holy Places) affirmed that any matter connected with the Holy Places, religious buildings or sites, or rights and claims of the various religious communities in Palestine would not be considered or resolved by any court in Palestine. It further determined that the high commissioner was the sole and final arbiter of which matters would be included in this category. Cust summed up the situation by advising that, under the British Mandate, the arrangements established in the firman of 1852, confirming the Status Quo of 1757 concerning the rights of the Christian communities in the Holy Places, should be scrupulously observed, and that each rite practiced at that time should remain unaltered.[15]

The general improvement of living conditions during the British administration led to an increase in Jerusalem's Christian population. The Anglican and the Protestant churches were the main beneficiaries of the British administration, and many new cultural and charitable institutions were founded during that period. The Church of Scotland took special pride in the impressive Church of St. Andrew that it built in 1931. The YMCA inaugurated its striking monumental building in the western section of Jerusalem in 1933. Several Protestant missions from the United States established themselves in the Holy City. But German Protestant institutions, which had expanded during the first two decades of the British Mandate, had to cease activity when World War II broke out, and their properties were vested with a Custodian of Enemy Property.

Relations between the Greek Orthodox Patriarchate and the mandatory authorities were excellent as were the Patriarchate's relations with the Anglican Church, whose representatives were permitted to hold services in the Greek Orthodox Chapel of St. Abraham near the Church of the Holy Sepulchre. However, the disastrous financial position of the Patriarchate forced the British administration to appoint a commission to investigate its affairs and to suggest a workable solution. Furthermore, the administration had to intervene to settle the differences between the Greek Patriarchate and its Arab Orthodox members.

The Jerusalem mission of the Russian Orthodox Church had been deprived of its financial support by the Bolshevik Revolution. The mandatory power decided to appoint an administrator for the Russian ecclesiastical property. During the British Mandate, the Rumanian Orthodox Patriarchate established a mission in Jerusalem.

The Roman Catholic Church in the Holy Land received important support from the Vatican when an Apostolic Delegate for Jerusalem and Palestine was appointed in 1929. Until then the Vatican representative had resided in Egypt, with his responsibility extending to the Holy Land. During the period of the British Mandate, several new religious orders and conventual congregations began their work in Jerusalem. To that period also belong several beautiful shrines, among them the Church of the Agony in Gethsemane and the Church of the Visitation in ʿEin Kārim. In 1927, the Jesuit Fathers opened a branch of their Biblical Pontifical Institute in Jerusalem. The Franciscans built both the Terra Sancta School, a landmark of central Jerusalem, and a monastery on Mount Zion near the Cenacle. The activities of the Uniate churches also expanded, and several of them entered new premises.

The Armenian Catholics, for example, built a church on the Via Dolorosa at the site of the Fourth Station.

The Divided City

When the Arab states rejected the Partition Resolution of November 29, 1947, and their armies invaded the territory that was to be the State of Israel, Jerusalem became the scene of fierce fighting. The outcome was a divided city.[16] In the course of the conflict, the Israeli forces, at considerable risk to their own security, were careful not to jeopardize the safety of the Holy Places within the Arab-held Old City. The Jordanian army's artillery caused extensive damage to churches in the Israeli sector of the city.

Among the basic principles laid down in Israel's Proclamation of Independence were the guarantee of equal rights to all citizens—without distinction of religion, race, or sex—and the solemn assurance that the Holy Places would be safeguarded. Consequently, when normalcy was restored to Jerusalem, Christian institutions renewed their religious activities in full. However, the heads of the religious communities of the Holy Land had their seat in the Jordanian sector of Jerusalem and were separated by an armistice line from their clergy and flock in Israel. The Israeli government did its utmost to enable church dignitaries, lesser clergy, and pilgrims to cross the lines in both directions at the Mandelbaum Gate. Only a thousand Christian faithful remained in the Israeli sector of Jerusalem; but the clergy was numerous, and soon friendly contacts, mainly of a cultural and scholarly nature, were established with them. The brief visit of Pope Paul VI to Jerusalem in 1964 was a meaningful event, though the Vatican was careful not to attach to the visit any political significance implying recognition of Israeli sovereignty over the city.

In the years prior to the reunification of Jerusalem in 1967, the most significant developments for Christians occurred in the Jordan-controlled Old City, where the heads of the churches resided and the Holy Places were situated. Under these circumstances, the Jordanian rulers considered themselves the lawful successors of the sovereigns of former regimes in all matters regarding the Holy Places and the regulations of the Status Quo. A new Jordanian constitution was framed in 1952. On paper, it gave equal rights to all citizens; in practice, it favored Arab nationalist aims, identifying itself mainly with the cause of Islam. Consequently, many Christians emigrated and the numerical ratio between the Muslim and Christian residents of the Holy City was altered.

To demonstrate Jordan's ability to master the difficult task of guarding the Holy Places, King ʿAbdallāh created a new post—Guardian of the Ḥaram al-Sharīf and Supreme Custodian of the (non-Muslim) Holy Places. In his eagerness to satisfy all parties involved, the king ordered not only that the

Status Quo be maintained but also that all the firmans of the Ottoman sultans and the traditional rights held by the partriarchs be examined and registered impartially in special gazettes, for the purpose of documentation, which anyone might utilize whenever necessary. It appeared that he was leaving an opening for a judicial investigation similar to the one that had been proposed in 1918 in the wake of World War I. In the end, however, the Christians refused to recognize the Supreme Custodian, and responsibility for the Holy Places later reverted to the district commissioner.

The Jordanian government was strict in maintaining order and succeeded in keeping the peace in trouble spots, such as the Church of the Holy Sepulchre and the Church of the Nativity in Bethlehem. On festivals such as Easter, the Jordanians stationed as many as 200 soldiers and policemen at the Church of the Holy Sepulchre to maintain order.

The Jordanian authorities also dealt with the repair and redecoration of the Church of the Holy Sepulchre. Perpetual disputes between the Christian communities over responsibility for repairs had created a situation obliging the mandatory government's Public Works Department, or in some cases the Municipality, to carry out urgent work. In 1951, the Jordanians initiated cooperation among the Christian communities on the subject of repairs, but negotiations dragged on for 11 years. Only in 1962 did the Catholics, Greek Orthodox, and Armenians set up a joint technical office to begin reinforcing and redecorating the building. Work proceeded slowly, partly because of its delicate character and the lack of access for vehicles, but also because of mutual suspicions. The unification of the city in 1967 found the work still in process.

In the 1950s, the Jordanian government issued several regulations that aroused serious concern among Christian church leaders. Strict control was imposed upon Christian charitable and educational institutions, and the purchase of real estate in Jerusalem was restricted. The severity of these provisions was somewhat mitigated in the face of vehement objections from Christian quarters.

Because the partition of Jerusalem prevented East Jerusalemites from using Catholic educational institutions in the western sector of the city, new Catholic schools had to be built in the Arab-held sector or existing ones had to be enlarged. A new Terra Sancta school for boys and a new Schmidt's school for girls were founded. The shrine of Dominus Flevit on the Mount of Olives also dates from this time.

The Greek Catholic Church, having an Arabic-speaking clergy, managed to expand under Jordanian rule, and its patriarchal vicar in Jerusalem was elevated to archepiscopal rank.

The Greek Orthodox Patriarchate ran into trouble when Patriarch Timotheus died and his successor had to be confirmed by the Jordanian government. The Arab Orthodox congregants demanded an effective role in the election of the patriarch and in the management of the revenues of the Patriarchate. Their move challenged the preeminence of the Hellenic element within the Patriarchate. The Jordanian government naturally sympathized with the Arab aspirations, but a compromise was reached when a new statute was approved by the Jordanian Parliament.

The Anglican Church underwent reorganization with the elevation of the Anglican bishop to the rank of archbishop. The Arab branch of the church was granted greater autonomy and placed under an Arab bishop, who also resided in Jerusalem.

The Lutheran Church had to reduce its activities radically during World War II because of its German connections. It could not resume its work in West Jerusalem, in Jewish surroundings, in the aftermath of the Holocaust. In East Jerusalem its activities were revived and new buildings were erected to replace those that were no longer available in West Jerusalem.

As the YMCA in West Jerusalem was no longer accessible to East Jerusalemites, a new building called Aelia Capitolina was erected in the Arab sector. A new Ophthalmic Hospital of the Order of St. John was likewise built in East Jerusalem. Several Protestant missionary societies, interested in assisting displaced persons and in proselytizing among them, also opened missions in East Jerusalem.

Reunited Jerusalem

The reunification of Jerusalem in June 1967 was an event transcending political or strategic considerations, stirring deep emotions in Israel and abroad. From the viewpoint of Christian interests, the new reality meant that the heads of the Christian churches of the Holy Land, having their seat in East Jerusalem, found themselves in territory under Israeli sovereignty, and the most important Christian shrines were now in Israel-controlled territory.

After the city's reunification, at a meeting attended by the heads of the Christian communities, Prime Minister Levi Eshkol affirmed that the Israeli government held it to be an essential principle of its policy to safeguard the Holy Places, while leaving their internal administration to the management of the heads of the churches concerned. On June 27, 1967, the Knesset passed the Protection of Holy Places Law, prescribing heavy penalties for the desecration or violation of Holy Places.

In an effort to normalize the newly emergent situation, the Israeli government gave compensation to Christian communities to repair churches and institutions damaged in the course of hostilities, regardless of whether the damage was inflicted by its own soldiers or by the Jordanians. Because of the presence of the Holy Places in the territory under its jurisdiction, the Israeli government was confronted with problems relating to the Status Quo. Consequently, it had to deal with the dispute between the Ethiopian and the Coptic churches concerning possession of the chapels of the Four Living Creatures and of St. Michael. Moreover, the government and its tribunals had to deal with a dispute concerning Russian ecclesiastical property between the Moscow-centered Russian Orthodox mission on the one side and the Russian ecclesiastical mission connected with the Church in Exile on the other.

Reunited Jerusalem under Israeli sovereignty witnessed an unprecedented building boom on the part of the churches. Among the edifices erected or restored were the Ecumenical Institute for Advanced Theological Studies on the outskirts of Jerusalem, the Armenian Theological Institute, St. Joseph's House on Mount Zion, the Center of the Lutheran World Federation on Mount Scopus, the hostel of the Greek Catholic Church, the new Maronite Monastery and chapel, the Christian Information Center at Jaffa Gate, and the Orthodox Church of St. Stephen. Extensive repairs were carried out in the Church of the Holy Sepulchre and in the Monastery of the Holy Cross. No less important than the impressive building activity has been the progress in cultural exchanges between Christian savants of the various Catholic and Protestant Biblical institutes and scholars of Israeli institutes of higher learning.

The decision of the government to extend Israeli law to the city in its entirety aroused opposition in international quarters and revived the question of the legal status of Jerusalem. The late Pope Paul VI often expressed himself in favor of internationalizing the city as a solution to the problem of the Holy Places and to preserve Jerusalem's universal character, although he did not exclude other solutions.

NOTES

1. For general orientation, see S. P. Colbi, *Christianity in the Holy Land; Past and Present* (Tel Aviv: Am Hassefer, 1969); and S. P. Colbi, *The Christian Churches in the State of Israel, A Survey* (Jerusalem: The Israel Economist, 1976). See also Anton Odeh Issa, *Les Minorités Chrétiennes de Palestine à travers les siècles* (Jerusalem: Franciscan Printing Press, 1977); S. Sayegh, *Le Status Quo des Lieux Saints; nature juridique et portée internationale* (Rome, 1971) (Latran Corona Lateranensis, 21); and W. Zander, *Israel and the Holy Places of Christendom* (London: Weidenfeld and Nicolson, 1971). E. Lauterpacht, *Jerusalem and the Holy Places* (London: Anglo-Israel Association, 1968), treats the problem of internationalization. During the period of the British Mandate an important memorandum was prepared by L. G. A. Cust, *The Status Quo in the Holy Places* (London: HMSO, printed for the Government of Palestine, 1929). On the Holy Places, see also D. Baldi, *Guida di Terra Santa* (Jerusalem: Edizioni di Terra Santa, printed in Turin, Marietti Press, 1973); B. Collin, *Les Lieux Saints*, 2d ed. (Paris: Presses universitaires de France, 1969); B. Collin, *Le problème juridique des Lieux-Saints* (Cairo: Centre d'études orientales, 1956); C. Coüasnon *The Church of the Holy Sepulchre* (Oxford: Oxford University Press, 1972); N. Moscopoulos, *La Terre Sainte* (Athens, 1957); and H. Vincent and F. M. Abel, *Jerusalem Nouvelle* (Paris: Gabalda, 1914–1925).

2. On the patriarchates in Jerusalem see A. Bertram and H. Luke, *The Orthodox Patriarchate of Jerusalem* (Oxford: Oxford University Press, 1921); N. Moscopoulos, *La question de Palestine et le Patriarchat de Jerusalem* (Athens, 1948); G. Fedalto, *La Chiesa Latina in Oriente* (Verona: Casa Editrice Mazziana, 1973); P. Medebielle, *The Diocese of the Latin Patriarchate of Jerusalem*

(Jerusalem: Typography Patriarchatus Latini, 1963); *Annuaire de l'église catholique en Terre Sainte* (Jerusalem, 1979) (sponsored by the Apostolic Delegation in Jerusalem); and K. Hintlian, *History of the Armenians in the Holy Land* (Jerusalem: St. James Press, 1976).

3. E. Hoade, *Historical and Geographical Outline of the Holy Land* (Jerusalem: Franciscan Press, 1974), p. 90.

4. Cust, *Status Quo*, pp. 3-4.

5. On the memoranda presented to the 1919 peace conference, see Zander, *Israel and the Holy Places*, pp. 57-62, 163-67, 181-94.

6. J. Prawer, *The Latin Kingdom of Jerusalem* (London: Weidenfeld and Nicolson, 1972), especially Chs. 10-12.

7. "Theoderich's Description of the Holy Places," in *Palestine Pilgrims' Text Society*, vol. 4 (London: Committee of the Palestine Exploration Fund, 1896) 4, p. 14.

8. "Ludolph von Suchem's Description of the Holy Land," in *Palestine Pilgrims' Text Society*, vol. 12 (London: Committee of the Palestinian Exploration Fund, 1895), pp. 97-110.

9. See Sir William Muir, *The Mameluke or Slave Dynasty of Egypt, 1260-1517 A.D.* (London: Smith Elder, 1896); and J. Drory, "Jerusalem in the Mamluk Period," in *Jerusalem in the Middle Ages*, ed. B. Z. Kedar and Z. Baras (Jerusalem: Yad Izhak Ben-Zvi, 1979), pp. 148-84.

10. On the Christian status in Jerusalem under the Ottomans, see G. Bateh, *Les Chrétiens de Palestine sous la domination Ottomane* (Rome: Pontificia Università Lateranense, 1963); and Ch. Wardi, "The Question of the Holy Places in Ottoman Times," in *Studies in Palestine During the Ottoman Period*, ed. M. Maoz (Jerusalem: Magnes Press, 1975), pp. 385-93.

11. See D. Hopwood, *The Russian Presence in Syria and Palestine 1843-1914* (Oxford: Oxford University Press, 1969).

12. On the Syrian Church, see Y. Koriah, *The Syrian Orthodox Church in the Holy Land* (Jerusalem: Syrian Orthodox Patriarchate, 1976).

13. On the Coptic Church, see O. F. A. Mainardus, *The Copts in Jerusalem* (Cairo, 1960).

14. On the Ethiopian Church, see K. Pedersen, *Ethiopian Institutions in Jerusalem* (Jerusalem: Franciscan Printing Press, 1975); and Archbishop Philippos, *The Rights of the Abyssinian Church in the Holy Places* (Jerusalem: Abyssinian Church in Jerusalem, 1959).

15. Cust, *Status Quo*, p. 11.

16. On the periods of the divided city and reunification, see especially Zander, *Israel and the Holy Places*.

7

THE INSTITUTIONAL STRUCTURE OF HETEROGENEOUS CITIES: BRUSSELS, MONTREAL, AND BELFAST

Emanuel Gutmann and Claude Klein

This chapter focuses upon the present-day institutional structure and the legal and constitutional provisions of Brussels, Montreal, and Belfast.[1] The political problems of these cities constitute one component of the wider conflict prevailing in their respective countries as a whole. Brussels and Montreal present the very core of the problem. Only in Northern Ireland the conflict does not center on Belfast, although it is presently most severe there. In all three cases the situation has deteriorated since the 1960s, and in none has a fully satisfactory solution or settlement been found.

In Belgium, since 1962,[2] extensive legislation, including the constitutional revision of 1967–71, has provided the legal groundwork for an accommodation between the two major language groups ("cultural communities") by a substantial change of the organizational structure of the state. This new and highly complicated structure, however, is in danger of collapse, solely because of the problems of Brussels, where, so far (1979), no final arrangement has proved acceptable. The determination of the "Brussels entity" as a separate region, its territorial boundaries, organizational and political structure, and the forms of lingual coexistence are all problems that have yet to be resolved. All attempts to freeze the lingual status quo by legal devices have failed to arrest the dynamism of social trends. The conflict about Brussels has not only been the principal reason for the nationwide deterioration in the relationship between the two language groups in recent years but has held up the definitive regionalization of the country and been the main factor of governmental instability since the mid-1960s.

The same phenomenon of a conflict focusing around a single city can be observed in Montreal. Jean-Charles Bonenfant of Laval University writes:

> Montreal occupies a special place amongst the problems of ethnic duality facing Canada. There are specialists who affirm that the drama of the Canadians takes place not so much in the whole of Quebec as in the agglomeration formed by this metropolis and its satellite cities.[3]

The internal conflicts in Montreal symbolize the struggle of the French-speaking Canadians more than any other issue. The city's French majority is attempting to reverse the process of cultural domination by the English, just as the Flemings in Brussels are trying to halt the process of Frenchification. However, in Montreal the struggle for a favored legal status for the French language is the main instrument employed by the majority in seeking to change its cultural and economic status, while the struggle of the Flemings in Brussels is, in effect, a rear-guard action to prevent their elimination from the city scene.[4]

In Brussels, Montreal, and Belfast, the city itself constitutes, in various degrees, the focal point of the conflict between two rival groups.

BRUSSELS

The Spatial Definition of the Brussels Urban Area

The various boundaries of and within the Brussels urban agglomeration and the language rights in the different types of areas in it are at present the central points of the Brussels problem. The new Article 3-C of the 1970 constitutional amendment states: ". . . Belgium comprises four linguistic regions: the French language region, the Dutch (Flemish) language region, the bilingual region of Brussels-Capital, and the German language region. . . ."[5] Brussels-Capital is distinguished legally from the other three regions because it enjoys a bilingual status, while the other regions have been defined as monolingual.

The principal conflict concerns extending or reducing the boundaries of the Brussels region. While the French-speakers demand an extension of the area of jurisdiction, the Flemings are opposed because Brussels lies entirely within the Flemish-speaking region, and any expansion of the city would be at the expense of Flemish territory. Moreover, because the resident population, as well as the population linked to the city by daily work, has been undergoing a process of Frenchification, Brussels, once a Flemish center, has changed into an overwhelmingly French city. Large sections of the population residing in boroughs on the outskirts of Brussels have been demanding that the capital's bilingual status be extended to its suburbs.[6] Hence the Flemings regard

Brussels as a kind of incessantly expanding "oil slick." Because they are powerless to halt the process of urbanization going on in the periphery of Brussels, they oppose any change of the boundaries of the Brussels-Capital region and resist any further language concessions to Francophones in the areas surrounding it.

The population of Brussels was estimated in 1973 as follows: Inner Center, 48,000; Brussels-City (commune or borough), 161,000; Brussels-Capital (19 boroughs), 1,075,000; and Brussels agglomeration (metropolitan region), 1,348,000.[7] Brussels is still undergoing a transfer to the French language. The figures testifying to the change are astounding, as reflected in the following listing of the declining percentage of registered Flemings in the population of Brussels-Capital: 1846, 66.5; 1910, 46.2; 1920, 37.8; 1930, 33.7; 1947, 24.2; and 1968, 13.5.

A recent, and rather controversial, survey established that although the mother tongue of 27.1 percent of Bruxelloises is Flemish, only 17.6 percent consider themselves Flemings and only 13.1 percent use Flemish as their major language.[8] Some 40 percent of the population are regarded as bilingual to varying degrees; about 3 percent claim to be "symmetrically bilingual." The language distribution in Brussels-Capital is quite uneven. Brussels-City had in 1968 about 20 percent Flemings, and their percentage ranged from 6 percent in some boroughs to more than 26 percent. But geographically speaking, no language frontier can be drawn through Brussels.

From the administrative viewpoint, Brussels-Capital and all its 19 boroughs maintain a completely bilingual regime. The application of this principle can well be seen in the Belgium educational system. In the rest of Belgium, since 1932, the language of the region is compulsory in primary and secondary schools, and since 1963, this principle was extended to kindergartens and higher education. In Brussels, however, legislation provides that the language spoken at home determines the language in which the child is to be taught. The law requires that the father's declaration as to the native language be checked by municipal inspectors, but because this check is usually a mere formality, many Flemish-speaking families contrive to send their children to French-speaking schools.

To implement the bilingual policy in Brussels, the government (and the municipality) actually grant the Flemish school system preferential treatment. For example, Flemish schools do not have to meet the Education Ministry's minimum for the number of pupils attending them, and the ministry maintains schools in sections of the capital where they would not exist by ordinary criteria. In fact, a number of Flemish schools have registered no more than a few dozen pupils.

With regard to the city's administration, all Brussels municipal employees are required to be bilingual, as are all civil servants who serve the public directly (in the post office, for example). The municipalities of Brussels-

Capital and the boroughs actually have two parallel linguistic sets of offices. Citizens are entitled to settle their affairs in their own language, and all official publications are printed in both French and Flemish. Legislation provides for exact proportional distribution of senior municipal appointments, including those of the social services, in Brussels-Capital and the 19 boroughs. The Flemings continue to claim that they are being discriminated against and seriously underrepresented.

While a modus vivendi concerning the so-called language problem has slowly been taking form in Brussels-Capital since the 1960s, the bone of contention has moved to those parts of the Brussels metropolitan area outside the city limits. Most of these are immediately contiguous to the Brussels-Capital boundaries in the Flemish-language districts of Brabant. Some are a little farther removed and located in the French-speaking districts of that province. In some of the boroughs of the Flemish-speaking periphery of Brussels, over 30 percent of the inhabitants spoke French by the mid-1960s; by the mid-1970s, most of these boroughs actually had a majority of Francophones.

Although the Flemings oppose any extension of the Brussels bilingual arrangements to these or any other boroughs, six of them were given the status of "boroughs of special facilities" (communes à facilités). These facilities comprise, first and foremost, instruction in French as first language and the use of French in written communication with government offices.[9] The enhancement of the language facilities and their extension to other boroughs in the Bruxelles metropolitan area are at the center of the intercommunal struggle in Belgium today.

Municipal Institutions

The present institutional structure of Brussels is exceptionally complicated, and growing more so. The number of authorities administering to Brussels, including the boroughs, exceeds 20, and according to one authority the city actually has 73 centers of executive power.[10]

The preservation of the outdated structure of 19 boroughs, and the reluctance or political incapability to establish a strong central municipal authority, are only one part of the explanation for the organizational maze that exists. More important is that the highly complex governmental and administrative structure introduced throughout the country in order to implement the policy of cultural autonomy and lingual regionalization is being mirrored in Brussels with a vengeance.

As a result of the constitutional revision of 1967–71, Belgium now has four linguistic regions (Article 3-B), of which Brussels, as a bilingual region, is one; three cultural communities (Article 3-C); and three (basically economic) regions (Article 107-D), of which Brussels is also one. Newly created also were "urban areas" (Article 108-B), the Brussels area being one of five in all, comprising the major agglomerations of the country in which language rights are specifically safeguarded in the constitution (Article 108-C); and "federations of boroughs" (Article 108-B), the only ones of their kind established so far being five such federations uniting boroughs peripheral to the Brussels urban area.

In addition, the old provinces (Article 1) continue to exist. Each one of these governmental units has a plenitude of organs, such as assemblies, councils, executive committees, permanent committees and other committees, chairmen, presidents, and governors—all of which create a most complicated network of legal competences and countervailing powers. There is now a cabinet minister for Brussels Affairs, as well as a ministerial committee on Brussels; and there is a special vice-governor of Brabant Province with special responsibility for the language laws concerning Brussels.

The Institutional Future of Brussels

The constitutional revision has provided the legal basis for the future regionalization of Belgium. However, no final agreement has yet been reached concerning the future of Brussels. It will, first of all, be necessary to decide whether the city is going to constitute one of the equal components of a Belgian-style federation, as seems to accord best with the present text of the constitution, or whether a special regime will have to be provided for it, a kind of *Reichsgebiet*, such as the District of Columbia or Canberra.

Whatever the specifics of the future federal solution, the question now being asked is whether it will be one of two or three units. The Flemings find it hard to accept Brussels as a region equivalent to Flanders and Wallonia. They are unwilling to countenance the notion of a "Bruxellor's nation," which to them would be implied in such an arrangement. As they view it, in a three-cornered federal structure, Flanders would risk becoming a minority of one against two.[11] Yet the tripartite structure seems to be becoming a political and administrative reality, with Brussels actually serving as the main countervailing force to progressively centrifugal tendencies evinced by the two other regions, that is, linguistic communities.

Second, there is the highly complex area problem of Brussels. The present containment of Brussels-Capital within the urban area (the 19 boroughs) is not viable from economic, administrative, or planning points of view. If the aggregative process of city building were to stop at its present boundaries, this would have most detrimental effects; indeed many have already been caused, as most impartial observers agree. Yet the location of the city and the composition of its population present what seem at this time to be insurmountable impediments to an optimal solution.

Finally, there is the exasperating administrative structure of Brussels, which is perhaps the most prominent expression of the foregoing constraints.

Some years ago, F. Perin, at that time minister for state reform, produced an ingeniously radical plan to solve most of the outstanding problems. Basically, his proposal was to integrate all existing administrative units of the Greater Brussels area into one city-region, which would make Brussels a unique entity in Belgium.[12] Such a solution would eliminate almost all existing structures, including the ancient 19 boroughs and all the special regional organizations. At the same time, the area of Brussels would be enlarged to include the widest possible periphery. Small wonder that the Perin plan was sharply criticized from almost all quarters.

After Perin's attempt, renewed efforts of a less far-reaching nature were made on the political level, but so far with little success. The so-called Egmont Pact of 1977 provides for a status quo over Brussels-Capital, including its 19 boroughs, but it introduces linguistic proportionality (rather than the unrealistic parity, in view of the extreme inequality between the two language groups in the city) and a considerably strengthened Brussels executive. Also significant is the provision of the Egmont Pact that the French-speaking inhabitants of the surrounding boroughs in the Flemish-speaking region would be accorded the same rights as the Flemish-speaking minority in Brussels, that is, practically equal standing. Further concessions were included in the Stuyvenberg Agreement of 1978 and in a subsequent bill prepared by the government of the day, but doubts on many sides, including legal impediments, have prevented a final, consensual accommodation.

More than one government has fallen over the Brussels issue. The December 1978 elections were prematurely called because of a renewed impasse over it, and the main Flemish party, the Volksunie, was heavily punished in the election by its usual supporters for having made too far-reaching concessions.

Brussels is still the stumbling block on the way to an agreed-upon new regionalized structure of Belgium.

MONTREAL

Montreal is not the only bilingual city in Canada, or even in the province of Quebec. In effect, there is almost no town in Quebec, large or small, that is not bilingual. However, this chapter examines only the question of Montreal, a metropolis with a strong Anglo-Saxon tradition that in recent years has been confronted with a powerful French resurgence.

The City's Boundaries

The problem of the city's boundaries is not parallel in Montreal and Brussels. The city of Montreal occupies only one part of Montreal Island and of a still wider area known as Grand Montreal. This entire area makes up an imposing metropolis, which contains about 44 percent of the total population of the province of Quebec and about 19 percent of the population of Canada, as the following statistics show:

Canada	22,500,000
Quebec	6,100,000
Grand Montreal	2,800,000
Montreal (city)	1,300,000

Montreal is the largest city in Canada (the second largest, Toronto, is only half its size).[13] Urbanization in Quebec is dominated by metropolitan Montreal, having over a third of Quebec's population, to a much greater extent than Toronto dominates Ontario. But a much more significant fact is that the city is the center of English-speaking Quebec and the only interface between the two language cultures in the province.[14]

The composition of Montreal's population has been changing over the years. Most conspicuous is the decline of the British minority for the last 100 years. There has, however, not been a compensating rise in the percentage of the French (see Table 7.1).[15]

TABLE 7.1: Ethnic Composition of Montreal, 1871–1971 (in percent)

	1871	1901	1911	1931	1941	1951	1961	1971
French	60	64	63	60	63	64	65	64
British	38	34	26	26	24	22	17	16
Jewish	—	2	5	6	6	5	4	4
Italian	—	—	1	2	2	2	4	6
Polish	—	—	1	1	1	1	1	1
Other	2	—	4	5	4	6	9	9
Total population (in thousands)	144.0	360.8	554.8	1,003.9	1,116.8	1,320.2	1,747.7	2,187.2

Note: 1971 figures are for Montreal census metropolitan area; the rest are for Montreal Island only.

Sources: *Census of Canada*, 1961 and 1971; and N. Lacoste, *Les Characteristiques sociales de la population du grand Montreal* (Montreal, 1958).

In spite of the very considerable diminution of the British element, however, the English-speaking sector has actually increased through the continued immigration of other ethnic groups, thereby reinforcing the linguistic duality of the city. In 1971, 63.3 percent of Montrealers spoke French at home, and 26.2 percent spoke English, of whom only 22.6 percent claimed it as their mother tongue. The French were more bilingual than the British, with about 40 percent speaking only French, while in 1931 only 29 percent of the French were monolingual. Apparently, it is now easier to get along with French alone, and as a result, intergroup communication actually becomes more difficult.

The problem of the relationship between the center and the outskirts is not as evident as it is in Brussels, but it is acknowledged. The English-speaking population appears to focus around several token centers (such as McGill University, for example) or the city's suburbs and consequently constitutes a majority in some boroughs. Also, the city of Montreal clearly tends to follow a policy of annexing its suburbs. The reason for these annexations is, first and foremost, pragmatic. It is hard to distinguish the city of Montreal from its suburbs. The whole area has become one metropolis, and the traditional administrative boundaries no longer reflect practical realities.

The recommendation of the Blier Committee in 1964 to establish a joint body, constituting a kind of federation of Montreal and neighboring areas to deal with major topics of common interest, was found wanting. Instead, the Montreal Urban Community (Communaute Urbaine de Montreal) was established in 1969. However, it should be noted that the structure of the organization is not related to the lingual heterogeneity in Montreal.

The organization of the city of Montreal is based upon a special charter drawn up in 1960. It provides for a 48-member council elected in 17 constituencies and a mayor who is chosen directly by the electorate. He is assisted by a six-member executive headed by a chairman (the mayor nominates the members of the executive from among the members of the council, with the latter body approving the list). Following an unwritten rule, the chairman of the executive is French-speaking, while his deputy is English-speaking. The post of executive chairman is regarded as one of supreme importance, second only to that of mayor.

The Language Problem

The true problem of Montreal is the confrontation between the English and French languages.[16] Until recently, English always appeared to have the upper hand. The reasons for this are basically as follows: Quebec's economy was always in the hands of Anglophones and they set the tone; the English-speakers possessed higher cultural standards, endowing the English language with a "positive" image, while French had a "negative" image; the French vernacular was of a low quality and bore a greater resemblance to a dialect (known as "Joual");[17] and English is the language of the majority in the Canadian federation (and of the neighboring United States). However, during the 1960s, there was a general awakening in Quebec,[18] commonly called the "Quiet Revolution," which led to a fierce conflict within the Canadian federation. Because this chapter does not intend to examine the Quebec problem as a whole, suffice it to say that in Montreal the conflict finds its expression in efforts to strengthen the status of the French language vis-à-vis English.

The status of the languages in Canada is defined by Section 133 of the Constitution (British North America Act of 1867) as follows:

> Either the English or the French language may be used by any person in the Debates of the House of the Parliament of Canada and of the Houses of the Legislature of Quebec; and both those languages shall be used in the respective records and Journals of those Houses; and either of those languages may be used by any person or in any Pleading or Process in or issuing from any Court of Canada established under this Act, and in or from all or any of the Courts of Quebec.
>
> The Acts of the Parliament of Canada and of the Legislature of Quebec shall be printed and published in both those languages.

In his famous study, *The Law of Languages in Canada*, Claude Armand Sheppard writes:

> The effect of Section 133 of the B.N.A. Act was to make the French language official through the Dominion. This section, in fact, gave protection, albeit restricted, to two linguistic minorities: the French in Canada and the English in Quebec. . . . However the real scope of Section 133 is very limited and does not guarantee the full equality of French and English.[19]

The protection is confined to limited spheres: Parliament, legislation, and the law courts. While these areas are significant in themselves, what is lacking is the citizen's right to employ the language in contacts with the administration and its departments. Above all, there is the problem of education. Sheppard writes, with justice, that the Constitution ". . . is totally unsatisfactory and does not even provide minimum guarantee to either the French or to the English minorities in Canada. Such linguistic rights as exist in Canada will be found to be based generally on custom, practical consideration, or political expediency."

Canada's federal law on official languages was enacted in 1968 and has been in force since 1969. It defines English and French as the official languages for everything connected with the Canadian Parliament and administration. The law requires bilingual publication of all federal documents and established the post of commissioner for languages, a senior official charged with implementing the regulations detailed in the law. At the same time, it should be noted that this law did not bring about a genuine revolution in Canada. Bilingualism in the sense of equal language rights is far from complete throughout the country, and the problems it engenders have only been partially solved.

In addition to this federal law, provincial legislation plays an important role in Quebec. Law No. 22 of 1974, which had aroused considerable controversy before and after its enactment, was replaced in 1977 by a new Official Language Act, Law No. 101, which is somewhat more liberal in some minor aspects to the minority language (English) than was the former, but on the whole is actually less so. The new law allows more exceptions, that is, more cases in which English may be used instead of French as the language of instruction. Otherwise, and basically, French is clearly defined in the new law, just as in the previous one, as the official language of the province of Quebec. It is called "the language of the instruction, the administration, business and trade and of the labour field." The law relates to the private employment sector as much as to the official bureaucracy. Generally, French must be used in all internal communications by the public administration. French is the language of instruction for all, excepting those one of whose parents has been educated in English.

It is too early to assess the working of the new law, particularly whether it has been instrumental in establishing a new equilibrium between the two language groups. It should however be added that the constitutionality of some of the provisions of the new law have already been challenged successfully in Quebec courts.

Montreal municipal regulations with regard to bilingualism are more liberal than those of the province. This has to be seen within the framework of the bilingual character of the city, which is more evident than that of any other place in the province of Quebec or of the province as a whole.

What are Montreal's municipal regulations regarding bilingualism?[20] In general, the provincial Official Language Act protects the public majority and minority alike by stipulating that "every person may address the public administration in French or in English, as he chooses." The Charter of Montreal includes a number of sections providing for bilingual arrangements and more such provisions appear in by-laws. For example:

- The Montreal Municipality specifies 417 different categories of officials; 416 of them must have "the ability to speak and write both languages."
- Under Section 734 of the Charter, the Municipality appoints two accountants, one English-speaking and the other French-speaking.
- Taxi-driver licenses may be issued only to "bilingual" candidates.
- The same requirement applies to policemen and guides.

Thus, from an administrative viewpoint, writes Sheppard, "Montreal is a completely bilingual metropolis." All minutes of the Municipal Council are recorded in both languages, and there is an indexing office that systematically translates all notices, by-laws, tenders, internal instructions, circulars, and so on. From this point of view, bilingualism does not appear to be a problem in Montreal, and in practice it operates quite well. However, there continues to be great tension over the access to English-language schools of the children of non-Anglophone immigrants and the status of French as the language within the private sector of the economy.

Educational Problems

The Montreal school system had, since it came into existence in 1845, been based upon a language-cum-religion separation between Catholic-French schools and Protestant-English schools. Later, some private English-speaking Catholic schools (named "Irish schools"), as well as several French-speaking Protestant schools, were founded. Lately, however, with the accelerated secularization of both language groups, the church has lost its place in the educational system, which is now based solely on the language criterion.

The problem involves mainly children of immigrants to the city—above all, Italians—who wish to attend English-speaking schools. In the past, according to Jeremy Boissevain, there have been cases in which Italian immigrants went so far as to convert so that their children could attend English-speaking schools.[21] This option is no longer open. The purpose of the new law is clearly to eliminate the phenomenon of immigrants choosing English schools and thereby joining the minority English-speaking group. However, there still exist legal and administrative loopholes, so that the system is far from totally separated.

Both sides are unsatisfied with the present situation, which accounts for the fact that the question of education has become the central language issue in Montreal. For a city that absorbs a substantial number of immigrants, the subject is an important one, as it might deter potential newcomers.[22] Yet in view of the program of Frenchification now being applied in Montreal and Quebec, this problem has yet to find its solution. Similarly, the use of French in the private sector of the economy far from satisfies the Francophones, whereas the English-speaking people are much worried by present policies. It will be interesting to see to what extent the legal provisions will change behavioral patterns in the years to come.

BELFAST

Demographical Data

Belfast is a reflection of the whole of Northern Ireland, and in effect no such thing as a Belfast problem exists independently of the Northern Ireland

(Ulster) problem. Belfast is the largest city in Northern Ireland. The most recent census (1971) showed the city to have a population of 362,000 out of a total population of 1,536,000 (or 23.6 percent). Its new boundaries as a county council (1973), however, contain 414,600 inhabitants, out of a total of 1,547,000 (26.7 percent), while nearly 600,000 persons live in the Belfast metropolitan area as of the mid-1970s (nearly 40 percent of the total population of Northern Ireland).

The fact that Northern Ireland's two next largest cities—Newtonabbey, with 58,000 inhabitants (itself a part of the Belfast metropolitan area), and Londonderry, with 52,000 inhabitants—each contains only about one seventh of Belfast's population gives added significance to whatever happens in that city. In addition, Belfast is the capital of Northern Ireland and its sole important industrial and commercial center.

Nevertheless, Belfast's population in the mid-1970s is close to what it was at the beginning of the century. In the course of 20 years, since the 1951 census, the city lost about one fifth of its inhabitants. Until the onset of the present disturbances in 1968 the reasons for this were mainly economic, but more recently there were major political and security considerations. Many Belfast residents preferred to move to the outskirts (Newtonabbey, founded in the northern section of Belfast's metropolitan region after World War II, has absorbed most of these) or to immigrate to England or overseas.

In its division along religious lines, Belfast's population does not differ from that of the other towns of Northern Ireland. However, while the ratio between the Protestants and Catholics in Ulster has long been 2:1 (with the Catholics fluctuating between 34 and 35 percent), the composition of the population in the various towns is far from uniform. In 1971, Catholics constituted slightly more than one quarter of the population of Belfast (27.5 percent), which is a significant decline from over one third at the beginning of the nineteenth century, but a slight increase over their 23 percent during the 1920s. As a rule, Catholics constitute a minority (sometimes an insignificant one) in northern and eastern Ulster near Belfast (County Antrim and County Down) and sometimes a large majority in the towns of western Ulster (for example, in Londonderry they make up two thirds of the population).

In Belfast itself, the Catholics are not spread uniformly through the city. On the contrary, the trend for years has been toward the concentration of Catholic residents in some district areas and of Protestants in others. This division along religious lines has become even sharper since the outbreak of the recent disturbances. Whether because of the destruction of their homes or because of bomb threats, most of the Catholic families have moved out of areas with a Protestant majority, and vice versa. The result is an increased concentration of each of the communities and geographical polarization.

If we define as "the Catholic city" those streets (or, more precisely, blocks) where the population is between 90 and 100 percent Catholic (in effect, most such streets are 100 percent Catholic), then the percentage of Belfast's Catholics living in "the Catholic city" rose from 56 percent in 1969 to 70 percent in 1972. Similarly, the percentage of Protestants living in "the Protestant city" increased from 69 to 78 percent.[23] Moreover, the measure of concentration was largest in working-class districts, while middle-class districts—which also experienced a trend toward segregation—did display some measure of continuing coexistence. Nevertheless, it should be emphasized that in spite of this mutual segregation, members of the two communities were not completely segregated, even though living in mixed districts involved considerable risks for those concerned.

The Essence of the Conflict

The assumption behind the above data is that the division between Catholics and Protestants is the dominant one in Northern Ireland. Indeed, inhabitants themselves perceive the matter in this way, and official publications (including statistics) also regard the Ulster conflict as interdenominational.

Historically, religion has been at the heart of the conflict in Ireland since the Reformation. But as far back as the seventeenth century, the antagonism between the English conquerors and the local population clearly shows that dimensions of nationalism, race, political loyalties, relations between the colonial rulers and their subjects, and economic stratification have also been part of the conflict. Nonetheless, the significance of religious adherence as a principal component of personal and group identity has not diminished. Every person in Northern Ireland is considered to belong to one of the two communities—Protestant or Catholic—and even though this identification is not recognized by law, no one remains unaffected by it. From this point of view, anyone who is not a Catholic is considered a Protestant (for example, Jews living in Northern Ireland are regarded as part of the Protestant camp).

No one today can seriously contend that the conflict is a theological one. Yet the people of Ulster are supposed to be members of two distinct religious groups with opposing political interests, aims, and aspirations. More broadly, they belong to two separate social entities whose places of residence are also distinctly separate.[24] The religious division has remained the strongest means of identifying the two communities, and it is for this reason that Northern Ireland is best considered as a biconfessional society.[25] At the very least, the denominational division constitutes the basis for other loyalties, as well as for political organization. However, the opposing camps do not view the conflict from the same perspective: The Catholics tend to view it in national terms, whereas the Protestants perceive it primarily in religious terms.[26]

It would clearly be a distortion to view the conflict in purely religious terms, as it does not relate to differences of doctrine.[27] Religion here is a basic component that defines two groups in which denominational identities coincide with political loyalties. The situation in Northern Ireland is clearly one of "reinforcing divisions," whereby two groups of a political and religious nature are segregated from one another by more than geography. According to one school of thought, Northern Ireland can be described as a pluralistic society that lacks a fundamental consensus, so that one group, by necessity, dominates the other.[28]

Least of all can the Northern Ireland conflict be regarded as one between classes, as class allegiances are less important than other identities for both Catholics and Protestants.[29] On political, constitutional, and economic issues, the citizens of Northern Ireland adopt views in accordance with their religious, not class, allegiance.[30] During the relatively quiet period in the 1960s, it was found that religion in Belfast had an influence six times greater than class.[31] At the same time, economic considerations played a significant role in stepping up the Northern Ireland conflict and remain important to this day. Far from strengthening class solidarity, however, economic factors have heightened the rivalry between members of the two opposing religious camps who belong to the same socioeconomic class.

Although many attempts have been made over the years to blur the national character of the conflict, there can be no doubt that it hinges on problems of political loyalties and national aspirations. It can be stated quite simply that the principal political issue in Northern Ireland is the nature of the political framework itself. A sizable minority repudiates the legitimacy of the existing constitutional framework and the premises of all governmental practices. What is involved is not the adversary politics between government and opposition usual in modern democratic states. Rather, conflict is essentially one of national identity, with the majority (about three quarters of the population) regarding itself as British and favoring links with the United Kingdom and the minority (about one quarter of the population) considering itself Irish, committing its personal and political loyalties to a neighboring state (Eire), and demanding the dissolution of Northern Ireland's union with the United Kingdom and its reunion with the Irish Republic.

Thus political and religious loyalties are interwoven in Northern Ireland. Almost all those who regard themselves as British and who favor a continuation of the constitutional link are Protestants (primarily Anglicans and Presbyterians), and practically all those who favor union with Eire are Catholics. When these two loyalties do not coincide, the religious affiliation is decisive. A sharp-eyed, sophisticated observer goes so far as to formulate the matter as follows: "In Northern Ireland, a person who adheres to the policies of the other religion—a Protestant Nationalist or Catholic Unionist—is for most practical purposes deemed, by the group he left, to have gone over to the other religion: which of course is worse than having been born in it."[32]

The Roots of the Conflict

Northern Ireland, then, is a country or province whose population is divided, with an overwhelming majority of close to three quarters facing a minority that does not much exceed a quarter. As far as representation is concerned, the majority has found no difficulty in preserving its hegemony by democratic means (one man, one vote) in the province as a whole, as well as in most of the towns (where the ratio is similar). Only a few towns have a Catholic majority (the most prominent being Londonderry), and there the Protestants have in the past taken advantage of their political status to gerrymander themselves a majority in the municipal councils. Some refer to a regime based on such a ratio as "a dictatorship of the majority," questioning whether it can be a genuine democracy;[33] others have called it "Protestant supremacy."[34]

In the existing state of affairs, the minority has no chance of achieving its aims. It can, of course, forfeit them, and for some time this is what the Catholics appeared to have done. But since 1969, many members of the Catholic minority have reached the conclusion that the only way to escape their status as a perpetual minority is to smash the existing structure, that is, challenge the very legitimacy of the political and constitutional framework and remove the border dividing Ulster's "six counties" from the rest of Ireland. From this conclusion, it was only a short step for a few Catholics to consider the use of force. Given the sense of deep division between the two camps and the irreconcilability of national aims, this move is really not so surprising, considering that violence is an old tradition in Northern Ireland.

On the other hand, there have been continuous efforts to overcome this profound cleavage and to soften the effects of the virtually unrestricted hegemony of the majority. The main aim of these efforts has been to weaken the opposition of the minority and reconcile it to recognizing the legitimacy of the regime. To date, however, no true progress has been made in this direction. After a long series of attempts to find a middle road between the rights of the majority and the demands of the minority, the Ulster problem is still at a total impasse.

For more than ten years nobody has been able to solve the problem, and no one is even capable of proposing a solution with any chance of success. Many observers are convinced that the problem is quite insoluble, although only a few are prepared to admit that publicly. One observer has written: "Many people speak of solving the political problem of Northern Ireland, but few attempt to state what the problem is. The reason is simple. The problem is that there is no solution—or, at least, not of the kind customary in those fortunate sections of the Anglo-American world where the regime rests upon a consensus."[35]

The Exercise of Power in Northern Ireland

From an historical perspective, the exercise of power in Northern Ireland is based upon the Westminster model (the politics of zero-sum game, or winner takes all), even though that system basically is oblivious to the existence of such social cleavages that seriously restrict the possibility of free play in a parliamentary democracy.

Genuine efforts have occasionally been made to accommodate the particular character and composition of Northern Ireland's society. One example was the early introduction of proportional representation by virtue of the STV (single transferable vote) system (also known as the Irish PR system) in the Government of Ireland Act. This system was abolished with regard to municipal elections in 1922 and with regard to elections to the provincial parliament in 1929.[36] The speed with which it was discarded by a government whose stable majority was unassailable, because it rested upon the solid support of the Unionist Party, highlighted the Protestants' reluctance to consider the needs of the Catholics, particularly in view of the fact that the Protestants' stable hegemony could never have been endangered even by proportional representation. Only some 50 years later, under the impact of severe and violent upheavals, was proportional representation reintroduced as a method of conciliating the minority in order to lay foundations for renewed cooperation between the majority and the minority.

One of the many paradoxes characterizing the present situation in Northern Ireland is that, although it is widely held (even by the British government) that the conflict in the province could be resolved by means of constitutional and structural arrangements, if only the correct formula were found, this view is not carried over into the sphere of municipal government. Yet objective observers (including the official Cameron Commission, appointed in 1969 to investigate the disturbances in Northern Ireland) clearly pointed to the crude and open discriminatory practices prevailing in cities with a large Catholic population (particularly in Londonderry, Armagh, Newry, Omagh, Fermanagh, and Dungannon) and concluded that this disparity in representation was one of the principal causes of the Catholics' sense of deprivation and discrimination.[37]

This criticism, and others of the same nature, led at first to appropriate measures, such as the dissolution of the Londonderry Municipality. But based as it was on a fundamental change in the rationale of local government, the far-reaching reform carried out in the early 1970s, including the drastic changes of the structure, functions, and geographic jurisdiction of all the municipal bodies in Northern Ireland, can be attributed only in very small measure to the lessons of the conflict. This reform practically abolished independent local government entirely, by transferring most of its powers to the regional branches of the central government. The true significance of this change was the conclusion that the intercommunal conflict does not allow for local independence or, for that matter, even democratic civil rule.

It is only with reference to these developments in municipal organization that one can comprehend the recent course of events in Northern Ireland as a whole, and in Belfast in particular.

Social and Economic Segregation

Before the municipal authorities in Northern Ireland were reorganized, their structure and organization resembled those of England and Wales, with two extremely important exceptions: (1) what are known in Britain as "the protective services" (police, civil defense, and fire brigades) were not entrusted to the local authorities (with the exception of Belfast's control of its own fire brigade); and (2) most educational matters were left to the central government of Northern Ireland at Stormont.[38] Within the customary two-tier structure of local authority, Belfast was considered an autonomous county-borough; and as in English county-boroughs, its council possessed the powers and fulfilled the functions of both a county council and a borough council. Prior to 1969, a similar status had been accorded to Londonderry's Municipality, but as mentioned, this was dissolved when severe upheavals paralyzed the activities of the council. (Unlike Belfast, in Londonderry the religious composition of the council was in inverse proportion to that of the population because of the unrestricted gerrymandering practiced there.) The municipal government was replaced by the Londonderry Development Commission, which, its name notwithstanding, was in fact an appointed municipal council whose principal task was the provision of existing services, not development.

From 1935 to the late 1960s, Belfast did not witness any serious intercommunal incidents. During World War II, the city was heavily bombed, principally because of its shipyards.[39] The city gained economic impetus from wartime and postwar industrial activity. At the same time, Belfast, together with the whole of Northern Ireland, remained at the bottom of the economic scale among the regions of the United Kingdom. The unemployment rate in the province was consistently three times as high as the British average, the average income was the lowest in the United Kingdom, and the area contained the largest number of households in the lower-income groups.[40] These circumstances did not heighten intercommunal class solidarity; on the contrary, the rivalry for jobs sharpened the conflict between Protestant and Catholic workers. In Belfast, for example, the larger industries—above all, the shipyards—were in practice closed to Catholics.

Another focus of tension, perhaps the most important, was housing. During the 1950s, most of the population of Belfast lived in housing considered substandard. In the early 1960s, an official estimate cited the need for 60,000 new housing units, 18,000 of which were to replace housing totally unfit for occupation. A memorandum of Northern Ireland's Ministry of Health and Local Government stated that the annual target should be 2,000 new housing units, and the situation was aggravated by the Belfast Municipality's failure to fulfill this goal. (As in Britain, Northern Ireland's local authorities were the agents of public housing—corporation or council housing—constructing the units and subsequently retaining ownership.) In 1956, the local authorities were also charged with slum clearance. Thus whoever controlled the local authorities in Northern Ireland held the power to allocate housing and, to a lesser degree, the means of livelihood to their supporters.

The Protestant mayors in the western regions of Northern Ireland, where there is a Catholic majority (Londonderry, Dungannon, and so on), used their powers to the advantage of their co-religionists. There can be no doubt that this fact set off the first disturbances in 1968–69. In Belfast, however, the Municipality hardly constructed any housing at all. Although Belfast had pioneered public housing before the war,[41] from 1945 until the end of the 1960s it built less than 300 housing units annually.[42] And, although Belfast's Municipality had been the object of severe charges of corruption and favoritism in housing as far back as the 1920s, allegations of flagrant religious discrimination (in favor of the Protestants) were on the whole feeble and unconvincing. On the contrary, some claim that the Catholics benefited from a degree of preference, because at least one of the aims of moving the population into new housing projects was to eliminate the hotbeds of extremism that flourished in the principal slums (the main source of recruits for the illegal armed groups).

In at least some of the new housing projects, the Municipality attempted to advance intercommunal integration by allocating them to a mixed population or by establishing enclaves of one community within a project populated largely by the other.[43] But when the disturbances erupted in the late 1960s, it soon became evident that the mixed quarters were the scenes of confrontation whenever tension rose, and neighborly relations could not overcome these outbursts. As a result, the communities were later segregated and new housing was allocated in proportion to each community's relative size and in proximity to existing communal concentrations.

There was also an element of electoral geography in this scheme. Mixed quarters could undermine the Protestants' absolute majority; hence, it was preferable to concentrate the Catholics in a limited number of constituencies (under the constituency system, an enlarged majority in any one constituency does not increase a group's overall representation).

At the beginning of the present disturbances, the favoritism toward Protestants in the western part of the province and the crying neglect of housing needs in Belfast and elsewhere led the Northern Ireland government to remove housing from the jurisdiction of the local authorities. Early in 1972, a Housing Executive was established in Belfast. By that time, the city's housing situation had deteriorated sharply because of the need to find alternative housing for people whose homes had been damaged in the hostilities or who had been subjected to intimidation in their neighborhoods.[44] The migration stemming from acts of hostility segregated Belfast's two communities even further. Working-class districts in particular witnessed the spontaneous exchange of populations.

Coinciding with the premeditated segregation in the new housing projects, most of Belfast's residential quarters underwent a three-stage process, as follows: Stage 1 included quarters with a large Catholic majority, mixed quarters, and quarters with a large Protestant majority. Stage 2 saw quarters with a large Catholic majority and quarters with a large Protestant majority. And stage 3 included exclusively Catholic quarters and exclusively Protestant quarters.

This growing segregation in housing led to the isolation of the two communities in other spheres as well. There was a tendency, particularly among Catholics, to find employment in their area of residence or close by. When violence is on the increase, people also prefer to do their shopping close to their homes. Segregation in education, self-imposed by the Catholics, has always been almost complete, at least on the primary school level and to a large extent at the secondary level as well. Catholic children attend either nonmaintained schools, completely controlled by the Church, or "voluntary maintained" schools, under predominant church control. The Protestants attend the controlled schools, which were part of the municipal educational system and now of the Education and Library Boards. As a result of the exchange of populations, segregation has become absolute, with no Catholic children remaining in the general, controlled primary schools.

Most of the single-community quarters, that is, the "Catholic city" and the "Protestant city," were progressively and in varying degrees taken over by the respective undergrounds, ostensibly in order to protect them from the opposing side; but at times these movements constituted themselves as quasi-governments. Intermittently over the course of the years, for example, the IRA (Irish Republican Army) was in de facto control of Belfast's Catholic quarters. This fact clearly restricted the activities of the civil authorities and the police. When the British army was called into Northern Ireland, even it was reluctant to enter the more violent of the exclusively Catholic quarters, so that the security forces found it increasingly difficult to maintain responsibility for iaw and order in them. In most places, the underground organizations of both communities also operate by means of front organizations, which, if not accorded official status, are at least not prohibited.

In addition to these organizations functioning in circumscribed areas, geographically there are general organizations operating throughout Northern Ireland, such as the Ulster Protestant Volunteers. At various times, particularly when tension was high, these or similar groups assumed government and municipal functions, thereby undermining the authority of the Municipality. (This is true for both Catholics and Protestants.) Thus the Municipality of Belfast ceased to function effectively, or functioned only sporadically, in vital but restricted spheres of activity. This development, together with the accelerated planning activity in Northern Ireland (above all as a result of the establishment of the Housing Executive) and the preparations for far-reaching reforms in the structure of local government throughout the United Kingdom, explains the extensive changes in Northern Ireland's municipal administration.

REORGANIZATION OF THE LOCAL AUTHORITIES

Since the mid-1960s, Northern Ireland has been intensely involved in preparing regional plans, physical as well as economic. This planning effort parallels similar endeavors in other parts of the United Kingdom. The first plan for the Belfast area was published in 1963 and contained a number of elements that remain guidelines to this day.[45] These include the need to determine the physical boundaries for the Belfast conurbation, which are to coincide with the city's urban area. Such boundaries were to constitute a line beyond which the city was not to expand. A number of towns in the Belfast region were earmarked to house residents forced or attracted beyond the city's boundaries and to absorb people from other parts of Northern Ireland who would otherwise relocate in Belfast.

From 1963 on, considerable planning work had been completed. A development plan was published for the Belfast urban area,[46] as well as for the city center.[47] These plans were worked out by private planning offices and adopted by the Municipality in 1970; but as a city-planning officer was appointed only in 1969, they were never implemented. The severe disturbances that erupted at the time put a stop to all work on reconstructing the city, and housing plans were disrupted because of the mass flight from one housing project to the safety of another. In the end, all work on housing was taken out of the hands of the Municipality (as has been described), leaving no trace of all these plans.

In the course of less than five years, Northern Ireland experienced four different forms of government. The semiautonomous Stormont regime, with an elected parliament and government (as introduced by the Government of Ireland Act of 1920), came to an end in March 1972, when the relatively moderate government of Northern Ireland objected to the British government taking over responsibility for law and order in the province. There ensued two years of "direct rule," without a local parliament or government and with the province's entire governmental apparatus functioning directly under a special minister for Northern Ireland affairs in the British cabinet.

Early in 1974, there was a renewed attempt at self-government under a new constitution that gave both the legislative body (called the Northern Ireland Assembly) and the government (renamed the Northern Ireland Executive) limited powers. But they still remained subject to the minister for Northern Ireland affairs in the British cabinet, while the British Parliament was empowered to legislate for Northern Ireland. The major innovation in this arrangement was the principle of "power sharing," whereby the provincial government was understood to represent "government by consent," that is, it would not remain content with a majority in the legislature but would rest upon "wider public support." The concrete expression of this principle was having representatives of more than one community in the cabinet. Elections to the provincial parliament were conducted under the Irish proportional system (STV). However, this arrangement survived less than four months, because the Protestant majority rejected it out of hand. At the same time, those Catholics who consented to serve in the cabinet were suspected by their co-religionists of being collaborators. The government fell in the wake of a two-week nonviolent general strike by the militant Protestant trade union that threatened to paralyze the province's economy. The strike was launched in protest to what the union regarded as a British attempt to achieve peace in Ireland by means of a puppet government in which the Protestant majority would not be properly represented.

After the failure of this short-lived attempt, "direct rule" was restored. In 1975, the Northern Ireland Assembly, chosen by proportional elections, was constituted in the hope that it (rather than the London government) would find a solution. The elections for the assembly reflected a substantial readiness for compromises on the part of the Catholics (even though their extremists boycotted the vote), but the Protestants displayed a hardening of attitudes. The attempt ended in total failure early in 1976, which indicated that, at least for the time being, there was no hope of finding a form of government for Northern Ireland that would be agreeable to both communities.

These developments are the background necessary to understand the far-reaching reorganization of local government in Northern Ireland. Even though discussion of governmental reforms began prior to the recent upheavals, as things turned out they fitted in well with the flow of events. The main reform was that services were removed from the sphere of the existing political party system and, to a large extent, from the control of the local authorities. As early as the mid-1960s, the government of Northern Ireland announced that it intended to initiate discussion of reforms in local government. Before the beginning of the disturbances, in December 1967, a first White Paper was published on *The Reshaping of Local Government: Statement of Aims.*[48] After extensive discussions, it was followed by a further publication: *The Reshaping of Local Government: Further Proposals.*[49] These proposals were based upon the need for modernization and efficiency, the abolition of miniscule local authorities and of the various categories of authorities, and the institution of two tiers of government (provincial and local administrations) in place of the three-tier structure (a county council between these two levels).

The government also published a document entitled *Administrative Structure of Health and Personal Services in Northern Ireland (Green Paper)*, whose principal recommendations were to centralize health and welfare services, that is, transfer jurisdiction over them to agencies of the central provincial government and, as far as possible, coordinate their spheres of operation.

Finally, in October 1969, the government announced the establishment of a central Housing Executive, which was to affect every future reorganization of local government for at least two reasons. The politicians of most local authorities displayed a keen interest in housing, while the newly founded Housing Executive required the assurance of a proper foundation for all services related to water supply, sewage, roads, licensing, local planning, and land availability.

It was against the background of these developments that the Macrory Commission was established, and its report, *Review Body on Local Government in Northern Ireland, 1970,*[50] laid the foundations for a general reorganization. Next came a plan for overall reorganization to increase efficiency and streamline services, while taking into account the existing state of affairs in Northern Ireland.

If the provincial government is included, Northern Ireland's administrative structure is theoretically two-tier, but in fact it is a three-tier network. The top tier is the central government of the province (known, for short, as Stormont), which is now entrusted with many of the powers and responsibilities that were previously in the hands of various local authorities. Some of its duties are carried out exclusively by the central authority, and some services are operated by area boards. These boards in effect constitute the third tier between the central authority and the local bodies. In the educational sphere, for example, there are five School and Library Boards (one for the Belfast region and four for the other regions). In the sphere of social services, the province is divided into four regions (Belfast being included in the eastern region), each with a board responsible to the appropriate department of the provincial government. The board members are nominated largely by the central department, with a minority appointed by the local authorities within the region.

The greatest change has taken place in the bottom tier of administration. The historical "six counties" of Ulster have been totally abolished. (They retain only geographical significance, for location on maps, although the mail also continues to follow the old divisions.) The 73 local authorities were also abolished, as was the distinction between urban and rural councils. These were replaced by 26 districts, one of which is Belfast (a completely urban district), whose boundaries were somewhat extended in the process. (A special demarcation board delineated the boundaries of all the districts regardless of previous boundaries.) Each district contains a central town or township (after which the entire district is named) and the surrounding countryside. With the exception of Belfast, whose population exceeds 400,000 inhabitants, the population of the other districts varies from 90,000 (Londonderry) to 13,000 (Moyle), with the majority of districts numbering between 30,000 and 75,000 inhabitants. This reconstitution put an end to the extreme differences in size among the old authorities.

Each district has its council, which is elected by the customary proportional method (STV), but possesses very limited powers, as welfare services have been entrusted to the provincial government and the area boards. The following list of tasks and responsibilities allocated to the district councils speaks for itself: environmental health; removal of garbage and cleaning of public places; parks and empty lots; cemeteries; sport, culture, art, and entertainment; building laws; licensing certain businesses for safety regulations; gas supply; markets and slaughterhouses; anchorages (other than ports); preventing nuisances (noise, pollution). In addition, the councils appoint representatives to central authorities, such as the Housing Executive, the Northern Ireland Fire Brigade Authority, and regional Health and Education Boards. The district councils are also entitled to be consulted on other services (urban planning, water supply, sewage) and are empowered to engage in transportation.

Thus the functions and powers of the district councils in Northern Ireland are far more limited than is customary in other parts of the United Kingdom after the recent reorganization.[51]

Belfast Following the Reforms

The Macrory Commission was aware that this reorganization would strike a blow at the "urban sensibilities" of Belfast (and of Londonderry) by transferring most functions and powers to the province's central government. As the report says, "before this indignation reaches boiling point," it would be well to recall that the old ceremonial privileges would not be affected (indeed, the chairman of the Belfast District Council was permitted to retain the title of Lord Mayor and to wear the appropriate ceremonial garb); that the District Council would play a prominent role in providing services; and that a similar fate had befallen the two largest cities in Scotland, Glasgow and Edinburgh.

In addition to the services transferred to departments of the provincial government, however, the city was also deprived of jurisdiction over other services. For example, the city's transport company was handed over to the Regional Transport Authority (1973), of which it constitutes a special subunit. Belfast's fire brigade was swallowed up by the Northern Ireland Fire Brigade

Authority. The generation, distribution, and supply of electricity (previously entrusted to four independent companies) were turned over to a single corporation, the Northern Ireland Electric Corporation (1973). Water supply and sewage now come under the Water Services Department of the province's Environmental Department, and their operational direction has also been entrusted to four regions (Belfast being the center of one of them in 1973). The Belfast district's Gas Department continues to produce and supply gas.

The physical planning of Belfast, like that of the other towns, is in the hands of the provincial government's Department of Housing, Local Government and Planning, which is empowered to publish any masterplan or other plans in the form of a binding decree. It is required to do no more than conduct consultations and hear objections from the general public. The District Council as such has an extremely minor influence upon this procedure.

Local urban government, as known in Britain over the course of a century, was in effect eliminated in Northern Ireland (and Scotland) in the early 1970s. The functions and powers left to the elected local authorities are minimal. It has been said in Belfast (and in Northern Ireland as a whole) that the elected authorities have been left with nothing but the parks and the cemeteries, and if the killing goes on at the present rate, all the parks will have to be converted into cemeteries.

Since the return to direct rule (1974) and as a result of the reorganization described above, there can be no doubt that the standard, efficiency, probity, and impartiality of services have improved beyond recognition. This improvement developed despite the fact that the security situation remained difficult and placed severe obstacles in the path of the reorganization policy. Almost all outside observers, as well as unbiased Belfast residents (however few these may be) are unanimous in admitting that there is no comparison between the present administration—which is bureaucratic and bears no parliamentary responsibility (that is, fundamentally undemocratic)—and the previous form of government. Special stress should be placed on the professional aspect of administering services, which is no longer subject to partisan considerations. In addition, the reorganization put an end (for the time being, at least) to the occasional complaints of discrimination that were voiced earlier. Neither the District Council (the city's council) nor the central authorities and their regional branches are now under attack in the context of the intercommunal conflict.

Conclusions

Belfast's experience makes it possible to draw a number of conclusions about cities whose population is divided into two unequal groups with opposing national and religious allegiances:

1. When the division of the population into different camps extends

throughout the country (region, province, and so forth), there is nothing unique about the situation within the city, and the conflict there is not substantially different from that prevailing in the country as a whole.

2. As long as the numerical discrepancy between majority and minority is fairly significant, changes in the numerical ratio between the two camps have no decisive influence on the character and vigor of the confrontation. Even when its dominant status is assured, the majority still displays opposition to any program (such as constitutional manipulation) that may prejudice its firm hegemony.

3. Segregation into separate residential quarters, whether forcibly or by free choice, may eliminate friction at the level of "neighborly relations" and affect the tactics employed in the intercommunal confrontation; but it is not a significant palliative at the level of the conflict itself and not a means of resolving the conflict.

4. Even though the majority takes advantage of its numerical superiority in local government to play according to the "democratic" rules of the game, it is aware of the highly flexible limits, which, if crossed, might risk its hegemony.

5. National and religious animosities not only overshadow class differences but to a large extent heighten rivalries between members of the same class (primarily workers).

6. Efficiency of public and municipal services, including the preservation of law and order, and the impartiality and fairness toward the minority, including its political representation, have a fairly marginal impact on the severity of the intercommunal confrontation. By themselves, they may temporarily alleviate the conflict but are incapable of resolving it. From this point of view, there is some difference between working-class people, whose view is only slightly moderated by these matters, and the middle classes, who are affected to a greater extent.

7. The demand for equality of municipal and social services is not related to the measure of representation.

THE THREE CITIES AND JERUSALEM

Each of the three cities discussed in this chapter is sui generis. Other ethnically heterogeneous cities in the Western world might have been discussed, but what these three have in common is not only that the conflicts based on their internal cleavages have recently been much aggravated and escalated in intensity but that they are basically parts of national or ethnonational confrontations. The specifics of these conflicts differ from each other vastly in almost all their parameters. So do those applying to the case of Jerusalem, which has not been discussed here, but does belong to the same category.

Whether the city serves primarily as a stage to effect the intercommunal conflict (Belfast, Montreal), or whether it becomes really its (main) target (Brussels), the conflict in and about the city always constitutes one facet of the wider, countrywide one. At the same time, the cities are of special significance for material, political, and symbolical reasons. This is even more so in Jerusalem, a city holy to three religions; and the millennia-old struggle over the city may not yet be over. Moreover, Jerusalem's more recent history includes times of violence, of division with a fighting line splitting it into two halves and disputed claims of sovereignty. At least since the reunification of the city in 1967, Jerusalem has not been the most conspicuous element of the Israel-Arab conflict, in contradistinction to the three cities in which the respective national struggles culminate.

Even with less emotional involvements prevailing in the three cities discussed here than in Jerusalem, their respective conflicts have hardly been contained; and although a good many solutions have been advanced for each, satisfying ones with some chances of finality seem so far to have been beyond human ingenuity. On the other hand, and in spite of the temporary containment of the Jerusalem conflict, the zero-sum attitude prevailing as a rule in the Middle East may yet call in question a settlement reached on all other issues outstanding between Israel and the Arabs.

The severity and intractability of these conflicts stem in each of the three cases from the fact that these are primarily ethnic or national conflicts, even though they are usually presented as language (Brussels, Montreal) or religious (Belfast) struggles. They all revolve around basic loyalties; and, more specifically, they have to do with the delicate equilibrium, or rather the tenuous imbalance, between some overarching or all-embracing national integration or solidarity and between ethnic (partial) separatism or particularism. But in Jerusalem no such dilemma exists, as no feelings of common national loyalty, such as may have encompassed diverse ethnic groups elsewhere, have existed there.

Under uncommonly auspicious circumstances or particularly well-contrived dispositions, such as fastidious adherence to equal treatment and strict observance of minority rights, such an intercommunal situation may be contained for a while and a mutually acceptable status quo be worked out. The sum of such experiences seems to point, however, to the ineluctable conclusion that even the most equitable and judicious of municipal services and administration cannot rectify what are in the eyes of one side, if not of both, involved, the political, that is, "national" wrongs. But because the determining factor in ordinary zero-sum situations at any given point in time is which of the conflicting sides basically supports the status quo and which is pressing for change, in what are conceived to be existential struggles, purely administrative considerations yield to the politics of power and prestige.

Even if it were possible—and in most cases it is not—to separate physically two rival communities in a city, or rather divide the city in order to solve problems on a level of personal convenience, such solutions are unacceptable, at least in principle, if only for symbolic, and perhaps ritual, reasons. This is particularly so if the city, as these all are, is also the capital of the country (or the province), because of the special significance that this entails. Paradoxically, and often at a great price, the very contentiousness serves as a unifying factor for the city in its physiognomical dimension.

The case of Belgium is the most obvious in this respect. The location of Brussels and the composition of its inhabitants function as major impediments that prevent the total separation of the two language sectors: None can quite do without the city.

Elsewhere the city's position is not quite so essential as a unifying center, even though both Montreal and Belfast are not only the major conurbations but the economic and cultural centers of their respective provinces. But the particularities of each of these two ought to be stressed. In Montreal the French are resolute to modify the existing language situation and all its legal and behavioral ramifications, and by augmenting the language rights of the majority at least meet their major grievance. The minority claims that the city as a whole will be affected adversely in this way; but a majority apparently concedes that any more far-reaching change by way of a separation of the province, by whatever precise constitutional formula, would be detrimental for the community at large.

In the case of Belfast, the full Irish solution of the Ulster problem would radically alter the city's status and fortune. Dublin would become the political and cultural center (much more so than it is even now) for the Irish-Catholic minority, which would join the majority in Ireland, while Belfast would be reduced to the status of a minor center for the non-Catholics and non-nationalists.

In all these cases the political (nonviolent) solution sought after is one in which the wolf will be satisfied and the sheep remain unmolested. In Jerusalem unity and communal coexistence are as vital and the geopolitical situation is as complex as elsewhere, but it is because of the unique international aspects and the diametrically conflicting claims of sovereignty that, so far at least, no mutually acceptable solution has been forthcoming. To meet the contingencies and peculiarities of this very special case, as yet nonexistent and unconceived arrangements will have to be devised.

Beyond the historical burden and the claims of rival interests and privileges of far and near states and people and churches, Jerusalem like the other cities is a living city with people of its own with their needs and rights. After everything is done to meet the diverse and conflicting demands of so many adversaries and full consideration is given so as not to prejudice the proper rights of all concerned, the wishes of the city's inhabitants, or at least of their majority, should not come least when the future of the city is at stake.

NOTES

1. These particular heterogeneous cities in the West have been chosen for research because of the salience and variety of their respective problems and the availability of pertinent information.

2. The year in which the law was enacted that laid down the linguistic boundary between the French-speaking and Flemish-speaking areas and that made the boundary permanent, not, as in the past, dependent on the results of the population census.

3. Jean-Charles Bonenfant, "Les études de la Commission royale d'enquête sur le bilinguisme et le biculturalisme," *Canadian Journal of Political Science* 5 (1972): 449.

4. Indeed, the Canadians refuse to concede any parallel between situations in the two cities. See Claude-Armand Sheppard, *Inventaire critique des droits linguistiques au Québec,* vol. 1 (Quebec: L'Editeur Official du Quebec, 1973), p. 63. According to his contention, there is no danger of the French being assimilated by the English in Montreal (while such a danger does exist for the Flemings in Brussels). However, Sheppard points out the danger of immigrants to Montreal joining the English-speaking group.

5. Robert Senelle, *The Belgian Constitution-Commentary* (Brussels: Ministry of Foreign Affairs, External Trade and Cooperation in Development, 1974).

6. This is, in effect, the heart of the conflict. See the Flemish case as presented in Manu Ruys, *Die Flamen* (Tielt: Lannoo, 1974), pp. 189–91. For highly interesting geographical studies documenting the process of Brussels' expansion, see E. Van Hecke, "La délimitation de l'agglomération morphologique bruxelloise à partir des données statistiques," *Courrier Helodomadaire du CRISP,* C.H. 623, November 30, 1973; and Bernard Jouret, *Définition spatiale du phénomène urbain bruxellois* (Brussels: Editions de l'Université de Bruxelles, 1972).

7. Van Hecke, ibid; p. 18. The Inner Center is a statistical area only, circumscribed by the Inner City Ring. Brussels-City is the historical core, which has today only minimal political and administrative significance. It is one of the 19 boroughs (or communes) that make up Brussels-Capital and has given its name to it.

8. "L'évolution linguistique et politique du Brabant (1)," *Courrier Helodomadaire du CRISP,* C.H. 466-67, January 16, 1970, p. 11. No unchallanged language data have been produced since the 1947 census.

9. In addition to the six "boroughs of special facilities" on the outskirts of Brussels, however, a number of boroughs in the two language regions—these called "linguistic frontier boroughs"—have been given special language facilities for the purpose of protecting their minority rights. The same applies to boroughs where German is spoken in the French-speaking eastern part of the country.

10. *Le Monde* ("Courrier de Belgique"), January 29, 1976.

11. M. de Vroede, *The Flemish Movement in Belgium* (Antwerp: Kultuurraad voor Vlaanderen, 1975), p. 91.

12. "Rapport politique presente par Francois Perin, Ministre de la Reforme des Institutions," March 15, 1976.

13. But the metropolitan area of Toronto has roughly as many inhabitants as that of Montreal.

14. Dale Posgate and Kenneth McRoberts, *Quebec: Social Change and Political Crisis* (Toronto: McClelland and Stewart, 1976), pp. 48–49.

15. Ibid., p. 49. The sources are *Census of Canada* for 1961 and 1971, and N. Lacoste, *Les Characteristiques sociales de la population du Grand Montréal* (Montreal, 1958), p. 77.

16. See Guy Bourassa, *Les relations ethniques dans la vie politique montrealaise* (Ottawa, Documents de la Commission royale d'enquete sur le bilingualisme et le biculturalisme, 1971). This book is a most important study of the ethnic problem in Montreal. On the language problem proper, see John R. Muller, ed., *Quebec Language Policies, Background and Response* (Quebec, 1977).

17. It is interesting to note that a similar problem existed in Flanders, where the existing Flemish dialects, considered as inferior, underwent a process of unification until they were transformed into genuine Dutch. Indeed, the Flemings now call their tongue "Dutch," or rather "Nederlands," instead of "Vlaams."

18. Though there are French-speaking minorities in other provinces, primarily Ontario, New Brunswick, Manitoba, and Nova Scotia. However, the 1971 census disclosed that outside Quebec only 45 percent of the Canadians of French origin use French regularly at home.

19. Claude Armand Sheppard, "The Law of Languages in Canada," *Studies of the Royal Commission on Bilingualism and Biculturalism*, no. 10 (Ottawa, 1971), p. 68. Section 133 is now the sole section of the constitution that can be amended only with the approval of the British Parliament in London. The rest of the constitution may be amended inside Canada itself.

20. There are a number of good studies on this question, including Sheppard, *The Law of Languages in Canada*, and especially the many studies prepared for the Gendron Committee and its multivolume report, *Rapport de la Commission d'enquête sur la situation de la langue française et sur les droits linguistiques au Québec* (Quebec: Government of Quebec, 1972). See particularly the volume *La situation de la langue française au Québec*. See also *Proceedings of the Sixth International Symposium on Comparative Law: Bilingualism and the Law* (Ottawa, 1969).

21. Jeremy Boissevain, "The Italians of Montreal," *Studies of the Royal Commission on Bilingualism and Biculturalism*, no. 7 (Ottawa, 1970), p. 40.

22. The Official Language Act requires that a minimum of French be taught in English-speaking schools, and that English be taught as the second language in French-speaking schools. The curriculum must ensure that pupils receiving their instruction in English acquire a knowledge of spoken and written French, and the minister of education may adopt the necessary measures to that effect. The minister of education must also take the necessary measures to ensure instruction in English as a second language to pupils whose language of instruction is French.

23. F. W. Boal, R. C. Murray, and M. A. Poole, "Belfast: The Urban Encapsulation of a National Conflict," in *Urban Ethnic Conflict: A Comparative Perspective*, ed. Susan E. Clarke and Jeffrey L. Obler (Chapel Hill, North Carolina: University of North Carolina, Institute of Research in Social Science).

24. John Magee, *Northern Ireland: Crisis and Conflict* (London: Routledge & Kegan Paul, 1974), p. 5.

25. Richard Rose, *Governing Without Consensus* (London: Faber, 1971), p. 248.

26. Ibid., p. 216.

27. Arend Lijphart, "Review Article: The Northern Ireland Problem: Cases, Theories, and Solutions," *British Journal of Political Science* 5 (1975): 87.

28. M. G. Smith, "Some Developments in the Analytic Framework of Pluralism," *Pluralism in Africa*, ed. Leo Kuper and M. S. Smith (Berkeley: University of California Press, 1969), p. 88.

29. Rose, *Governing Without Consensus*, p. 389. With regard to Belfast, this is extensively and thoroughly documented by I. Budge and C. O'Leary, *Belfast: Approach to Crisis* (London: Macmillan, 1973), pp. 228–48.

30. Rose, *Governing Without Consensus,* p. 381.

31. Budge and O'Leary, *Belfast*, pp. 221–24.

32. Conor Cruise O'Brien, *States of Ireland*, 2d ed. (London: Panther, 1974), p. 16, note 2.

33. Lijphart, "Review Article," p. 94.

34. D. P. Barritt and C. F. Carter, *The Northern Ireland Problem*, 2d ed. (London: Oxford University Press, 1972), p. 157. Other scholars, however, conclude that the degree of democracy in Belfast is greater than in many towns in England and the United States and that Belfast should be regarded as "an unstable democracy," not as "a stable oligarchy" (Budge and O'Leary, *Belfast*, pp. 197–98).

35. R. Rose, *Northern Ireland: Time of Choice* (Washington, D. C., American Enterprise Institute for Public Policy Research, 1976), p. 139.

36. N. Mansergh, *The Government of Northern Ireland* (London: Allen & Unwin, 1936), passim; Cornelius O'Leary, "Ireland: The North and the South," in *Adversary Politics and Electoral Reform*, ed. S. E. Finer (London: Anthony Wigram, 1975), pp. 175–83.

37. *Disturbances in Northern Ireland: Report of the Cameron Commission*, Cmd. 532 (Belfast: HMSO, 1969).

38. R. J. Lawrence, *The Government of Northern Ireland* (Oxford: Clarendon Press, 1965), pp. 25–26, passim.

39. During the 1950s, the Harland and Wolff shipyards were the largest in the world. They employed over 10 percent of the industrial workers in Northern Ireland and almost 20 percent of those in Belfast.

40. M. A. Busteed, *Northern Ireland* (London: Oxford University Press, 1974), pp. 7, 8.

41. Budge and O'Leary, *Belfast*, p. 145.

42. Busteed, *Northern Ireland*, p. 36.

43. Budge and O'Leary, *Belfast*, p. 164.

44. The Northern Ireland Community Relations Commission, *Flight*, CRCOP, 5, September 1971; *Intimidation in Housing*, Research Paper, February 1974.

45. *The Belfast Regional Survey and Plan 1962*, The Matthew Report, Cmd. 451 (Belfast: HMSO, 1963).

46. *Belfast Urban Area Plan*, vol. 1, *Main Report* (1969).

47. *Belfast Central Area: A Report to the Belfast Corporation* (1969).

48. Belfast, Cmd. 517, HMSO, 1967.

49. Belfast, Cmd. 534, HMSO, 1969.

50. Belfast, Cmd. 546, HMSO, 1970.

51. A detailed description of the present administrative structure in Northern Ireland, including the provincial administration and that of the local authorities, can be found in Northern Ireland Office, *Northern Ireland, Discussion Paper 3, Government of Northern Ireland: A Society Divided* (London: HMSO, 1975).

8

LOCAL GOVERNMENT FOR HETEROGENEOUS POPULATIONS: SOME OPTIONS FOR JERUSALEM

Daniel J. Elazar

The Middle East has a long tradition of religiously and ethnically heterogeneous populations living side by side, so intermixed within particular localities that simple territorial separation has not been a means for them to maintain their particular ways of life. This is especially true within the region's cities that have been settled on a high density basis, further intensifying the intermixing.

Even the system of separate quarters or neighborhoods has been more a fiction than reality in many cases. While certain neighborhoods have been predominantly inhabited by one group or another, rarely have they been exclusively so. Thus the famous four quarters of the Old City of Jerusalem are formally labeled Jewish, Christian, Muslim, and Armenian; and, indeed, each group had (and now has) its central node in "its" quarter, but in reality members of every group lived in every quarter. In fact, since the Jews came to constitute the largest single group in old Jerusalem by the mid-nineteenth century and an absolute majority shortly thereafter, they were to be found in numbers in every quarter of the city. So, too, in predominantly Muslim cities, Muslims lived in the minority quarters as well.

At the same time, and perhaps because of this, the Middle East also has had a tradition of managing heterogeneity both to sustain the separate groups

This study was prepared under the auspices of the Jerusalem Institute for Federal Studies. I wish to express my gratitude to Naamah Kelman, then of the JIFS staff, for her aid in its preparation.

and to keep the peace. The management of heterogeneity in the Middle East has been most successful under imperial regimes that have been able to keep the peace or strongly encourage local authorities to do so in order to preserve good relations with the imperial rulers. The great problem of the contemporary Middle East is how to develop similar techniques and institutions for managing heterogeneity within a democratic framework.

This chapter presents the results of a survey of local arrangements for managing heterogeneity under democratic politics; the survey was conducted to bring the relevant experiences of other cities to bear on the Jerusalem case. Underlying this survey is the assumption that the Jerusalem Municipality has a central concern with long-range planning that will accommodate the several non-Jewish minorities within a city with a substantial Jewish majority, essentially within the present municipal boundaries. A second concern is to accommodate the different factions within the Jewish majority. The alternatives surveyed in this report are all potentially useful in dealing with both concerns.

The sum and substance of this investigation is that the city of Jerusalem has done as well or better than any other local government in dealing with its heterogeneous population in a democratic fashion, by judiciously adapting older devices common in its region to new conditions in a way that is fully consonant with democratic expectations. While there may indeed be institutional devices that Jerusalem could profitably adapt from other cities, there is much that Jerusalem can teach the rest of the world.

The Jerusalem authorities have managed to achieve what they have in an ad hoc manner, without seeking formally to institutionalize the steps they have taken in the past 13 years. This effort to adopt patterns customary in the Middle East and give the adaptations the force of custom rather than law is notably consonant with the region's general approach to many problems. It is also a useful way to deal with the ambivalences of the city's non-Jewish minorities, who have strong primary loyalties to Jerusalem yet want to maintain their respective ways of life as separate communities. They are willing to cooperate quietly with the authorities but are not willing to acknowledge fully their status as citizens of a united city under Israeli jurisdiction.

The city authorities have sought to bend the law where necessary to avoid having to take formal steps that might prove troublesome to accommodate the diverse populations of the city. While this is particularly noticeable in the reunited sections, it has also been traditionally true in other parts of the city, for example, the ultra-Orthodox Jewish neighborhoods. Many of the most successful efforts are not easily visible because they have no formal expression.

No doubt this is true of other cities as well. It is possible that those involved in managing the diversity of Jerusalem could learn something from Brussels or Singapore or other cities, but the learning would not involve any new overall approach.

Jerusalem's authorities have developed an indigenous approach that has been working. However, while the ad hoc method has worked for now, some day it probably will have to be systematized and institutionalized, in part, if not substantially, if only to provide a sufficient framework to ensure democratic decision making. There is an understandable reluctance to hasten that day because of the conflicts that any such attempt would provoke in the current political climate. Moreover, there is a strong tradition in the Middle East of subtle rather than formal institutionalization in precisely such circumstances as a means of avoiding open conflict.

Nevertheless, it is well for all parties concerned to have some idea of the lines along which formal institutionalization has the ability to manage heterogeneous populations. Some of the alternatives examined have become conventional arrangements within a particular country. Indeed, this may be their best recommendation. While we have not avoided seeking the unusual, we have tried not to err by ignoring what is routine and conventional elsewhere but which would be new in the Israeli context.[1]

It should be noted that relatively little attention has been paid by political scientists and urbanologists to the problem of managing mixed populations within a local setting. Most studies have focused on extralocal units of government, that is, state-local systems or national forms of accommodation. This indicates that perhaps the successful local arrangements of heterogeneous populations have grown unplanned, products of a period of evolution. If this is indeed the case, it is of great significance to Jerusalem, whose city authorities have opted for such a course of action.

The alternatives for local government of heterogeneous populations will be examined under five headings:

- City-county arrangements (standard counties, contractual relationships, consolidational city-counties, federated counties)
- Federated municipalities (borough systems, federations of existing municipalities)
- Neighborhood-district programs
- Functional programs (special districts, interlocal arrangements, functional arms of general-purpose governments, functional service entities)
- Extralocal models (consociational arrangements, federacies)

All of the arrangements explored here are solutions developed in response to the specific problems of particular localities. Hence, the prospect of simply duplicating or transplanting any one of them is limited. However, if the examples are viewed as models or options open to local governments, they may well be a source of or stimulus for ideas that can be applied to Jerusalem.

Each of the five arrangements can be viewed from one of two perspectives and its application structured accordingly. The conventional wisdom suggests that they are designed to foster either centralization or decentralization.

Thus the amalgamation or merging of several local units to create a unified county or metropolitan government is usually understood as a form of centralization, while the development of neighborhood districts is usually seen as decentralization. A different perspective (or different continuum), namely, noncentralization, can be more valuable for understanding the same structures and institutions and used to design the relationships that animate them.

Noncentralization implies the distribution of real powers among several centers that must negotiate cooperative arrangements with each other in order to achieve common goals. A noncentralized system contains both a strong general government and strong constituent units, each legally and practically accountable to each other and their citizens. A noncentralized system differs from a decentralized one in that the overarching government can be quite strong indeed, provided that the units over which it exercises authority are also protected constitutionally in some significant way.

The government can decentralize as well. A noncentralized system differs from a centralized one in that, no matter how strong the overlapping government may be, there are constitutional limits imposed on the extent to which it can constitutionally concentrate governmental power and functions. In sum, noncentralization requires the development of partnership in the sharing of power, even where powers are divided as clearly as possible.[2]

Both of these divergent theories struggle with the same questions of accommodating interest groups and equitable and efficient distribution of services. For Jerusalem, noncentralization appears to be the most feasible approach. Centralization is not likely to accommodate its heterogeneous population, and simple decentralization is not likely to satisfy either the aspirations of minorities or the requisites of proper administration.

CITY-COUNTY ARRANGEMENTS

A county in the modern sense (as distinct from premodern English or European forms) is a unit of local government established by state authority to provide services to a specific territory.[3] Where counties exist, they are generally organized on a "wall-to-wall" basis, that is, the entire territory is divided into counties so that no area is left uncovered by county government, whether or not it has municipal government. Within each county there are likely to exist urban and rural areas, incorporated and unincorporated. Cities, towns, or boroughs may incorporate under state law as municipalities, but they remain within the borders of their county and under its jurisdiction in those functional areas assigned to it. This basic structure is a well-established Anglo-American phenomenon that allows various government bodies to have separate and distinct jurisdiction in the same territory.

The entire area within the county's jurisdiction receives the range of services provided by the county government except where special arrangements are made for municipalities to provide their own parallel services. Thus, in the case of law enforcement, a country may agree to provide its services to the unincorporated areas while the cities within it maintain their own internal police forces. In only a few cases does a county formally relinquish jurisdiction; it reserves the right to send in the sheriff at any time, but the tacit agreement not to do so is rarely, if ever, violated except, perhaps, in situations of "hot pursuit."

Even in counties where such special arrangements are common, the county governments provide at least minimum services for all those under their jurisdiction, regardless of where they live. Thus a county will usually be responsible for public welfare services throughout its area. The key to standard city-county arrangements ("city" for the purposes here refers to incorporated municipalities) is that, although cooperation does exist, the provision of services does not necessitate cooperative arrangements. Each county has its own functions to perform and has the necessary powers to do so because the city-county system is based on a division of functions.

The Standard County (U.S. Model)

The traditional U.S. system of counties[4] facilitates the provision of services by the county equally to all units within its jurisdiction under the conditions outlined above. Unincorporated areas rely upon the county, plus special districts and arrangements (see below), to provide services, while incorporated areas provide most of their own services. Special districts are designed and created for explicit service functions and their boundaries are drawn to reflect the appropriate service-shed. This quality makes the special district a highly flexible instrument of local government. The standard county system allows for an almost unlimited number of such service districts within its territory; the single limitation is the human capacity to absorb and staff so many diverse governmental authorities.

With the trend toward metropolitanization and the expansion of settlement beyond established city limits came the development of new city-county relationships. Inasmuch as this study is not concerned with suburbanization, per se, the following analysis is confined to the impact on structure, institutions, and relationships for governing of populations spread among a number of adjoining municipal jurisdictions.

The growth of urban settlement has brought in its wake increased power for both municipal and county governments as the tasks of both have been expanded. Counties, once basically instrumentalities for rural government, have gained more and more responsibility in urban affairs and, increasingly, "home rule" (a U.S. term for local autonomy). Many states now make provision in state law for a county's residents to adopt a county charter (basic law) conferring municipal powers. This is usually done without in any way limiting or interfering with the municipal powers of the cities within the county. Home rule counties provide comprehensive services for their residents as a matter of course. In such cases, city-county relationship also undergoes a change. Three major new forms of relationship have developed.

Contractual Arrangements

Contractual arrangements[5] involve a county government providing services to municipalities within its boundaries on a contractual basis with each city choosing the "package of services" it desires from the complete set offered. The Lakewood plan in California is an example of this type of relationship. Los Angeles County (population 7 million) can provide by contract up to 58 different services to cities within its borders. The state legislature has created a uniform local retail and use tax, making it financially attractive for municipalities to incorporate to maintain their local autonomy and, at the same time, contract with the county for services rather than providing them unilaterally, usually at a greater cost.

The program, set up in 1954, presently involves 74 cities, each purchasing from 4 to 42 of the available services at a uniform rate. Newer cities purchase more at the onset and tend to contract for less as they develop their own local administration. Significantly, Los Angeles County also includes the city of Los Angeles, with more than 2.8 million people, which provides most city services independently. The flexibility of the Lakewood plan enables the county to accommodate a wide range of city sizes and develop whichever city-county relationship is appropriate to each municipality, even as it continues to serve as the overarching government in certain spheres for all its residents.

Consolidation

In a few cases, particularly where suburbanization has occurred in a single county, the central city and the county have been consolidated into a new political entity.[6] In the nineteenth century, when unlimited city growth was a desideratum, unincorporated territory in the county, and often other municipalities as well, were usually annexed by the central city, sometimes with provisions for neighborhood control of schools, police, zoning, and public assistance on a ward basis, precisely because of the heterogeneous immigrant populations then to be found in large U.S. cities. Today, the process is often reversed; and in such cases, a broadened county government authority supersedes that of the city, which is absorbed within it. The previously unincorporated areas fall under the new government while the previously incorporated areas within the county may choose to remain independent or become part of the new arrangement.

Those incorporated areas that choose to remain independent maintain their separate identities and provide their own municipal services but transfer their traditional relationship with the county to the new entity. In some cases, they contract with the consolidated city-county for new metropolitan services as well. Under such consolidation arrangements, three categories of services are developed: traditional county services, which are provided for the entire jurisdiction; municipal services, which are provided for the urbanized area of the county only, either by the new government or by the separate municipalities that remain outside of it; and metropolitan services, which are the province of the new authority.

A prime example of county consolidation can be found in Nashville-Davidson County, Tennessee, whose residents voted for consolidation in 1961.[7] In its case, four suburbs and municipalities voted to remain outside the new Davidson County merger. They remain independent but linked to the new entity in the manner described above. At the same time, consolidation extended the city services formerly provided by Nashville for its residents alone to the unincorporated urbanized areas surrounding the former central city.

Federated County Systems

Under the federated county system[8] a two-plane system is formed. The existing county administration is expanded in scope and powers to become the overarching government, and the existing municipalities become the constituent units of government in the new federation. All preserve their respective integrities and basic functions; but some functions are transferred to the county in toto and others are made joint tasks, thereby establishing a cooperative relationship between the two planes. In the federated county, the constituent units need not be symmetrical in size or character, although the arrangement is not feasible where there is one single city of overwhelming size plus many smaller ones.

Dade County, Florida, is a prime example of the federated county. It consists of 27 municipalities (including Miami and Miami Beach), 19 having fewer than 10,000 people, covering a 2,054-square-mile area. Miami, the largest city, has a population of 334,000 or approximately 25 percent of the county's 1.3 million total. In this instance, the county became the new areawide government, with the municipalities functioning like states in a federal union. The new area provides transportation, police, fire, health, welfare, and recreation services. Other functions remain in the hands of the municipalities. The division of functions between the metropolitan council and the municipalities involves a certain level of formal cooperation. For example, rather than all phases of a function being assigned to one plane or another, both planes share in its implementation. Thus refuse collection is the responsibility of the municipality but refuse disposal is a "metro" task.

Were a county system to be instituted in Israel, there appears to be no reason why the present city of Jerusalem could not be reconstituted as a county possessing full municipal powers, with the possibility of territories within it incorporating as municipalities in the manner of the standard U.S. county described above. The links between the county and the municipalities within it could be hierarchical, federal, contractual, or some combination of all three with special districts utilized to fill any service area gaps.

FEDERATED MUNICIPALITIES

A federated municipality[9] differs from a federated county system in that, rather than relying upon an existing structure, a new two-tier structure is created to serve a particular metropolitan region. The new structure takes one of two forms: Either both tiers are designed anew from scratch (the borough system) or the existing municipalities become units of a newly formed overarching government. Although some functions are clearly allocated to one tier or another, increasingly the key to successful relationships in the federated municipalities is cooperation, formal and informal, both in allocation of power and provision of services.

The Borough System

The London borough system is the oldest and perhaps the classic example of two-tier local government organization.[10] Under its recent reconstitution, the total area under the jurisdiction of the Greater London Council (GLC) was enlarged, the boroughs were restructured, and their boundaries redrawn. Today the GLC encompasses 32 boroughs. London is too large to serve as a model for Jerusalem; several of the boroughs are larger than the total population of Jerusalem.

Much the same can be said of the Toronto (Canada) plan, which has become the most cited post-World War II model of a metropolitan borough system. In Canada, the decisions to federate or otherwise reorganize cities and metropolitan regions are made by the provincial government and forced upon the local authorities (unlike such changes in the United States, which require local voter approval). Toronto was restructured twice, first in 1953, when a metropolitan city was constituted embracing 13 local authorities, and then again in 1967, when the 13 were combined into 6 boroughs. The federated city covers 241 square miles and contains 1.2 million inhabitants. The largest borough is slightly smaller than Jerusalem. Each borough elects a mayor and city council who deal with the municipal responsibilities allocated to it. The elected borough officials are also members of the Metro Council.

The Metro Council has been successful primarily in the field of major construction of public works: new roads, schools, highways, subways, and water and sewage facilities. Its accomplishments are the result of the low pressure politics of the metropolis, weak involvement of interest groups in areawide issues, lack of factioning into parties on the Metro Council, and general cooperation with the Metro Chairman. Even though its population is relatively heterogeneous ethnically, it may be politically too homogeneous to be a reliable model for Jerusalem.

A number of European examples of municipalities are divided into boroughs where a strong central government has divided the city symmetrically for different purposes. Paris, for example, is divided geographically and symmetrically into arrondissements. Only recently were the city's voters granted the right to elect a mayor for the city as a whole. Other examples are capital cities that are controlled directly by central government for reasons of state.

Federation of Existing Municipalities

Under this arrangement, the new entity is created by union of the existing municipalities.[11] In Winnipeg, Manitoba (Canada), where the population of 500,000 more closely approximates that of Jerusalem, the cities retained their historical boundaries while the Manitoban provincial government created a new metro government to embrace them. These efforts were the result of city bureaucrats' pressures for a presumably more efficient and equitable areawide service administrative body. Since then, it should be noted, Greater Winnipeg has been consolidated and redivided into boroughs. Nevertheless, the original arrangement bears consideration if only because one of the major cities in the metro region, St. Boniface, is French, while all the rest are English-speaking and ethnically mixed.

Israel has provided its own examples of highly successful local federated arrangements, which, while developed for a different scale, deserve consideration. The country's kibbutzim and moshavim are federated into regional councils, some of which have been suburbanized in recent years and have become urban service authorities. In addition to the standard governmental functions, the regional councils have major economic responsibilities as operating arms of the settlements federated within them. This economic role adds to their strength.

At the same time, their record in dealing with heterogeneity is distinctly mixed. Almost without exception, the regional councils are organized around either kibbutzim or moshavim of the same political trend or camp. The two forms of settlement are rarely mixed within the same regional council, nor is it common to build regional councils around settlements of different political movements. This is most particularly a reflection of the intimacy of the connections among kibbutzim, which make it difficult for them to work with settlements outside their own world. Nevertheless, there is one regional council in the Galilee that federates Arab villages and Jewish moshavim. In short, regional councils have done rather well in handling country-of-origin differences among Jews but poorly in handling ideological heterogeneity. They have come to be constituted on a movement basis only, even at the expense of scale factors and geographic neatness.[12]

For Jerusalem's purposes, the federated city arrangements have less utility than the various county-based arrangements because they require more symmetry of size and population among units. Jerusalem's situation, on the other hand, is essentially asymmetrical in the size of its neighborhoods, in the composition of their populations, and in their fundamental interests. Jerusalem, as a "county" embracing "cities" of different sizes, shapes, and scope, would do better to accommodate these asymmetries.

NEIGHBORHOOD-DISTRICT PROGRAMS

Neighborhood-district programs[13] developed primarily in the larger U.S. cities during the 1960s to accommodate black, Puerto Rican, and some white ethnic demands for more control over the services provided them. As such, it is one of the few options discussed in this chapter that was specifically developed to deal with local government accommodation of ethnic heterogeneity.

The most outstanding characteristic of neighborhood-district programs is the fact that the municipal government, which is usually a large one, uses them simply to provide a subgovernmental framework through which to respond to citizens' demands. The municipal government itself remains intact, undergoing no basic structural change. Instead, a neighborhood office is set up to manage special-interest programs, to mobilize support for them, and/or to absorb public responses. Funds, personnel, and/or technical assistance are made available to local groups to initiate projects within their neighborhood appropriate to their specific needs.

During the 1960s, U.S. experiments in community development and citizen participation did initiate some interesting programs for various neighborhood organizations. Relying on funding from the federal government and subsidies from private foundations, community groups could determine and design programs to meet some educational, housing, and health needs, to mention just three fields. For example, housing in some sections of New York City's Harlem was redeveloped through efforts of its residents. New building complexes went up and old ones were rehabilitated with the community board deciding on questions of location. The board also contracted for builders and other related technicians. In other cities, block associations hired private police protection and organized neighborhood clean-up campaigns. In

Philadelphia, one community group developed an intricate system of health maintenance programs and services. These examples reflect the dissatisfaction of city dwellers with municipal services.

The level of success of these programs was dependent upon some combination of the amount of federal funding available and the political sophistication of the community in securing and utilizing those funds, either with their own people or by hiring professionals to work for them. Success was also determined by the flexibility of the government framework in allowing local residents to initiate and explore ideas. In that sense the concept's strength was also its weakness. The less permanent and defined the local arrangement was, the more it was left to citizens to perpetuate these programs. Almost inevitably, the lifespan of the activity was short. By 1973, even the political science literature had come to consider this alternative outmoded. Political and social scientists have shifted their attention toward more structured programs for accommodating pluralistic needs in urban settings.

Considering the aforementioned results, this alternative does not seem to be too promising. Neighborhood institutions of this kind are at the mercy of city hall for help in any form. In the United States, this help usually was provided only after outside intervention, particularly on the part of the federal government. In essence, all concerned were responding to the new ideology and not to a new balance of power embodied in legally defined governmental structures that could also protect and ensure the needs of its citizens. While the neighborhood-district system sought to involve minorities, the lack of a permanent governmental structure with real powers of its own thwarted the system as a permanent form of accommodation.

Israel has a wide range of informal mechanisms that take cognizance of the religious and cultural needs of special neighborhoods, but until recently it has not pursued this kind of formal decentralization. The neighborhood committees common in certain of the larger cities, especially Jerusalem, are advisory rather than operational bodies.

FUNCTIONAL PROGRAMS

Under this arrangement, existing general-purpose local governments are augmented by special-purpose authorities and departments and/or formal intergovernmental arrangements. In effect, new administrations are created as part of the overall network of local government. In some cases, these are designed to serve specific geographic areas—neighborhoods within the city (or cities) plus areas outside. In others, they are designed to serve particular populations within the common whole. Unlike the neighborhood-district approach, where the formal arrangements are undefined, these programs are highly specialized.

Special functional authorities serve as adjunct organizations to already established local governments, either as units within the government or as a unit that overlaps several local governments. The boundaries of a park district may be coterminous with the county borders; a school board may be fully independent while limited to each city; a water district may cut across general government boundaries. A functional authority may serve a distinct geographic area tailored to the function itself, for example, a sewage treatment district defined by topography and drainage network; a distinct ethnic group, regardless of the geographic location of its members, for example, the Montreal system of Catholic and Protestant school boards; or a particular population based upon geographic area, for example, a metropolitan airport district that can tax all potential users within its jurisdiction regardless of the municipality in which they reside.[14] The following specific arrangements can be detailed.

Special Districts That Function as Independent Governments

This form of special functional authority[15] is an entirely separate local governmental unit that has the power to tax and spend, make and execute policy, and administer programs. It is built around a particular "service-shed" or "user-shed," that is, the area or population appropriate for the function involved. Local funding may come from a general tax on all those within the district boundaries or from users alone. Thus the special district may overlap several general-purpose governments to accommodate its users or properly fill a particular function. Special districts are generally governed by a small council elected by residents or users that appoints a professional manager with substantial powers.

Interlocal Networks of Accommodation

In some cases, rather than separate or overarching authorities, municipalities have developed special intermunicipal links[16] to handle common tasks such as planning, law enforcement, and joint services. These links range from long-term formal contracts to informal but regular contacts. While they are generally confined to singular metropolitan regions, they can even cross state boundaries when the patterns of urbanization call for it. These networks guarantee the juridical and functional independence of a substantial number of municipalities working together to provide regional programs. They also encourage outside governments (national or state) to rely on interlocal decision-making mechanisms rather than intervene directly into local affairs on the grounds that local jurisdictions are too limited to handle them.

Long-Term Contractual Links

Long-term contractual links[17] are favored in cases such as Brussels, Melbourne, and Sydney, where the urbanized area actually consists of a significant number of independent municipalities of roughly equal size and the city bearing the common name, if there is one, is actually no larger or more politically significant than any of the others.

In the major metropolitan areas of Australia, the cities whose names are attached to the entire area remain within their original boundaries, much as the city of London remains confined to its original square miles, and are surrounded by newer municipalities. Like Brussels, and unlike London, they have remained independent and linked, if at all, through functional arrangements. The major difference is that the state governments in Australia intervene directly in municipal affairs in a multitude of ways. This is principally because of the country's population configuration, whereby some 90 percent of the total population in most states live within one metropolitan area. The state government must function as a kind of metropolitan authority, or it will have little to do.[18]

Council of Governments (COGs)

The COG[19] is a U.S. device stimulated by the federal government in an effort to achieve metropolitan areawide coordination for planning services with areawide implications and handling the distribution of federal grants for those services. All COGs are technically voluntary bodies; however, because they are required by Congress to make local governments in metropolitan areas eligible for certain federal aid programs, they have become universal in the United States.

COGs have taken two forms. In most cases they are constituted by representatives from each local government within the metropolitan areas. The resultant council is principally a forum for the expression of municipal interests and the hammering out of a joint policy to meet federal requirements—a kind of United Nations General Assembly or arena for bargaining rather than decision making.

Metropolitan Pueblo, Colorado (pop. 118,000), has developed a second option. Because the entire metropolitan population is contained within the county, either within the city of Pueblo (pop. 97,000) or closely adjacent to it, its COG was organized to include all seven members of the city council, all three county commissioners, and one representative from each of the two independent school districts and the water district serving the metropolitan area. As a result, any decision taken in the COG reflects the will of the constituent governments and is then ratified automatically by each body sitting separately. The Pueblo COG has established four planning bodies subordinate to it, one for physical planning and development, one for planning technical services, one for industrial development, and one for health and welfare planning. They develop plans and monitor programs within the community in the name of COG, thus providing an additional measure of areawide planning and coordination.

Israel has developed its own system of federations of cities for specific purposes (fire protection, education, drainage, and sewage disposal), which function on the same principle. Such federations are constituted as permanent separate authorities whose governing bodies are constituted by representatives of the constituent units and whose budgets are contributed by those units on a shared basis.[20]

Regional Planning Commission

These are bodies that serve multiple local jurisdictions, often crossing state and even national boundaries, principally to develop lines for comprehensive regional physical planning and economic development. They are generally not governments in the formal sense, but rather arms of some government—state, provincial, or local. They may even be only semipublic if local interest demands that kind of arrangement.

The Regio Basiliensis, serving the Basel region (which includes the cantons of northwestern Switzerland, southern Alsace in France, and southwestern Baden-Wurtenburg in Germany), is one of the best examples of how a semipublic regional planning commission has succeeded in serving metropolitan regional interests cutting across three national states and a substantial number of federated states (in Germany and Switzerland).[21]

Backed by the canton of Baselstadt and the great industrial firms of Basel, it has dealt with such problems as a work force that commutes across those national boundaries daily, the construction of a Swiss-owned and -operated airport on French territory, the maintenance of a German railroad station on Swiss territory, and many other such problems. It is a major factor in promoting cooperation in the Rhine River Valley. Its success has come precisely because it is a local body rather than an instrument of a state. A similar instrumentality exists in the Geneva area serving Switzerland and France, and more are being developed in other European frontier regions.

Functional Arms of a General-Purpose Government

Services are sometimes provided to heterogeneous populations through specialized functional arms of a general-purpose government in which the various groups are represented. The Montreal school system is a dual one in which two distinct school boards, Catholic and Protestant, administer schools. The citizens choose the school system of their choice and their school taxes are allocated accordingly.[22] (The Jews came under the Protestant system by their own choice, having turned down a possible opportunity to develop a third system many years ago.)

Delhi, the Indian federal capital, has an even more complicated variation of this system, involving private as well as public initiatives. Four separate school systems function in Delhi: the one sponsored by the Delhi government is the Hindi-speaking public school system; the Indian federal government provides a separate school system for its employees' children in which the language of instruction is English, so as to include families of non-Hindi-speaking civil servants and to facilitate a basic stability in the education of children of parents who may be transferred often in the course of their careers; there are schools sponsored by linguistic groups identified with the various states of India (the state of Gujarat maintains a school in Delhi for Gujarathi speakers and the South India Education Society, a semipublic body, for children from the several states where Tamil is spoken); finally, there is a private school system that employs English as a language of instruction. Similar, but less elaborate arrangements prevail in other major cities in India.[23]

In Jerusalem the municipal Department of Education serves the state schools, state religious schools, independent schools, and private schools through subdivisions within the department.

Functional Service Entities

In multilingual areas, separate universities are frequently established to provide instruction in different languages and to serve as focal points for group cultural development (and often as centers for political expression as well, given the nature of things). Brussels, Montreal, and the major cities of South Africa have such arrangements. Likewise, there are separate hospitals in Quebec for French- and English-speakers. In many countries, religious organizations are responsible for providing social services to their constituencies with government support. All these are examples of quasi-public institutional arrangements for the maintenance of heterogeneity with government backing. In such cases the services are formally private but should be considered public nongovernmental or "communal" in character.

Functional service arrangements offer many positive ways of solving the problems indigenous to heterogeneous cities. These programs ensure the interests of various populations and in certain cases supply them with quasi-governmental institutions that serve as vehicles for self-expression and transcend the geographic problem by servicing the target population wherever it may be located.

EXTRALOCAL MODELS

It has already been noted that most discussions of political organization dealing with heterogeneous populations focus on extralocal political contexts. In a few cases, those extralocal arrangements may be relevant to the Jerusalem situation. Three such sets of arrangements are particularly worthy of consideration.

Consociational Arrangements

Consociational arrangements[24] are semiformal, based in every case on many years of evolving accommodation among ethnic, religious, and/or ideological groups, which reflect fundamental commitment to structural pluralism within a particular polity. In the Netherlands and Switzerland, the various ethnoreligious groups have developed ways of preserving their integrities through such devices as percentages of representation on national bodies, separate spheres of influence, and independent organizations supported by government funds.

Consociational arrangements often rely on some of the specific devices described in this chapter, and is as much a matter of attitude as of formal government structure. The Netherlands has reached a remarkable level of stability within its borders through consociational arrangements. Lebanon, on the other hand, once regarded as a model of consociationalism, has been unable to restrain conflict-provoking tendencies—several of them external in origin—although it may be through the consociational model that peace and unity are restored in that country.[25] Austria and Switzerland continue consociationalism and federalism very successfully, and Belgium is moving toward federalism to give its consociational system a firmer foundation.

Observers have noted that in many ways Israel is also built on consociational lines.[26] Jerusalem itself is governed by a regime that has many consociational elements, which can be extended to new groups as appropriate. Consociationalism needs time to develop properly because it requires a basic consensus regarding the virtue or necessity of intergroup power sharing. Jerusalem itself is an example of this. Its consociational form has emerged out of literally centuries of intergroup accommodation and has been sharpened by the policies pursued by the present municipal government. It was the prior existence of tacit consociational arrangements that shaped the approach of the Jerusalem authorities toward East Jerusalem after 1967 and that made this approach a workable one for all parties, even if the Arabs were unwilling to accept a formal role in the city's governance.

Federacies

Federacies,[27] or associated state arrangements, have become increasingly popular in the postwar period. There are presently more than 20 of them. They have been developed principally as a means for asymmetrically linking ethnically or linguistically different territories that are geographically separated. Federacy is based on mutual agreement as reflected in a federal bargain. In this case the essence of the bargain is that both the greater and the lesser partners shall remain substantially separate in their institutions, but that the lesser will be permanently attached to the greater for certain common purposes.

The relationship between Finland and the Aaland Islands is a good example of federacy. The Aaland Islands off the Finnish mainland constitute the smallest of Finland's 12 provinces. The population is Swedish, but for historical reasons they continue to be part of Finland, even though the islanders' language and social and cultural institutions are Swedish. Since 1920, they have been granted autonomy as a province in internal affairs. Special features of the relationship include complete taxing and budgeting power. Unique is their "native locality right." This law affords them the freedom to maintain their own provincial politics, control the ownership of property on the islands (to prevent its alienation from the Aalanders), regulate settlement by outsiders, and be released from the obligation of national military service. The Aalanders continue to speak Swedish and maintain Swedish-language schools.

Consociational arrangements can be used to provide a context for the division of services to heterogeneous populations. They require mutual commitment to a certain level of cooperation based on bargaining and compromise on the part of all parties involved. Federacies, on the other hand, require a minimum of cooperation because there is a geographic basis for separation of functions, power structures, and the allocation of services.

Capital Districts

In a number of countries, the capital districts[28] are set aside with special arrangements for their governance. In some cases they are ruled directly by officers of the capital government but divided intentionally into neighborhoods with administrations of their own. In others (Australia, India, and the United States) they are organized as federal districts. Should the character of the overall settlement between Israel and its neighbors take a certain turn, one of these models may be worth further examination in conjunction with others suggested in the previous pages.

IMPLICATIONS FOR JERUSALEM

As has already been suggested, Jerusalem has done as well as or better than any city in the modern world in the development of means to govern heterogeneous populations. This point deserves emphasis. Jerusalem's success in this regard reflects a combination of intelligent and far-seeing leadership. It judiciously utilized and built upon principles of accommodating ethnic heterogeneity that are indigenous to the Middle East and western Asia. There, civilization is built upon the determined existence of varied ethnoreligious communities that, out of necessity, have had to live together within the same territory and under the same political jurisdiction. In the past, these arrangements rested upon an autocratic base, or more properly, were able to exist only within an overarching autocratic framework. One of the great achievements of the city fathers of Jerusalem has been to transform that framework into a democratic one and to adapt older models to a democratic society.

What has emerged is something that comes closer to consociationalism than to any other form of accommodation. In Jewish Jerusalem, this consociationalism has been substantially institutionalized within the municipal governmental structure. This has been less true for Arab Jerusalem because of the Arabs' reluctance to accept formal institutionalization. Still, it would be a mistake to underestimate the degree to which informal consociational devices have been institutionalized.

Were the situation to be left as it presently stands, that is, were Jerusalem to cease to be a matter of contention in international politics and simply be accepted by one and all as an integral part of Israel in all of its sections, then the present consociational framework would probably become further institutionalized within the municipal structure through the existing electoral processes.

Because this is not the case, it becomes necessary to consider how such institutionalization can be achieved under circumstances that are likely to prevail as as result of any settlement of Israel's conflict with its neighbors. In part, such speculation is idle, as the shape of the larger settlement will do much to determine its expression in relation to Jerusalem. However, it is appropriate to assume that Jerusalem will remain an undivided city and under Israeli control—exclusive for most of the city and perhaps shared for certain sites or parts. This may mean the development of a territorial formulation along with consociational ones. Indeed, the expansion of Jerusalem's boundaries in 1967, which has led to the development of outlying Jewish neighborhoods within the municipal jurisdiction, probably makes such territorial expression necessary for the Jewish population as well as for the Arabs.

Any solutions proposed could probably utilize some combination of several devices and mechanisms discussed in this chapter. For example, Jerusalem could be established as a capital district within Israel; this would give it an organic law of its own, including provisions for extraterritorial status for certain sites or residents within its boundaries. As a capital district, it would become the equivalent of a county within which separate municipalities could be established. Then most municipal services would be provided to the municipalities by the capital district government on a contractual basis, and the municipalities' primary function would be to provide political expression for specific populations or neighborhoods within the larger whole. In addition, various functional authorities could be established to serve those communal needs that are not clearly geographically defined. The council governing the overall district could be elected on an area basis, that is, by dividing the entire jurisdiction into districts and electing all or most council members from them.

A less far-reaching solution could be accommodated within contemporary Israeli law. This already provides that residents of a particular municipality who are not citizens of the state can vote in municipal elections, while municipalities themselves can request the establishment of submunicipal governments for particular neighborhoods. Thus special neighborhoods chosen for their internal uniqueness or outlying character could be given the status of urban quarters (the technical term under Israeli law) and allowed to elect councils of their own while still remaining part of the larger Jerusalem municipality.

Should the political circumstances change, other combinations are also possible, which might emphasize federal and/or confederal structures and relationships. Jerusalem could conceivably be reorganized as a federation of quarters or, in most extreme form, as a confederation of separate cities, united for shared municipal purposes. Few if any Israelis would recommend either of the latter two courses of action, as both would not only involve some ceding of Israeli sovereignty over the united city but would also introduce great complexity that might prove to be a hostile environment.

The point is that many options do exist and that, while it will be necessary to be inventive, the inventions do not have to emerge out of whole cloth, but rather can build upon models that have been tested and found workable.

NOTES

1. These alternatives are treated in the literature through one or more of the following strains of political science thought: structure of governments, public policy, and political behavior. Recent political science literature emphasizes the latter two, stressing different trends depending on what is current and fashionable. Material identifying and examining the actual structure of government is harder to find in the current literature, which has emphasized behavioral policy problems sometimes to the exclusion of such basics.

There are some gaps in this survey. Belgium and Australia are mentioned only briefly. Almost no attention is given to Asian frameworks. This is because of the shortage of published material available and can be corrected only through more extensive research.

2. Daniel J. Elazar, *American Federalism: A View from the States*, 2d ed. (New York: Crowell, 1972); and idem, "Harmonizing Government Organization with the Political Tradition," *Publius* 8, no. 3 (Summer 1978): 49–58.

3. John C. Bollens and Henry J. Schmandt, *The Metropolis: Its People, Politics and Economic Life* (New York: Harper & Row, 1970), pp. 107–13; Clyde F. Snider and Samuel K. Gove, *American State and Local Government* (New York: Appleton-Century-Crofts, 1965), pp. 359–416.

4. Bollens and Schmandt, *The Metropolis.*

5. Ibid., pp. 358–64; Winston Crouch and Beatrice Dinerman, *Southern California Metropolis* (Berkeley: University of California Press, 1963), pp. 201–5; and Richard M. Lion, "Accommodation Par Excellence: The Lakewood Plan," in *Metropolitan Politics: A Reader,* ed. Michael N. Danielson (Boston: Little, Brown, 1966), pp. 272–80.

6. Bollens and Schmandt, *The Metropolis,* pp. 302–7; Daniel F. Grant, "A Comparison of Predictions and Experiences with Nashville Metro," *Urban Affairs Quarterly,* September 1965, pp. 38–42, 47–48; William L. Havard, Jr., and Floyd L. Cordy, *Rural-Urban Consolidation: The Merger of Governments in the Baton-Rouge Area* (Baton Rouge: Louisiana State University Press, 1964); Bruce D. Rogers and C. McCurdy Lipsey, "Metropolitan Reform: Citizen Evaluations of Performances in Nashville-Davidson County, Tennessee," in *The Study of Federalism at Work,* ed. Vincent Ostrom, *Publius* 4, no. 4 (Fall 1974): 19–35.

7. Brett W. Hawkins, *Nashville Metro: The Politics of City-County Consolidation* (Nashville, Tenn.: Vanderbilt University Press, 1966).

8. Bollens and Schmandt, *The Metropolis,* pp. 324–39; Edward Sofen, *The Miami Metropolitan Experiment,* rev. ed. (Garden City, N.Y.: Anchor Books, 1966).

9. Joseph F. Zimmerman, *The Federated City: Community Control in Large Communities* (New York: St. Martin's Press, 1972).

10. Frank Swallwood, *Greater London: The Politics of Metropolitan Reform* (Indianapolis, Ind.: Bobbs Merrill, 1965).

11. Bollens and Schmandt, *The Metropolis,* pp. 336–39.

12. All too little has been written on the regional councils in Israel. The best sources of information are to be found in the publications of the Center for the Study of Rural and Urban Settlement in Rehovot. A general treatment of the subject matter can be found in the center's *Regional Cooperation in Israel* (Hebrew) (Rehovot, 1972). For more specialized work at the center, see Erik Cohen and Elazar Leshem, *Survey of Regional Cooperation in Three Regions of Collective Settlements* (Hebrew) (Rehovot, 1972).

13. For the strongest argument on behalf of this approach, see Milton Kotler, *Neighborhood Government: The Local Foundations of Political Life* (Indianapolis, Ind.: Bobbs Merrill, 1965). See also Alan A. Altshuler, *Community Control: The Black Demand for Participation in Large American Cities* (New York: Pegasus, 1970).

14. Leonard J. Fein, *The Ecology of the Public Schools: An Inquiry into Community Control* (New York: Pegasus, 1971).

15. Robert B. Hawkins, Jr., *Self Government by District: Myth and Reality* (Stanford, Calif.: Hoover Institution Press, 1976).

16. For a survey of such movements, see *Advisory Commission on Intergovernmental, Substate Regionalism and the Federal System* (Washington, D.C.: U.S. Government Printing Office, 1974), Vol. 3, Ch. 3, "Intergovernmental Service Agreements and Transfer of Functions," pp. 29–52. For the workings of such arrangements and their theoretical rationale, see the articles included in Vincent Ostrom, ed., *The Study of Federalism at Work, Publius* 4, no. 4 (Fall 1974); and California Governor's Task Force on Local Governments, "Report: Public Benefits from Public Choice," Robert B. Hawkins, Jr., Chairman (Bloomington, Ind.: Workshop in Policy Theory and Policy Analysis, Indiana University).

17. Emanuel Gutmann and Claude Klein, "The Institutional Structure of Heterogeneous Cities: Brussels, Montreal, and Belfast," this volume.

18. C. P. Harris, "Regional and Local Government," in *Australian Federalism,* ed. Russell Mathews, *Publius* 7, no. 3 (Summer 1977).

19. Bollens and Schmandt, *The Metropolis*, pp. 364–72; Advisory Commission on Intergovernmental Relations, "Improving Urban America: A Challenge to Federalism" (Washington, D.C., September 1976).

20. There are no studies of these bodies, only the periodic reports of the Israel state comptroller on each of them.

21. On the Regio Basilensis, see Susan J. Stock, "Toward a Europe of Regions: Transnational Political Activities," *Publius* 4, no. 3 (Summer 1977); and Steven Schechter, "Sharing Jurisdiction Across Frontiers," in *Self-Rule/Shared Rule*, ed. Daniel J. Elazar (Ramat Gan: Turtledove, 1979).

22. Stephen Schechter, Montreal "Metro" field notes, 1975. See also Gutmann and Klein, "The Institutional Structure of Heterogeneous Cities."

23. Daniel J. Elazar, New Delhi field notes, January 1977.

24. On the theory of consociationalism, see Arend Lipjhart, "Consociational Democracy," *World Politics* 21, no. 2 (January 1969): 207–25; Arend Lipjhart, *The Politics of Accommodation: Pluralism and Democracy in the Netherlands* (Berkeley: University of California Press, 1968). On Austria, see Rodney P. Stiefbold, *Segmented Pluralism, Consociational Democracy and Austrian Electoral Politics: A Theoretical and Empirical Case Study of Austria under Great Coalition, 1955-1966* (Ann Arbor, Mich.: University Microfilms, 1973).

25. Leonard Binder, ed., *Politics in Lebanon* (New York: Wiley, 1966); Daniel J. Elazar, *Israel: From Ideological to Territorial Democracy* (Jerusalem: Jerusalem Institute for Federal Studies, 1978); R. Hrair Dekmejjan, *Patterns of Political Leadership, Egypt, Israel, Lebanon* (Binghamton, N.Y.: State University Press, 1975).

26. Jacob Landau and Emanuel Gutmann, "The Political Elite and National Leadership in Israel," in *Political Elites in the Middle East*, ed. George Lenczowski (Washington, D.C.: American Enterprise Institute for Public Policy Research, 1966), pp. 163–99; and Daniel J. Elazar, "Israel's Compound Polity," in *Israel at the Polls*, ed. Howard R. Penniman (Washington, D.C.: American Enterprise Institute, 1979), pp. 1-39.

27. R. Michael Stevens, "Asymmetrical Federalism: The Federal Principle and the Survival of the Small Republic," *Publius* 7, no. 4 (Fall 1977): 177–203.

28. Donald L. Rowat, *The Government of Federal Capitals* (Toronto: Toronto University Press, 1973).

CHRONOLOGICAL TABLE

c. 2000 BC	Canaanite settlement in Jerusalem
c. 1750	Jerusalem mentioned in Egyptian Execration Texts
c. 1300	Jerusalem mentioned in Amarna Letters
c. 1100–1000	Jebusites rule Jerusalem, a foreign enclave within Israelite settlement
c. 1000	Jerusalem made capital of United Monarchy under David
c. 965–30	Reign of Solomon, builder of the First Temple; First Temple period begins
c. 930	End of United Monarchy; Jerusalem remains capital of Judah
586	Destruction of Jerusalem and the First Temple by the Babylonians; First Exile
538	Edict of Cyrus; return from Exile; Persian period begins
520–16	Building of Second Temple completed by Zerubbabel
332	Conquest by army of Alexander the Great; Hellenistic period begins
301	Ptolemies of Egypt
198	Seleucids of Syria
167	Antiochus Epiphanes IV desecrates the Temple; Maccabean revolt
164	Temple rededicated by Judah Maccabee; Hasmonean period begins
63	Roman general Pompey enters Jerusalem; Roman period begins
37 BC–AD 4	Herodian period; Temple rebuilt and walls surrounding Temple Mount erected
A.D. 6	Judea becomes a Roman province governed by procurators
66–70	First Jewish Revolt; Jews liberate Jerusalem
70	Destruction of Jerusalem and Second Temple
132–35	Second Jewish Revolt led by Bar Kokhba; Jerusalem recaptured

	135	Roman colony of Aelia Capitolina
324		Christian Emperor Constantine the Great; Byzantine period begins
	335	Church of the Holy Sepulchre complex dedicated
	614	Persians under Khusraw II occupy Jerusalem
	629	Byzantines under Heraclius reconquer Jerusalem
638		Jerusalem capitulates to Arab-Muslim conquerors; Arab-Muslim rule begins
	660–750	Umayyad rule; dynastic capital in Damascus
	691	Dome of the Rock built by Caliph ʿAbd al-Malik
	c. 705	Al-Aqṣā Mosque built by Caliph al-Walīd
	750–878	ʿAbbāsid rule; dynastic capital in Baghdad
	878–905	Ṭulūnids (Turkish descent) of Egypt
	905–41	ʿAbbāsid rule returns
	941–74	Ikhshīdids (Turkish descent) of Egypt
	974–1071	Fāṭimids of Egypt
	1071–98	Seljūk Turks
	1098–99	Fāṭimids return
1099		Crusaders conquer Jerusalem; establish it as capital; Latin Kingdom of Jerusalem begins
1187		Saladin, Ayyūbid Sultan of Egypt (Kurdish descent), reconquers Jerusalem
1229–44		Christians regain possession of Jerusalem by treaty between al-Malik al-Kāmil, Ayyūbid Sultan of Egypt, and Frederick II; Second Crusader occupancy
1244		Crusader Jerusalem falls to Khwārazmians, in employ of Ayyūbids of Egypt
1244–53		Ayyūbids of Egypt and Syria
1253–54		Mamluks of Egypt (Turkish and Circassian descent)
1254–60		Ayyūbids of Syria
1260		Mamluks defeat Mongols at ʿAyn Jālūt and annex Jerusalem and the rest of the country to their rule; Mamluk period begins; Jerusalem subordinate to Damascus, later directly to Cairo
	1291	Defeat of Crusaders at Acre; final fall of Crusader Kingdom
1516–17		Ottoman Turks defeat Mamluks; Ottoman rule begins; Jerusalem subordinate to Damascus, Sidon, Istanbul
	1831–40	Egyptian occupation under Muḥammad ʿAlī and Ibrāhīm Pasha

1852	Firman regulating Status Quo in Christian Holy Places
1863–64	Founding of Jerusalem Municipality
1917	Jerusalem surrenders to British forces under General Allenby; British occupation begins; Jerusalem administrative capital
1920	Civil administration under High Commissioner Sir Herbert Samuel
1923	British Mandate for Palestine ratified
1928–29	Wailing Wall controversy and commission
1936–39	General strike and great revolt by Arabs of Palestine
1937	Royal (Peel) Commission Plan recommending partition; Jerusalem to remain part of British mandatory
1939	White Paper; Palestine to be made independent state within ten years; Jerusalem to be capital
1947	UN Partition Plan; Jerusalem to be international zone
1948	Foundation of State of Israel
1949	Jerusalem partitioned between Israel and Jordan by Rhodes Armistice Agreement after it was divided in 1948 war
1967	Jerusalem unified after June War when eastern (Jordanian) sector annexed by Israel

INDEX

ABOUT THE EDITOR
AND CONTRIBUTORS

TEDDY KOLLEK has been the mayor of Jerusalem since December 1, 1965. Born in Vienna, he came to Palestine in 1934 and held a variety of posts, including head of the U.S. desk in Israel's Foreign Office, minister of the Israel Embassy in Washington, D.C., director general of the Prime Minister's Office, and chairman of the Israel Museum in Jerusalem. He holds an honorary doctorate from the Hebrew University in Jerusalem

JOEL L. KRAEMER is chairman of the Department of Middle Eastern and African Studies at Tel-Aviv University. Kraemer received his Ph.D. in Arabic and Islamic Studies from Yale University, where he served as assistant professor in the Department of Near Eastern Languages and Literatures. He and his family have been living in Israel since 1971.

ALISA MEYUHAS GINIO is senior teacher in the Department of History of Tel-Aviv University. She received two degrees in History from the Hebrew University in Jerusalem.

DANIEL RUBINSTEIN, a native of Jerusalem, holds his degree in Sociology and Oriental Studies. Since 1966, he has been the political correspondent and in charge of Arab affairs for the daily newspaper *Davar*.

UZI BENZIMAN is a seventh-generation Jerusalemite and a graduate of the Hebrew University in Modern History and Political Science. A journalist for 18 years, he writes the diplomatic column for the daily newspaper *Ha'aretz*. He is the author of *Jerusalem, City Without Walls*, which was published in Hebrew and Arabic in 1973; it describes the decision-making process that led to the unification of the city in 1967 and the situation in the city since it was reunified. He is now completing a book on the peace negotiations between Israel and Egypt.

ISRAEL KIMHI is the head of the Policy Planning Division of the Municipality of Jerusalem. He is a lecturer in the Department of Geography and the School of Urban Studies at the Hebrew University in Jerusalem.

BENJAMIN HYMAN is the deputy head of the Town Planning Division of the Municipality of Jerusalem. He holds a degree in Economics and Sociology from the Hebrew University and an M.Sc. (economics) in Urban and Regional Planning from the London School of Economics.

SAUL P. COLBI graduated from the Law Faculty of Rome University and practiced law in his native Trieste before settling in Palestine in 1939. As an expert in canon law, he was head of the Division of Christian Affairs in the Israel Ministry of Religious Affairs from 1948 until his retirement in 1975. He is the author of several books on Christianity in the Holy Land and is a commander of St. Gregory the Great and a commander of the Merit of the Italian Republic.

EMANUEL GUTMANN teaches Political Science at the Hebrew University in Jerusalem and was chairman of the department from 1971 to 1975. He wrote his dissertation at Columbia University in New York City on the development of local government in Palestine. He also has taught at the Victoria University of Manchester and has lectured widely in Western Europe and the United States. He is now working on a study of religion and politics in contemporary Western Europe.

CLAUDE KLEIN is the dean of the Faculty of Law at the Hebrew University in Jerusalem, where he has been a faculty member since 1968. A native of France, he received his doctorate from the Faculté de Droit, Strasbourg. He has written several books, and was a visiting professor at the University of Pennsylvania and Temple University in 1977–78.

DANIEL J. ELAZAR, a native of Minneapolis, Minnesota, received his doctorate in Political Science from the University of Chicago. He is the Senator N. M. Paterson Professor of Political Studies and head of the Institute of Local Government at Bar-Ilan University in Israel, president of the Jerusalem Institute for Federal Studies, chairman of the Center for Jewish Community Studies (Jerusalem and Philadelphia), and senior fellow of the Center for the Study of Federalism at Temple University. He is the author or editor of 20 books and a member of the Israel State Commission for Local Government Reform and chairman of the Subcommittee on Structure of Local Government.